D0872207

ONSTAGE
WITH
GRIEG

ONSTAGE WITH GRIEG

INTERPRETING HIS PIANO MUSIC

Einar Steen-Nøkleberg

TRANSLATED BY WILLIAM H. HALVERSON

INDIANA UNIVERSITY PRESS / BLOOMINGTON & INDIANAPOLIS

Publication of this book is made possible in part with the assistance of a Challenge Grant from the National Endowment for the Humanities, a federal agency that supports research, education, and public programming in the humanities.

Publication of this book was also assisted by grants from Grieg-Jubileét Bergen 1993; Norsk Kulturråd, Oslo; and an anonymous donor.

Originally published as *Med Grieg på podiet: Til spillende fra en spillende* (Oslo: Solum Forlag, 1992).

The paper used in this publication meets the minimum requirements of American National Standard for Information Sciences—Permanence of Paper for Printed Library Materials, ANSI Z39.48–1984.

Manufactured in the United States of America

Library of Congress Cataloging-in-Publication Data

Steen-Nøkleberg, Einar, date
[Med Grieg på podiet. English]
Onstage with Grieg : interpreting his piano music / Einar Steen-Nøkleberg ; translated by William H. Halverson.
p. cm.
Includes index.
ISBN 0–253–33248–6 (alk. paper)
1. Grieg, Edvard, 1843–1907. Piano music.
2. Piano music—Interpretation (Phrasing, dynamics, etc.). I. Title.
ML410.G9S7413 1997
786.2'092—dc20 96-34512
MN

1 2 3 4 5 02 01 00 99 98 97

CONTENTS

Contents

PREFACE

Of course it is presumptuous to write a book about the interpretation of Grieg's piano works! We already have so many books about this composer—about his life, his art, and his works. It is not my intention that my writing be compared with them or compete with them in any way. One of my explicit goals is to avoid scholarly analyses. For the most part I have also tried to avoid biographical details about Grieg, and I have quoted him and others as seldom as possible because I wish the music, Grieg's notes, to be the focus of this book. Whether Grieg was in Berlin or Copenhagen or Lofthus or Bergen when he wrote a particular piece is not of great importance for its interpretation. Whether he was sick, depressed, or tired—or in particularly good humor—when he wrote a piece also strikes me as being of only secondary importance. Some of these considerations may be of value for those who study Grieg's works, but if so I happily refer them to other books, other works about the master, for sources of such information. Obviously I have benefited from most of what has been written about Grieg—books, editions of his works, articles, and the like. But the main point of departure, the most important source of what is found in this book, is the progressive mastery of Grieg's piano works—an effort that must be pursued almost like that of an actor attempting to master a role.

Learning the pieces by heart as early in the learning process as possible sharpens one's powers of observation: the score and the composer's performance instructions are imprinted in the performer's mind. Practicing the works in this way brings one closer to Grieg's process of composition. It is also necessary to practice these pieces constantly over a period of many years.

I have made it a point to play each work as I have written about it. Thus the difficulties about which I write are all real, and I think I am in a position to give advice to others who are dealing with the same difficulties. I would not have felt ready to write this book if I had not performed all these works several times in the concert hall, sometimes as individual pieces and sometimes in a series of concerts encompassing Grieg's entire production in this genre. One's own experience—good luck and bad onstage—tells one where the shoe pinches. My own practice and occasional mistakes are the basis for the counsel given here. The logic of the concert hall is different from that of any other situation. Performing artists talk about the two worlds they have to master and live in, one "onstage" and another "off stage." Off stage is the locus of our everyday lives, where, among other things, we practice and prepare ourselves for the concert situation. It is important to remember that one's mind and body function differently in these two worlds. I have tried to distinguish between the suggestions that are applicable when one is practicing and those that can be used—and are explicitly recommended—during a public performance. My experience both as a performer and as a teacher is that one needs *simple* ideas onstage. As a rule, complex analytical observations cannot be taken into the performance situation. They can be helpful as part of our preparation, but at the moment of performance they are likely to inhibit us so that we do not achieve what we had intended.

This book, then, is a compendium of suggestions from one player to another concerning the interpretation of Grieg's piano music. In the interest of conserving space, many of them are expressed in a few imperious-sounding words—"do not slow down here," "play this measure *pianissimo.*" Readers should mentally precede these remarks with the thought "it is advisable to" and not regard my advice as a set of hard-and-fast directions. These recommendations arise from my own experience, but they should be tempered by individual players' taste and judgment The form is deliberately simple, for my goal is to give practical instruction rather than a theoretical discourse regarding this music. I have deliberately avoided grading the pieces with respect to difficulty. Obviously some of them are technically demanding—several of the *Peasant Dances* of Op. 72, for example, as well as *Brooklet* (Op. 62, No. 4), *In the Mountains* (Op. 19, No. 1), and of course the *Piano Concerto.* But truly artistic interpretations of the technically simpler *Lyric Pieces* or the transcriptions of folk tunes in Opp. 17 and 19 are also exceedingly rare. There is little correlation between technical difficulty and interpretive difficulty.

I have also assiduously avoided making any comments about the relative quality of the various pieces, for such judgments are very much a matter of personal taste. Complex structures and textures such as those in many of the pieces in Op. 72, for example, appeal greatly to some listeners and less or not at all to others. Grieg's own wife is reported to have said that she didn't understand those dance tunes and didn't really like them! Others, however, consider Op. 72 among Grieg's finest achievements as a composer. At the opposite extreme, some pieces with a very simple structure have become popular because of an exceptionally beautiful melodic line, a distinctively folklike feeling, a charming atmosphere, or a bouncy rhythm.

The main purpose of this book is to establish a standard of interpretation for Grieg's piano music consistent with the composer's intentions. Of course there is room for differences among performers in the interpretation of these scores, but Grieg's performance indications are sufficiently explicit to enable us to distinguish between professional and amateurish interpretations. The latter clearly do not belong "onstage."

The book would certainly make tedious reading for non-pianists. My hope, however, is that it will be of interest and value for those who want to study and perform Grieg's piano works. My observations and suggestions are not intended for those who are already experienced performers of Grieg's works. Indeed, they may disagree violently with some of my ideas. Every composition is capable of various interpretations, depending in part on the particular bent of the performer. I wish primarily to show young players who would like to get acquainted with Grieg how to learn his works in order to play them, enjoy them, and in some cases perform them publicly—thereby carrying on a long tradition.

One thing is clear: a lyrical, dreamy, and poetic element is fundamental in Grieg's musical language and must never be neglected when we play his works. If it is, something essential dies in his endlessly beautiful music. The prominent folk-music strain appears especially in the form of pedal points, special rhythmic effects, and syncopated accents. I have attempted to draw attention to these things as they occur. With respect to *rubato*, one ought not go much beyond what Grieg has explicitly indicated. It should not be employed on the basis of the performer's feelings but in a manner consistent with the changing harmonies and modulations. I have tried to give suggestions regarding interpretation with specific reference to the placement of the harmonies on the circle of fifths.

Do not read this book cover to cover. Use it as a reference. Read the part that is relevant to whatever you are working on at the moment. Enjoy!

Einar Steen-Nøkleberg
Oslo, Norway

CHAPTER

1

Four Piano Pieces, Op. 1

Edvard Grieg's fame as a composer rests to a considerable extent on his piano works. No fewer than 36 of his 74 opus numbers are compositions for solo piano—including his immortal *Concerto in A Minor*—and five more are works for piano four-hands or for two pianos. Grieg was himself an accomplished pianist and concertized extensively throughout Scandinavia, the rest of Europe, and the British Isles. The piano was his instrument, the one he knew the best and loved the most, and both his intimate knowledge and his love for the piano are evident in his music.

Not surprisingly, Grieg's first opus was a collection of piano pieces. After a number of preliminary attempts at composition, some of which were in response to assignments received during his student days in Leipzig, in 1861 Grieg wrote "4 Stücke für das Pianoforte." He was eighteen years old at the time. This series of pieces aroused considerable attention in the community associated with the conservatory—among his teachers, his fellow students, and others who heard them. Naturally, the fact that they were written by a student is reflected in their melodies, their harmonies, and their formal characteristics, but their sound craftsmanship impressed everyone who heard them. They are successful character pieces in the spirit of Schumann and Mendelssohn, but with respect to harmony Grieg goes beyond his predecessors.

The first piece could have been given the subtitle "Song Without Words."

No. 2 could have been called "Elegy" (but with a very special middle section). Grieg himself gave No. 3 the subtitle "Mazurka," and No. 4 is "a la polacca." They are rich and lush piano compositions. The first piece features arpeggiated triads with the melody played by the thumb in the manner made popular at the time by Sigismund Thalberg. (Thalberg had been given the nickname "old arpeggio" because of his predilection.) No. 2 is especially interesting harmonically, with extensive chromaticism and sometimes ambiguous harmonization, which clearly points to the mastery that lies ahead. To be sure, the middle section—*Allegro capriccioso*—is somewhat Mendelssohnian in character, but it possesses a kind of burlesque and Nordic sound. It holds the promise of better things to come! No. 3 has something of a "salon music" sound, but this mazurka nonetheless initiated something that Grieg loved and returned to many times later. Just think about the many pieces in waltz time in the *Lyric Pieces*. There is a line that goes forward from the mazurka all the way to *She Dances*. The last piece in Op. 1 is unique in Grieg's production: it is his only polonaise.

Grieg was in a setting that was supportive of pianists when he wrote Op. 1, and presumably he himself was also in good performing condition. These are not easy pieces! In the same year that Grieg wrote them—1861—he reported that he made his debut, i.e., he played, for the first time, a complete evening concert as a solo performer. The place was Karlshamn, Sweden, and the program included compositions by Moscheles, Mendelssohn, and Schumann. This concert may have had much to do with the pianistic shaping of the pieces. The piano comes into its own.

No. 1. Allegro con leggerezza

Play No. 1 in a "Schumannian" style, warmly, with a cellolike sound in the right thumb (see Ex. 1.1*). It is important for the player to have a completely

Ex. 1.1

*The measure numbers used in this book correspond to those in *Edvard Grieg: Complete Works*, vols. 1, 2, 3, and 10 (New York, Frankfurt, and London: C. F. Peters, 1977–86).

free arm, using sideways movements in the wrist to help move the thumb downward and to support the fifth finger as it moves upward. Leading with one's arm in this way yields a rounded and pleasant sound. Now and then there is a duet between the right hand and the lower voices (see Ex. 1.2),

Ex. 1.2

which should be emphasized. The first part of the piece—about the first page and a half—is cellolike, with the melody in a low register. In the middle of the second page the melody moves up into the treble clef, where it is played with the fifth finger. Try to play the notes with an upward movement on the fifth finger. That way you will get a more "singing" tone.

In the recapitulation the melody appears only in the soprano voice, thus creating a delicate, bright reply to the dark color of the opening measures. In many of Grieg's pieces, a rest can be perceived as the goal—as if the music continued right on into the rest, which then becomes a continuation of the melodic line. This phenomenon appears already in Grieg's first piece (see Ex. 1.3).

Ex. 1.3

Another characteristic of Grieg's music that we encounter in this early piece is the dramatic turn mediated by a Neapolitan subdominant chord. The use of *rubato* is governed by the Romantic principle "take and give back," i.e., if you speed up in one place you must later "give back" what you have taken with an imperceptible *ritardando*. Look, for example, at Ex. 1.4, where in the space of four measures the preceding *a tempo* is followed by *stringendo*, *più lento*, and *ritenuto*. Try to execute a *rubato* such that the four measures take approximately the same amount of time whether they are played *a tempo* all the way through or, as in Ex. 1.4, with a *stringendo* at the beginning and a *ritenuto* at the end. An ideal *rubato* creates a feeling of balance despite the freedom of tempo being exercised.

Ex. 1.4

No. 2. Non allegro e molto espressivo

Grieg indicated that the first part of this piece is to be played "very expressively and not slowly." The mood could be described as one of "elegiac lament." It is clear that Grieg wished to demonstrate the compositional technique of handling several simultaneously moving voices, and he accomplished it in an exemplary manner. Primarily he used contrary motion, but occasionally also parallel motion in thirds and sixths for contrast (see Ex. 1.5).

Ex. 1.5

A classical prescription for voice-leading specifies about 80 percent contrary motion and 20 percent parallel motion as the ideal. In terms of this aesthetic principle, No. 2 measures up very well. The multi-voice aspect is illuminated by advanced and close harmonies. The harmonies change so often that the piece must not be played too fast; otherwise the overall effect can be unsettled and episodic. In the *ritardando* in measure 12 it is good to linger a bit, precisely because the harmonic progression is so dense. Forget about rhythm here. Think about the changing chords. Take enough time to hear them and to make them heard. The tempo that you think reveals the harmonic progression is the best one for the interpretation. Here, too, you should use a flexible form of *rubato*. Three times we go up to G, and then to A. The natural intensity of this line requires a kind of release in the last part of the first phrase (see Ex. 1.6).

Ex. 1.6

Now to the brilliant *Allegro capriccioso* section. Here, for the first time in Grieg's music, the little trolls are lying in wait—especially in measures 25 and 26 (see Ex. 1.7). The trolls' incursion here fits nicely into the whole, but

Ex. 1.7

it also points beyond the immediate context and into the future. One can discern, even this early, what Grieg later called "his only success"—namely, his breaking with the Mendelssohn and Schumann traditions, choosing instead to derive his inspiration from the folk music of his homeland. It is precisely these moments in the second piece—the measures reproduced in Ex. 1.7—that elevate Op. 1 from a very talented beginning—the graduation composition of an exceedingly gifted young man—to a work exhibiting a flash of genius. Grieg must have been pleased with this middle part, for it is peppered with unexpected rests and clever little embellishments (see Ex. 1.8).

Grieg is truly reveling in the music, not least as he triumphantly turns the recapitulation into a dramatic, ponderous section marked *pesante*. It is temperament, it is conviction, it is a proud eighteen-year-old's self-confidence. Grieg feels that he "has it," that he has "nailed it," that he is going to surpass his teachers. He is convinced that he will soon leave Leipzig and find other pathways that will lead right to the pinnacle. All of this is in the *pesante* section, as shown in Ex. 1.9.

Play it, therefore, with supreme conviction and pianistic aplomb. After he

Ex. 1.8

Ex. 1.9

is finished with the *pesante* section, Grieg rounds things off with the most convincing conclusion one could imagine. It contains chromaticism, parallel motion, hidden syncopation, pedal points, inverted pedals—everything that a school, a seat of learning, might wish to have demonstrated in the way of craftsmanship. And the craftsmanship is organic, an integral part of the whole. Op. 1, No. 2 is a true masterpiece!

No. 3. Mazurka

This mazurka requires a good pianistic technique. The intricate runs in triplets must be supple and clear, rippling and cascadelike in order to sound their best. Practice them, therefore, with a view to evenness and precision at first, then with suppleness and a flexible *rubato*. Pay special attention to the sixteenth-note octaves in Ex. 1.10. To be sure, these octaves occur only in

Ex. 1.10

groups of four, but that is why it is essential to keep the wrist as relaxed as possible in order to make them elegant. They should not stick out, i.e., should not be too loud just because they are precise. On the other hand, if we think of them as being too pliant they can easily get lost altogether. So practice them with a flexible wrist and loosen up your hand before you begin.

If the mazurka is to be played *con grazia*, as Grieg wished, I think it is essential to think of these elements. Otherwise the piece as a whole tends to get choppy. The accompaniment in the left hand is nicely worked out; it is simple, but it has a fine countermelody (see Ex. 1.11).

Ex. 1.11

In the middle section Grieg plays with the mazurka rhythm, treating two measures in 3/4 time as if they were three measures in duple time—a rhythmic feature that, in a totally different context, he will use again in the *Norwegian Peasant Dances*. The old hemiola pattern of an earlier day has reappeared in modern garb. The pattern in measures 25–26 (Ex. 1.12) reappears a number of times—for example, in measures 37–38.

Ex. 1.12

Rubato as employed in the mazurka rhythm has a certain tradition: a dotted eighth note followed by a sixteenth note is sometimes notated with a sixteenth-note rest in place of the dot (in Chopin's mazurkas, for example). The sixteenth-note rest lengthens the beat by just a touch, so we can have a kind of swinging, extended rhythm at these places. The simplest and easiest way to achieve this is to raise the wrist slightly. This notation occurs a number of times in the piece—in measures 77–79 (Ex. 1.13), for instance—and is a rhythmic subtlety worth observing.

The mazurka points forward to *She Dances*, and as in that lyric piece it is wise to play as lightly and lucidly as possible. Don't stomp around in heavy boots. A nimble left hand, especially in the octave accompaniment (see Ex. 1.14), yields the desired effect.

If the mazurka is played lightly—like a ballet—it will be successful. This

Ex. 1.13

sempre cre - scen - do

Ex. 1.14

piece always reminds me of a surprise meeting I once had with a world-renowned Russian pianist. I was young and had by no means played all of Grieg's piano music at the time. He said, "The *Mazurka*? Don't you play it? Why, it's one of his best pieces!" It was something to think about, something to practice, something to work toward. Grieg was living in a conservatory environment when he composed the piece, and he wrote it as dutifully, as carefully, as convincingly as he was able. The notational details, the performance indications, the dynamic variations are so numerous and minute that they can shackle the performer. Try to unlock the music by studying the dynamic markings as thoroughly as you can. Observe as many of them as possible while you are practicing—but then tear yourself away from them. Don't let them fetter your imagination, your temperament, or your capacity to listen, for these are absolutely essential at the moment of performance. A roguish elegance is more important than slavish adherence to every little dynamic nuance indicated in the score.

No. 4. Allegretto con moto

We are still in an elegant salon, and even though Grieg has not indicated it in the score, both the first section and the recapitulation have polonaise rhythms ("a la polacca"). The piece is elaborately constructed, with such devices as pedal points, contrasting melodies, syncopation, and chromatic harmonic progressions. When Grieg repeats a motive or passage, he usually introduces some small changes. We see this when the opening motive is repeated: measure 24 is slightly different from measure 4, the first iteration, even though the harmonic conclusion is still on B. There are also some small changes in the recapitulation, where, in measure 71, Grieg has added a chromatic twist in the middle voice: B–A♯–B. Similar small changes occur in the other pieces of Op. 1 as well. Variation of this kind is a mark of compositional craftsmanship. In later works—in the *Lyric Pieces*—the restatements are very often identical to the original statements, but it is clear from Op. 1 that Grieg's later tendency to use identical restatements was not a result of ignorance. The kind of variation exhibited in Op. 1 is something he consciously abandoned later in order to make the music simpler and more tranquil, to bring it closer to the folk tune and the Nordic temperament. Op. 1, however, does exhibit tiny variations of this kind, and naturally we must be aware of them—even if we have to rack our brains to keep them all in mind! The piece is tightly constructed, and it is essential to play the chords with great precision. Even the polonaise rhythm surely can have a bit of a swing to it: there is no reason why the rhythm of the first phrase, for example, must consist of eight beats of exactly the same length. Perhaps the sixteenth notes should be a shade slower in order to give the whole phrase a certain swing. This is just by way of a small suggestion. It must not be exaggerated, and perhaps it can be done differently at different places when the same pattern reappears. In the *Lyric Pieces* there are many opportunities for falsetto effects. Very often when the motive is repeated *subito piano*—or, as in Ex. 1.15, *subito pianissimo*—it contains a little chromatic modulatory shift.

Ex. 1.15

A *subito pianissimo* effect of this kind generally requires a little time. It is a good idea to strike the key upwards in contrast to other notes. The middle section of No. 4 is a harplike, steady stream of chords and melodies that fragmentarily correspond to one another. The steady flow of sixteenth notes is similar in some ways to that of the first piece in this opus. The basic idea, the compositional technique of the two pieces, is related. Bring the melody out as clearly as possible; make it warm, make it legato. As the chords are being played evenly, they can stand in relief, i.e., dynamically undergird the melody. In several places Grieg has written such instructions as *ritardando*, *a tempo*, *stringendo*, *agitato*, and *molto ritardando*. There are so many instructions that one has to conclude that the piece should be played *rubato*. It remains only to do it as *organically* as possible. Remember: "take and give back." Playing the piece with and without *rubato* should take approximately the same amount of time!

Grieg was very fond of dialogue between the broken fragmentary chords—a pattern that appears in his later works as well. We are emphasizing something permanently "Griegian" when we let the various melodic voices call back and forth to one another. An example of this occurs in the middle section, measures 35–38 (see Ex. 1.16).

Ex. 1.16

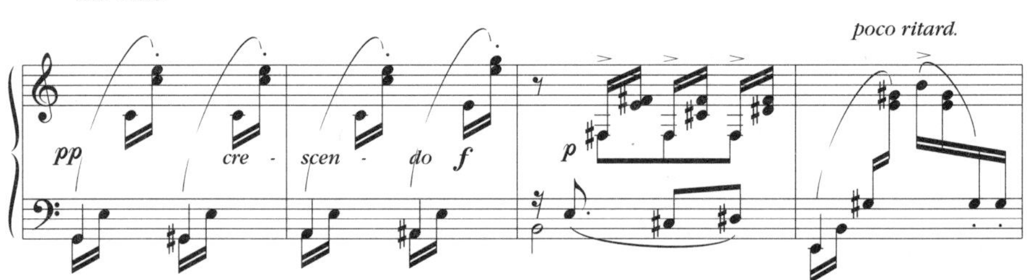

The elegant coda, which begins at measure 84, is built on a pedal point on B. To be sure, the B is not sounded continuously, but it occurs at regular intervals throughout the coda, and from measure 102 onward it is always present. In between we are treated to the most ingenious harmonic—chromatic—elaboration of the motives, especially in the left hand (see Ex. 1.17).

Ex. 1.17

Technically, it is desirable to have time to accentuate each individual chord clearly and to articulate the right hand and its ties. The ending is reminiscent of Schumann—like a clock striking. The pedal point on B gives it a kind of midnight mood: the clock—the device that measures time—intervenes and stops the progress and gradually brings the whole experience to a tranquil conclusion. The pedal point is on B, the fifth degree of the chord, and a 6/4 effect as well as a certain folkish coloring result from the very fact that the tension is not released via a D^{5}_{3} chord.

Grieg's final pedal indication also yields an effect reminiscent of folk music: the B is to be held over into the first beat of the last measure (see Ex. 1.18), which emphasizes the fifth of the final chord (which also has the fifth

Ex. 1.18

in the top voice) more than the Classical-Romantic tradition would have prescribed in creating a conclusion. Grieg's teachers would have stressed the root of the chord. Grieg stressed the fifth. That is very Norwegian.

CHAPTER

2

Poetic Tone Pictures: Six Piano Pieces, Op. 3

Grieg is twenty years old and is now living in Copenhagen, Denmark. He has just written his Symphony in C minor, which would later become the subject of considerable discussion. He took no chances: he pronounced his symphony unsuitable for performance. He did, however, take the two inner movements, arrange them for piano four-hands, and have them published as *Two Symphonic Pieces*. But he considered his symphony a student work. It was during this period that he wrote the *Poetic Tone Pictures*, which were published by the Chr. E. Horneman firm in Copenhagen.

The title that Grieg gave these six short pieces is very fitting, for "tone pictures" were to become the most important part of his production. This appellation is also the most important clue for pianists who play his works—not only with respect to Op. 3, but for the interpretation of his music in general. It is hardly possible to perform Grieg's works adequately without a poetic approach, a poetic frame of mind. Grieg himself was poetic to the core. Bereft of the poetry, his music collapses and loses its most important element. The interpreter must be capable of painting tone pictures. Grieg's character pieces are never very concrete. They must be interpreted creatively and with great imagination. Then they come to life!

Poetic Tone Pictures: Six Piano Pieces, Op. 3

Grieg dedicated these pieces to his friend and mentor Benjamin Feddersen, but he leaves us guessing as to exactly what pictures he had in mind. There are tender passages, but there is also humor and temperament in Op. 3. We find singing melodies, miniature scherzos, solid, almost marchlike rhythms, short fanfares set up in contrast to nocturnelike moods or spirited virtuosity. As you practice the pieces, try to visualize pictures that you think are appropriate for each and invent titles for them. Give *names* to the pieces! I won't tell you the names I have given them, for that might limit you. Give them names of your own choosing, names that you feel are appropriate. The picture, and the corresponding manner of playing, must be poetic. Outward brilliance is not the most important thing in these short pieces. Variation in tone and subtle *rubato* transitions are more important. These pieces easily fall apart if you make the tempo variations too pronounced. In some places Grieg has indicated that the tempo should be a little faster or slower—but just a little! Not metronomically, but nonetheless within one and the same basic tempo or related tempo in each piece. After all, music is not mathematics, so you have absolute freedom of movement within a given tempo, but if you go too far—take too many liberties—you destroy the framework for the poetic tone pictures.

No. 1, Allegro ma non troppo

The seeds of Griegian distinctiveness are evident in the very first piece in Op. 3. The two introductory measures can be characterized as harmonic, and in measure 3 the soprano voice introduces a well-balanced Schumannesque-Mendelssohnesque melody containing many slurs (see Ex. 2.1). Slurs play an important role later in the piece as well. Start with them as you strive to achieve a melodic and beautiful phrasing.

Measure 7 introduces a lively, humorous motive that has something of the character of a *slått,** i.e., a Norwegian peasant dance (see Ex. 2.2). The points of similarity are the accents on the second beat, which is characteristic of the *springar*, and the plagal cadence, which creates a certain modal effect. C♯ produces tritone tension, i.e., a Lydian tinge relative to G. All in all we feel that we are on Norwegian soil. The development is nicely worked out from a compositional point of view, with a bass line that descends stepwise, as in the introduction. This device appears again and again in Grieg's music, so you must never forget the bass line. The excitement builds *con fuoco*, but keep it

**Slått* (pl. *slåtter*) is the generic term for a Norwegian dance tune of instrumental character. The principal types of *slåtter* are the *gangar*, the *halling*, and the *springar*, though other names are used for these subtypes in various regions of the country.

Ex. 2.1

Ex. 2.2

under control. The piece is not without its hazards: *forte con fuoco* easily becomes too fast, and the *piano dolce* that follows, too slow. Obviously a mood of serenity must prevail in the graceful melody in *piano*, but the difference in tempo between the two passages must not be *too* great. The piece is simply constructed, alternating between series of slurs and lively little sixteenth-note figures reminiscent of fish—like the figures in Schubert's famous song *Die Forelle*. If we were to guess what fish belongs in this picture, we would have to say that it is a very poetic Norwegian fish that now and then shakes its tail. Such an association sounds silly "off stage," but "onstage" it is quite apt.

No. 2, Allegro cantabile

The second piece in Op. 3 is like a beautiful song, with a delightful melody in the upper voice that "sings" a fine duet with the bass line. The upbeat is simply a chord, as if we were tuning our instrument to B♭ major. The principal melody starts on D in measure 1 (see Ex. 2.3). Measures 2 and 3 are

Ex. 2.3

identical except that G is changed to G♭ in measure 3, giving the line a minor cast. You might want to play a little more softly and delicately the second time, at the point where the harmony makes this downward shift. The second part of the first section is a development of the first; you can open up the sound and let it flow, both dynamically and with respect to tempo. The ending also has a repeated passage, and here I recommend that the second iteration, measure 50, be a little softer—like an answer to measure 49.

The middle section, starting in measure 21, is a little *scherzoso* that Grieg marked *più vivo*. The right hand was more prominent in the first section, but here the left hand absolutely has to take the lead. It should be clear and distinct. The denser and softer you make the accompaniment in the right hand, the more precise and even it will be and the greater will be the effect. As the piece moves forward via sequences, it also grows, and we come at length to a little *forte* in measure 32. Measures 33 and 34 deserve close attention. Note first the articulation: the staccato in the right hand is interrupted by the slur between the third and fourth eighth notes. Measure 33 should be in strict tempo, and measure 34 should be extra soft (see Ex. 2.4).

Ex. 2.4

The transition to the recapitulation is shaped like a wave (see Ex. 2.5). The recapitulation itself is almost identical to the opening, but the harmonies modulate to the left side of the circle of fifths. Toward the end of the piece, Grieg takes the harmonies toward the subdominant—the minor subdominant, as a matter of fact—and this can be given a little emphasis with a special *piano* effect in measure 45. Treat the chromatic ascending line in the bass in the next measure as a contrast to the little *leggiero* run that follows in the right

Ex. 2.5

hand in measure 47. The *leggiero* run should be played with the fingers flat, but be careful not to make it too fast.

A gradual rounding off at the end of the piece concludes with an elegant *pianissimo* arpeggio. Pay attention to Grieg's original pedal marking, which sustains the low B♭ as the root of a B♭ major chord (see Ex. 2.6).

Ex. 2.6

Try to play the melody in as supple and songlike a manner as possible. Grieg has written *cantabile*, and the melody needs to be as *legato* as we can possibly make it—in contrast to the open staccatos in the middle section.

The middle section is marked *più vivo*, but be careful not to overdo it. If the *più vivo* goes too fast and differs too much from the tempo of the outer sections, the piece gets excessively choppy and loses some of its tender, poetic character. It becomes episodic and divided instead of poetic and unified.

No. 3, Con moto

This piece surely is a Norwegian burlesque. The rhythm is important and has several different aspects. The left hand dances: ♪𝄾♪ in 6/8 time. The right hand has a dotted rhythm: ♪𝄿𝅘𝅥𝅯 ♪, a pattern that Grieg used often; we will see it again in many short pieces as well as in *Ballade*, Op. 24. And it always presents the same difficulty: it is easy to flatten out the pattern, to lose some of the tension, to make it sound like two eighth notes with a grace note in between. That is not the way to think of it. The effect is always much better—there is more suppleness—if the rhythm can be maintained, i.e., if the performer consciously feels the rest or the dot (in this case the rest). If you find it difficult to do so, slow the tempo a bit.

In addition to the two subrhythms, there is an overarching "walking" effect, almost *alla marcia*, in striding, dotted quarter notes, i.e., two beats per measure. Try to keep the accompaniment subdued despite the rhythmic interest. The simple triplet in the upbeat with which the piece begins returns many times and is a modest little thing; nonetheless, it deserves attention. It easily gets lost, becomes indistinct. I recommend using the fingering 1–2–3–1 at the beginning of the piece. Later, when the E♭ is to be sustained, use 1–2–3–4, with extra activity in the fingers.

Think upwards after the attack to maximize clarity. Grieg has placed accents on the first beat in measures 2 and 4, creating an upbeat, or preparatory effect, in measures 1 and 3. Measures 5 and 6 have accents on the first beat; measures 7 and 8 have no accents. Then comes another series of rhythmic progressions, i.e., measure 9 is preparatory to measure 10, and the second half of measure 10 prepares for the second part of measure 11, where the accent is on the fourth eighth note, as is also the case in measure 12. Measures 13 and 14 have no accents, but there is a firm *sforzando* on the last chord. Observe these accents carefully because they are placed irregularly and result in plastic phrasing. Irregularly placed accents became a distinctive characteristic of the music of Grieg, a technique he used more and more frequently as he matured and which occurs most frequently in his later works. Irregular, amusing accents add much to the playing of Grieg! There is no doubt that he put them there deliberately and wanted them to be observed.

The middle section is a mixture of jovial merry-making, clear triads, and teasing, descending staccato runs. These runs occur against a backdrop of sustained notes in the melody, as in measures 18–19. Note the melodic progression in the middle voices in measures 22, 23, 24, 25, etc., and be careful to emphasize it. There are many unexpected accents in this section as well as in the transition passage preceding it. We have accents that alternate between the left hand and the right hand as they play a charming duet (see Ex. 2.7).

The recapitulation, starting on measure 37, is like the opening, but perhaps one can make the *fortissimo* a little louder this time—or, to put it the other way around, hold back a bit at the beginning. I would recommend that you not take the *fortissimo* at the beginning too literally: make it *forte* rather than *fortissimo*.

No. 3 is by no means an easy piece to play, especially with respect to vertical precision. When all the voices are really made to sing together, though, the result is a wonderful pianistic sound. It's a challenge!

Ex. 2.7

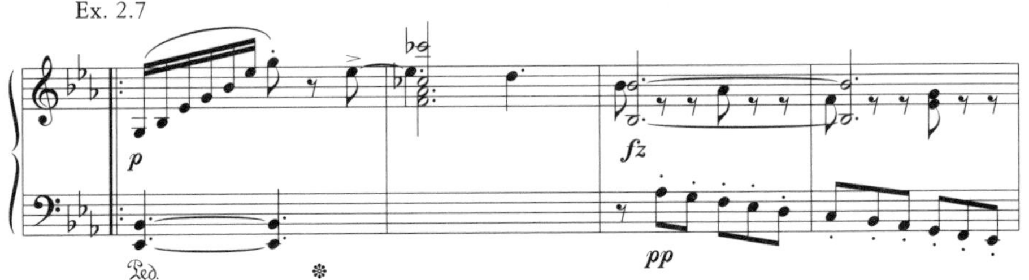

No. 4, Andante con sentimento

Grieg wrote only one piece that he called *Notturno*, namely, one of the *Lyric Pieces* (Op. 54, No. 4), but the mood of No. 4 of the *Poetic Tone Pictures* is very much like that of a nocturne. The motives are characterized by slurs and embellished slurs, and even the melody is similar to the principal theme of *At Your Feet* (see Exx. 2.8a and b). Broken chords appear throughout the piece. But there is a consistent melody line formed by the lowest notes, and for that reason it is important that they be played with sufficient sonority. If they aren't, the sound can be left suspended in the air without a harmonic undergirding.

Exx. 2.8a and b

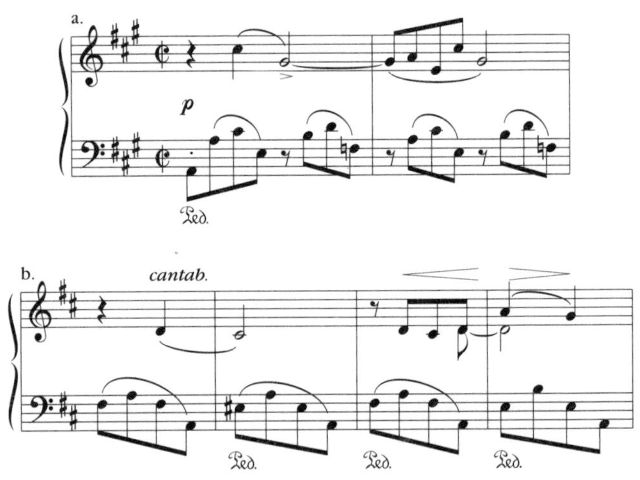

In the middle section Grieg has written *crescendo e stringendo* (measure 14), but don't overdo it. Don't exceed the bounds of an essentially uniform tempo. You can also create fine lines—for example, in measures 3, 4, and 5 and in the long chain of upward-moving syncopations in measures 6, 7, and 8. Make these hang together, but be careful to preserve the tempo. This is another piece where it is easy for the tempo to get out of hand. A gradual broadening that starts in measure 11 culminates in the accented triplets in measure 17 (see Ex. 2.9). Be careful about the relationship between the triplets in the right hand and the duple pattern in the left in measure 25 (see Ex. 2.10).

Ex. 2.9

Ex. 2.10

After having clambered to the top of the mountain in measure 18, G♯–F♯–E can be played with a gently relaxed wrist before heading back down again and into the recapitulation. Practice to achieve as even and complementary an eighth-note rhythm as possible in this piece. One should have the feeling at all times that the several voices, though traversing different patterns, are resonating to the same beat. The *rubato* should be like a rubber band that is stretched and then relaxed. It should never exceed these bounds. The melody and accompaniment should be played with the flat cushion of the fingers so as to produce as gentle a sound as possible.

No. 5, Allegro moderato

Now it is the *Norwegian* Edvard Grieg who comes into full view once again. The first eight measures resemble Schumann and Mendelssohn, but starting in measure 9 the rhythm in the left hand becomes almost *halling*-like.* We hear fifths, augmented fourths, and even a Lydian appoggiatura on B. Grieg has put Leipzig behind him and is on his way to the lofty heights of folk music! However, despite that exciting fact we must try to keep our balance and examine the piece as objectively as possible. The principal melody is

* See footnote, p. 13.

characterized by gentle phrasing and periodicity. First there are two one-measure periods, then a two-measure period. This is important! Articulate the counterrhythms clearly, i.e., from unaccented to accented beats in eighth-note rhythms, and even with a suggested accent on the upbeat to emphasize the syncopation (see Ex. 2.11). This pattern demonstrates Grieg's desire to characterize the motives in his own unique way.

Ex. 2.11

In measures 9–10, the harmonies of late Romanticism are juxtaposed with open fifths in the bass that Grieg derived from Norwegian folk music (see Ex. 2.12).

Ex. 2.12

Note the irregularities toward the end of the piece: in measure 58 there is a *sforzando* on F, but in the last measure the F is not accented. These two ways of handling the F refer back to similar instructions regarding the two G♯'s in the first part of No. 4 of this opus.

The open fifths in the left hand, starting in measure 9, convey a feeling of Norwegianness. The lively middle section, marked *vivo* (measure 19), sparkles with virtuosity. The *vivo* marking does not mean that it has to be played extremely fast. It is more important to have rhythmic precision, more important to have time to bring out the little embellishments, chromatic and otherwise, with which Grieg has enriched his melody. The open fifths in measure 9 are only a hint of what is to come, and in measures 41 and 42 Grieg shows us what he really has in mind. Here we get the fifths A–E and E–B simultaneously, in a direct allusion to the fiddle and the swinging rhythm of the Norwegian *slåtter*.* We can't help but feel that we are in touch with the

*See footnote, p. 13.

young Grieg, that the forces stirring within him are about to spring forth and conquer the world. Put some vigor and enthusiasm into your performance at that point. Think about *Brooklet* (Op. 62, No. 4)!

No. 6, Allegro scherzando

If *Brooklet* is concealed in No. 5, No. 6 is nothing less than the mountain stream itself. *Allegro scherzando* is playful and mischievous, but its intricacies require a little time. If you play it too fast they get lost in the shuffle. Pay careful attention to the chromatic alterations and turns. Make sure that they come out, for it will add to the characterization and rhythmic verve. It will actually make the piece *seem* faster and more whimsical.

Technically, the sixteenth notes should first be practiced as evenly as possible, with very precise fingering. To achieve a vibrant sound play these sixteenth notes with the whole finger—i.e., with the downward movement proceeding entirely from the knuckles—and with a relaxed and swinging arm. Keep your hand a bit firm on the staccato eighth notes, with bright, lively fingertips and a compact, lower-arm staccato. The piece will sound even more supple and bewitching if you play the descending chromatic run with your hand turned slightly to the left, i.e., counterclockwise (see Ex. 2.13). In the long, fast ascending runs, on the other hand, you can turn your hand slightly in a clockwise direction (see Ex. 2.14). The concluding run (measures 33–36) has a captivating double rhythm: groups of 3 + 3 notes (giving a feeling of four beats to the measure) are superimposed on an underlying 6/8 rhythm. Play it at a tempo that allows you to retain the feeling of rivalry between these two rhythmic patterns.

Ex. 2.13

The piece as a whole is a little *perpetuum mobile*, but even so it should not be played so evenly that it has the character of an etude. It is wise to start out with an even and well-defined tempo, but it is equally important musically to have dynamic shadings and tiny, imperceptible transitions—for example, in the transition in measure 14 (Ex. 2.15), where you can take a little extra time. It is not necessary for the listener to be aware of it, but the performer should feel

Ex. 2.14

Ex. 2.15

it. The same goes for the passage from measure 16 to measure 17, which is purely and simply a transition. In measures 5–8 (see Ex. 2.16), 11–12, and other similar passages, make sure that the sixteenth notes in the accompaniment remain soft and unobtrusive. Note the weak-beat accents in the left hand in measures 34 and 35.

Ex. 2.16

Play lightly and delicately. Both in this piece and in the middle section of No. 5, first practice playing steadily and evenly—quite loudly, perhaps—until you have thoroughly mastered the notes. Next, exaggerate the accents, the asymmetries, the slurs in the phrasing, and the dynamic effects. Then begin to increase the tempo gradually, perhaps with the help of a metronome. In this way the dynamic shadings and effects will seem natural and will fall into place. The same procedure should be used if you already have the piece in your repertoire and are just coming back to it. Avoid practicing it *pianissimo* and with too many nuances at first, for the result is likely to be music without a firm foundation—and a performer who lacks confidence. As a practical matter, try following this formula every day for three or four weeks and see if it works. You will be well rewarded for the time you spend on the young Grieg's early demonstration of his talents.

CHAPTER

3

Humoresques, Op. 6

The Norwegian buds that appear in the musical language of Op. 1 and in the six "poetic tone pictures" of Op. 3 burst into full flower in the *Humoresques*. Here Grieg took the plunge and composed four piano pieces based entirely on the Norwegian temperament and indigenous musical characteristics. Both the motives and the harmonies, though original, are inspired by national models. He was at the crossroads that he himself later characterized as his "only success," i.e., he chose to distance himself from his Classical-Romantic training and to compose works based entirely on the Norwegian folk-music tradition. Grieg had been inspired by an inner circle of friends, especially Rikard Nordraak, the composer of the song that was to become the Norwegian national anthem and the very embodiment of Norwegian national fervor. Grieg was caught up in Nordraak's national zeal. It was in this mood of enthusiasm for Norway that he wrote the four *Humoresques*, Op. 6, and dedicated them to Nordraak.

The title *Humoresques* presumably means "folk-like pictures." With respect to a later opus—*Pictures from Folk Life*, Op. 19—Grieg used the terms interchangeably, sometimes referring to the pieces of Op. 19 as "humoresques" instead of the title he had given them. Understanding what Grieg meant by the term "humoresques" can help the performer in the interpretation of Op. 6, for if Grieg occasionally called his *Pictures from Folk Life* "humoresques," then it also makes sense to think of the *Humoresques* of Op. 6 as some sort of "pictures from folk life".

No. 1, Tempo di Valse

Notwithstanding the title Grieg gave to this piece, its rhythm and notation are reminiscent of the mazurka in Op. 1. It is a spirited and powerful piece, but—as so often in Grieg's music—it is not altogether straightforward. Grieg sometimes notated a dotted rhythm with a dotted eighth note followed by a sixteenth note, at other times with a sixteenth rest in place of the dot. The latter pattern is of course well known from its frequent use by Chopin and others in waltzes and mazurkas, and we have already encountered it in the mazurka in Grieg's Op. 1. The tradition says that the dot can be prolonged slightly if it is notated with a rest. Technically, these passages should be played with a slight but loose elevation of the wrist: this will slow you down a little, and the rhythmic result is delightful. Grieg has indicated accents on the third beat. Thus the dotted rhythms notated with rests—most of which occur on the second beat—contrast sharply with them. The overall rhythmic picture becomes plastic and intricate, but take care that the metric pattern doesn't "wiggle away from you." You must never lose the feeling of the underlying beat.

The next section is friendlier and more flowing. In measures 11, 12, and 13 the accent is on the first beat, but they are counterbalanced by the last measure of the period (measure 14), in which both the second and the third beats are accented. In the repeat that follows, Grieg has specified accents on all three beats of measure 18! Pay close attention to the notated accents and their placement. For example: in measures 19–22 (marked *pianissimo*) there is a natural little accent on the first beat. When the passage is repeated *fortissimo* in measures 27–30 the accent is on the second beat, but it returns to the first beat in the fourth measure (see Ex. 3.1).

Ex. 3.1

The melodious passage that follows calls for fluid, horizontal phrasing so as to produce a lyrical feeling. The rhythmic element is extremely important in the *Humoresques*. You must maintain rhythmic control at all times. Don't let the music run away with you. The most important thing is to feel the basic tempo as an underpinning. The figurations must conform to that tempo. As in the *Poetic Tone Pictures*, it is wise to work toward a manner of playing that is not too rigid but that maintains the same basic tempo throughout.

The passage in G major in measures 19–20 (Ex. 3.2) has a natural tendency to get a little too slow. On the other hand, the passage in measures 51–58, leading up to the *fortissimo* in measure 59 (see Ex. 3.3), easily gets too fast. Don't play it as if you were following a metronome, but do maintain the feeling of a single underlying pulse.

Ex. 3.2

Ex. 3.3

There is something tranquil and melodious about the middle section, starting in measure 35. Note the Lydian G♯. The dynamic marking in measure 91 is *fff*, and one might ask whether *fortissimo* wouldn't be sufficient. Be that as it may, it is important for the sake of clarity to take time to bring out the echolike triplets in the left hand in measures 92, 94, 95, and 97. You also need time to execute the various dotted rhythms.

Then you come to *con fuoco*, *stringendo*, and *molto allegro*. But how fast can you play the *molto allegro* measure 103? You must have the whole piece in mind as you plan your tempos. Start with the concluding section. Work it up to as fast a tempo as you can manage while still maintaining good articulation and the contrasting rhythms between the hands. Then work backward via *stringendo* (measure 101) and *con fuoco* (measure 99) to a basic tempo, which of necessity will be somewhat slower. This tempo will be the best one for the rest of the piece. Work it out systematically in this way. Don't start out by establishing a tempo at the beginning of the piece that is too fast for you to accelerate as you approach the end. Obviously there is room for *rubato* in accordance with the performance style of the individual artist, but an outline such as that given here should be a useful point of departure for most performers. The triplets have the greatest danger of becoming indistinct. Practice, therefore, with good finger activity and with a firm feeling of key contact in each note. Practice also with an accent on the last note of the triplet group. It can even be helpful to practice with a quick break between the second and third notes of the triplet—to make you aware of the note that most easily gets lost (see Ex. 3.4).

Ex. 3.4

The section in G major, starting in measure 19, is like a peaceful body of water, but let the peace be expressed primarily in the volume, not so much in the tempo.

One especially effective passage occurs in measures 51–66, where a diabolical *pianissimo* is followed by a dramatic *crescendo* to *fortissimo* in measure 59 and *sforzando* in the trills (measures 63–66). The movement from the first to the second measure of this bewitching intermezzo should be made with a relatively low wrist on G, then raise it on the D after the bar line. Prepare for the downbeat in measure 52 by putting the fifth and fourth fingers together as you move from the last note of measure 51 (see Ex. 3.5).

Ex. 3.5

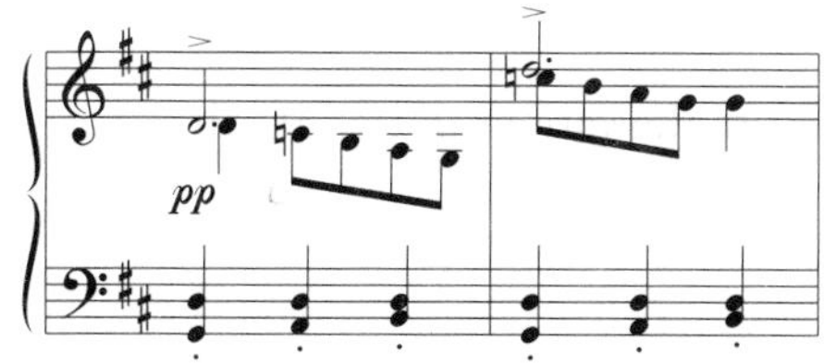

The passage should be played without the damper pedal, unadorned; the soft pedal may be used sparingly. The double stops in measures 59–63 are intricate. Practice them with two fingers held down; i.e., hold the interval E–A with 5–3 and play the D–F♯ several times with 4–2. Then reverse the procedure, holding down 4–2 while repeatedly playing 5–3. Lift the fingers, but keep the arm loose. As you are playing, remember to loosen up whenever there is a rest. Accent the first beat the most, i.e., use the free weight of your arm. The trills should be started with the whole arm *sforzando* in order to achieve a powerful effect. The trill may be played somewhat less forcefully than the attack, however. In the recapitulation it is possible to have a little more rubato in measure 67ff. than in the opening. Note what happens in the left hand: the music gradually becomes denser and more elaborate until, in the *finale*, it imitates the triplets. It is the left hand that is in control: it leads, and the right hand follows.

No. 2, Tempo di Menuetto ed energico

Grieg wrote two versions of this piece. The original is in G♯ minor; the later one is in A minor, and is easier to sight-read. The G♯-minor version is more colorful, and, by comparison, the piece sounds tame in A minor. The Danish edition of the piece, published by Horneman & Erslev in A minor, has a footnote reading, "Should preferably be played in G♯ minor." In Grieg's next opus—the *Piano Sonata in E Minor*—the third movement is marked *a la menuetto* and is akin to the present piece. As in the sonata, however, this is not a minuet in the Classical sense. It is a familiar designation that Grieg borrowed and applied to a piece of music that has more in common with the sagas than with courtly ballrooms. In both the sonata and this *Humoresque* it may be advisable to maintain a slightly broader tempo than would be appropriate for an ordinary minuet. The music will sound more solemn, more somber, more "old Norse." The theme is derived from the folk song "Alle mann hadde fota" (All men had legs), and Grieg has developed it in a masterful way.

In his preface to the *Norwegian Peasant Dances*, Op. 72, Grieg wrote that he was trying to "raise these works of the people to an artistic level." The same may be said of the present piece: a folk song, which in its original form is very ordinary, is placed in a brilliant setting and made into something beautiful and significant. The piece is simple but varied, with rather heavy octaves in the bass and *leggiero* triplets. Sporadic imitations, *staccato* passages, and the two chords marked *pianissimo* in measures 40–41 and 83–84 provide perspective. It is as if we are hearing a sound behind the real *Humoresque*, music from a distant world—a world that has vanished into the mists of time. Imagine an opera where the chorus is concealed behind the stage. Suddenly the choir can be heard in the distance offering a commentary upon what has transpired. This may sound silly "off stage," but "onstage" it makes sense.

Pay special attention to the chord-playing in this piece, maintaining good precision in the harmonies as well as in the melodic line. The phrasing should be governed by the accent mark on the second beat of measure 2: the first beat leads to the accented note like a long upbeat. The same pattern continues through measure 4. Then follows a long period, extending from measure 5 to the second beat of measure 8. A similar period occurs in the next section (measures 13–15), but at its conclusion (measure 16), beats one and two are both accented. Measures 17–20 are more animated, and these four successive measures have accent marks on beats one and three. In measures 21–28 there are accents only in the left hand, independent of a free figuration in the right hand marked *dolce*. In measures 29 and 30 Grieg has indicated accents on the first beat, but in the next two measures the accent is on the second beat. This pattern is repeated in measures 33–36, and then comes the imitation section with different accents in the left and right hands—on the second beat in the right and the third in the left.

What a complicated maze of accents to remember! Pay close attention to them so that from the very beginning you capture the bouncy asymmetry that Grieg has built into the phrasing. The resulting jerkiness brings the piece to life in a way that an ordinary pattern of accents would not. Starting in measure 17, keep a movable, leading, and pliant arm. Be careful about the rhythm at the micro level: make sure that the triplets are precise relative to the eighth notes in measure 19 and to the dotted rhythm in measures 21–22 (see Ex. 3.6).

Ex. 3.6

Two chords played as if from afar are followed by a lovely duet between the hands, in thirds with slurs (see Ex. 3.7).

Ex. 3.7

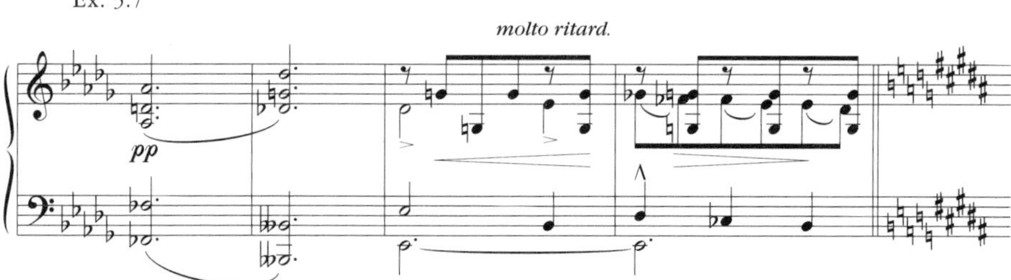

The next section (measure 44ff.) has an eighth-note pattern in the left hand. Make the *crescendo* as even and gradual as you can, leading with the right hand. The descending octaves in measures 56 and 57 should be as smooth and "doughy" and rounded as possible. The repeat is identical, but you might want to vary the expression a bit the second time.

The Coda is marked *pianissimo* and should be a little lighter. Play the accompaniment in the left hand with a light skipping motion (see Ex. 3.8).

Ex. 3.8

The eighth-note chords in measures 107 and 109 should be played as precisely as possible and should be carefully coordinated with the sixteenth-note tremolo in the left hand (see Ex. 3.9). The last G♯ in the left hand tends to get lost, but obviously Grieg intended for it to be heard. Notwithstanding the precision and the *pianissimo* dynamics, one should be able to hear the imitation that passes from the right hand to the left hand and then back to the right hand in measures 107–109.

Ex. 3.9

At the end the music just dies away, *quasi pizzicato* (see Ex. 3.10).

Ex. 3.10

No. 3, Allegretto con grazia

This lovely, captivating little piece could almost be called a "hit" tune. It is the most frequently played of the four *Humoresques* and one of the most popular pieces in Grieg's entire corpus. Because the piece is so well known, it is advisable to work out the overall sonorities and phrasing with great care. Try to produce a slender sound, which is produced with a light, floating, movable arm and an open hand. The phrasing is characterized by discreet, clever little *rubatos*. The endings of the phrases are of prime importance, i.e., each phrase must be allowed to conclude naturally: it must be given time to breathe, time to catch its breath. Indeed, care in ending the phrases should be your chief concern in this piece. Thus, for example, in the first four measures one should first establish a steady crescendo, then create a falling line in measures 3–4 leading to an "exhale" on the last quarter note in measure 4. A mathematician would say that the end of the phrase is lengthened slightly, but to a musician it is just a natural rounding-off.

The ingratiating theme (see Ex. 3.11) could have been an oboe solo—or perhaps you could think of it as something that might be played on a *lur*, an indigenous Norwegian instrument similar to an alpenhorn. The theme is followed by an apt reply (see Ex. 3.12).

Ex. 3.11

As in many of the *Lyric Pieces*, various passages are repeated without alteration. Compared with Opp. 1 and 3, this practice marks a forward step

Ex. 3.12

in Grieg's mastery of the folk-music idiom. It is a move toward greater authenticity, not a sign of impoverishment. Although the use of exact repetitions corresponds to the character of the folk music from which Grieg derived his inspiration, it poses a challenge for the interpreter. You have to be creative, to interpret the passage a little differently each time, just as a singer would subtly alter the melody with each stanza of a song to fit the mood of the text. A verbatim repetition of a passage should never be *exactly* like a previous iteration of the passage but should introduce subtle rhythmic and dynamic differences to heighten interest.

The middle section in B minor, measures 17–24, is marked *fortissimo*, and the same dynamic marking occurs again in measures 38–39. These passages should not be played too loudly or brashly, however. Rather make them intense. In practice it works best to think in terms of an intense *forte* rather than to pound away *fortissimo*. If the music gets too wild, its basic character changes, and then all is lost.

The conclusions of the phrases are always important. Consider a few examples. The last beat in measure 4 is long: hold it out; similarly in measure 6; and in measure 8 lengthen the last chord by half a beat. Measures 24 and 26 have phrase-ending rests; take time to hear the sixteenth rest in measure 24 (see Ex. 3.13). The eighth rest in measure 26 is twice as long: take time to hear it as well (see Ex. 3.14).

Ex. 3.13

The rests become even more numerous toward the end of the piece; the next to the last measure has a rest that is equivalent to three and a half eighth notes. Count it out to the very end, all the while maintaining an attentive, expectant attitude. The sequence in measures 34–36, on the other hand,

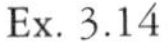
Ex. 3.14

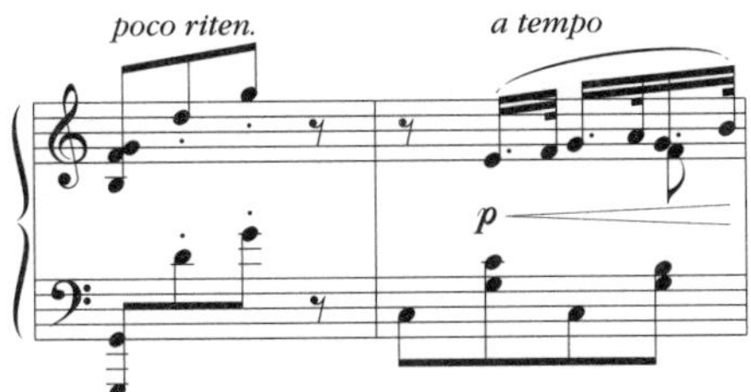

should be treated as a unified whole (see Ex. 3.15) and played so as to produce a long line, in contrast to the snippets that have preceded it.

Ex. 3.15

The modulation in measures 29–31 (see Ex. 3.16) lends itself to varying *rubato* each time it is played. The first time through you might create a long line, i.e., understate the modulation. The second time, do just the opposite: emphasize the chromatic progression B–B♭–A in the tenor voice (delayed resolution to A), and take time to do so.

Ex. 3.16

The coda has a pentatonic ring that is reminiscent of the *langeleik*, an indigenous Norwegian folk instrument similar to a zither (see Ex. 3.17). Play it clearly, with a hornlike accent on the A in the left hand. In the third measure from the end, play with a mischievous, graceful flair—melodiously, but with an almost *staccato* touch on the final eighth note. At the very least, avoid extending it into the rest.

In approaching this *Humoresque*, work out the left hand, then work out the piece as a whole. Make a clear distinction between dotted rhythms and undotted eighth and sixteenth notes. Be clear about the places where the rhythm is dotted and where it isn't (see Ex. 3.18).

Ex. 3.17

Ex. 3.18

It is important that the grace notes not be turned into thirty-second notes. First play the melody without the grace notes; then add the grace notes, playing them almost simultaneously with the notes to which they are attached. In measure 2, for example, play the D and the C almost together. When this starts to feel natural, separate them slightly. The point of practicing this way is to make the grace note short enough.

There is a "question and answer" feeling between the principal theme and the secondary theme. In general the individual phrases can be played off against each other in a sprightly manner—producing, if one is lucky, a feeling of flirtation between the two. Let there be coquetry between the phrases! The result will be truly charming, and your audiences will love it. The subtleties are achieved in the first instance through varied finger articulation rather than a too-heavy touch. It requires a lot of work, but it all pays off in the end. The key is *subtlety.*

No. 4, Allegro alla burla

The *Allegro alla burla* brings Op. 6 to a rousing conclusion. The *alla burla* (in the manner of a burlesque) implies reckless abandon, almost wildness. The tempo should be a little faster than in No. 1, and the concluding section—the coda—should be the most virtuosic of all. It is important to think in this all-inclusive way if one is performing all four *Humoresques* as a set. In addition to planning the tempo variations within No. 1 you must be aware of the differences between the *finales* in No. 1 and No. 4: the latter should be more brilliant in both tempo and power. That means that in No. 4 you can bring to bear all the technique, clarity, rhythmic and dynamic intensity—indeed, all the bravura—you can muster.

No. 4 calls for careful attention to tempo in its own right. How fast can you handle the last seven measures of the piece—*fortissimo con fuoco*—without sacrificing clarity and control? The answer will determine your tempo in the concluding measures. Establish the tempo of the *più Allegro* section (measure 134), then the *finale* as a whole and the rest of the piece. The *Allegro alla burla* at the start will necessarily be somewhat slower than the *Più Allegro*. If you are not satisfied with the main tempo that follows from this procedure—i.e., if you think it is too slow—the only recourse is to practice some more! Work on the *finale* evenly and regularly. Using a metronome, practice it both slow and fast, keeping the arm loose and relaxed. It will be only a matter of time until you can handle a faster tempo. Then go back to the beginning, *Allegro alla burla*. Put some animation into the left hand. Make the half notes diabolically *tenuto* and the quarter notes as short as lightning (see Ex. 3.19).

Ex. 3.19

The rhythm of the principal theme is very important. Articulate it as clearly as possible with the fingers. It will help to pull the forearm slightly on each quarter note. Measures 3–5 lead up to an accent on the first beat of measure 6, and the next four-measure period is constituted the same way. But then comes the burlesque: one measure has the accent on the third beat, the next on the second (see Ex. 3.20). The accents continue thereafter to be hilariously irregular, sometimes on the third beat, sometimes on the first, etc. The overall effect is music that is animated and energetic.

Ex. 3.20

In the delightful middle section (measures 21–38) it is as if one were looking up from the dance and the noise, from the trivialities of everyday life. You see the landscape, the placid lake where everything is reflected as in a painting. Use a light, graceful style, emphasizing the upper voice. The tempo should be swaying, supple, devoid of accents—finally! The danger here is that you may get lost in dreams and allow the tempo to get too slow. An asymmetrical division of the musical line is followed by a staccato section that slowly becomes more and more robust (see Ex. 3.21).

Ex. 3.21

In No. 4, as in No. 1, it is wise to keep the tempo within certain limits throughout the piece. Just as the B♭-major section (starting in measure 18) has a tendency to lag, the somewhat chromatic run in measure 37—perhaps because of the hemiolas—tends to go too fast. These are the two extremes so far as tempo hazards are concerned. A conductor would hold the performer in check, but a solo pianist has to be both conductor and performer at the same time. Practically speaking, the slow note values must set the pace and keep everything orderly, and the eighth notes—which may have a tendency to speed—must line up accordingly.

Even when the music is marked *fortissimo*, it is important to pay attention to Grieg's phrasing: measure 126 is marked *fortissimo*, and the following measure is *fortissimo* with three accents. The accent marks in measure 127 are intentional—not a slip of the pen—for this measure is followed by one in which there are no accent marks and then by one in which these instructions appear again. This discussion of accents may sound pedantic and make for tedious reading, but in my experience in concert and with students the piece easily lapses into excessive evenness—sometimes because it is played with a steady stream of accents, at other times because there are no accents at all. The features that give life, vivacity, and a burlesque quality to this piece—indeed, give it its distinctive character—are these rhythmic dislocations and their irregular but plastic placement. Because it is difficult to memorize them in addition to the notes and the dynamics, it is all the more important to note them so carefully that they force their way into your consciousness. They are of critical importance for the shaping of the piece.

The section marked *pianissimo* in measures 55–59 can be very effective, but one must be careful to maintain its clarity. Watch the articulation of the long held notes in the middle voices. Spend a lot of time practicing what Liszt called "tied exercises," i.e., hold G–D and strike C more actively. This exercise will get your fingers used to articulating even in an uncomfortable position. After you have achieved a fast and solid mastery of the piece you can go on to feel the resting point in the middle voice. That, in turn, gives freedom to the other fingers, just as putting all your weight on one leg produces a feeling of lightness and freedom in the other. This technical mind-set can help you articulate well despite the uncomfortable hand position required by this difficult passage. Despite its difficulty, the *pianissimo* section is very effective, and in the *crescendo* that follows, you have an opportunity to express your temperament to the hilt in clearly articulated triads and irregularly placed accents. Throughout this part it is best to play with a loose arm and an open hand (see Ex. 3.22).

Ex. 3.22

The B♭-major section (starting in measure 68) is as distinctively Norwegian as any music ever written, with a seductive *springar*[*] rhythm in the left

[*]See footnote, p. 13.

hand and inverted pedal points in the right (see Ex. 3.23). Thereafter the music dies away into a lucid, dry *pianissimo*. The transition, in dotted half notes marked *pianissimo* and *ritenuto*, is especially exciting and is somewhat similar to the *pianissimo* chordal passage near the end of *Humoresques* No. 2.

Ex. 3.23

In the recapitulation, the middle section, starting in measure 101, is in G major instead of B♭ major. Some editions call for the right hand to be played an octave higher, yielding a light and captivating sound. To put the sonority of the whole piece in a broader perspective, think of the high notes in the right hand in contrast to the low-register notes in the left hand in measures 85–86.

The bravura character of the concluding *Più allegro* section perhaps deserves a little extra attention: *staccato* in the left-hand quarter notes, then slurs and eighth-note and triplet figurations. The right hand has clearly marked little slurs over 2 + 2 eighth notes to begin with—but note the pedal point in the left hand and the inverted pedal point on D in the right hand. Make these pedal points as *tenuto* as possible despite the articulation. Grieg calls for accents on the first beats in measures 135, 136, and 137. Then come two measures without accents, then four measures with an accent on the first beat of every other measure. Measure 144 is marked *fortissimo con fuoco*, and in measures 145 and 147 the accent is on the second beat. At the end, Grieg calls for an accent on each quarter note in the left hand, thereby increasing the dynamic and rhythmic excitement in a brilliant final flourish.

The *Humoresques* are a thoroughly delightful, audience-pleasing set. When played clearly and rhythmically—with style, drive, and entertaining accenting—they are a success. The fundamental rhythms set the tone, and the others add a bit of spice. To perform onstage requires strong character on the part of the pianist. Don't be too "nice" when you play these pieces: a good dose of crankiness—unfortunately, perhaps—is better than a meek and mild nature. Practice to gain the sense of security and discipline that will enable you to do your best. When all of this falls into place, playing the *Humoresques* is sheer delight.

CHAPTER

4

Funeral March for Rikard Nordraak

Rikard Nordraak, who is best known around the world as the composer of the Norwegian national anthem, was one of the most ardent representatives of Norwegian nationalism. Grieg, like many others, felt that the death of this exceptionally talented young man from tuberculosis at the age of twenty-three was a national tragedy. There had been every reason to expect that Nordraak would become a composer, a truly significant artist. Grieg wrote the *Funeral March* in 1866 the day he received word of his friend's passing. Thus it is not an occasional work in the usual sense of the word, but a composition that grew out of a genuine, spontaneous feeling. The composition was so much a part of Grieg that he requested that it be performed at his own funeral as well. And it was.

Try to create a sagalike atmosphere in your performance. The melodies have an Old Norse flavor—not exactly the same as in *Ballad* (*Lyric Pieces* Op. 65, No. 5), although certain parts of it are similar. Make the rhythm as precise as possible and keep the chords as coordinated as you can in order to achieve the dignity that the piece requires.

Measures 1–2 (Ex. 4.1) are part of the melody, but the rhythmic pattern is equally important. Measures 3–4—which are in C major, in contrast to the preceding A minor—can be given a somewhat more melodic tinge. Measures 5–6 could be still more *cantabile* in the upper register (see Ex. 4.2).

Ex. 4.1

A dramatic, anguished theme enters in measure 9—a theme that expresses deep commitment, feeling, and involvement. Employing bold harmonies, modulations, and chords, Grieg attempted to give musical expression to the national sorrow over Nordraak's passing, but at the same time to commemorate the perspectives and the possibilities of this rich talent (see Ex. 4.3).

Ex. 4.3

The middle section, in A major, has a forlorn, Norwegian-sounding melody with medieval chords, dominants with minor triads and mediant chord progressions (see Ex. 4.4). This section concludes with an almost plagal cadence (see Ex. 4.5). A majestic fanfare creates contrast. Imitate trumpets and horns (see Ex. 4.6).

The touch in the first part of the funeral march should above all be precise, whereas the melodic passages should be somewhat smoother while still conveying a sense of profound seriousness. The tremolo figures are written out, and they should be played exactly as written. This is much better than treating them as ordinary tremolos. The tremolo in measure 10 (see Ex. 4.7) may be played with both hands, thereby achieving a more impressive dynamic effect.

Ex. 4.4

In measures 11–12, the right hand has a passage with a stirring sound like that of brass instruments. Try to keep the melody *legato* in contrast to the insistence of the lower voice, marked as it is by sixteenth notes, eighth rests, and silence between the eighth notes. Measures 19–24 may be given a more articulated character, after which there is still another fanfare. Strike the keys with firm fingertips and a live arm. Maintain strict rhythm, absolute *staccato* and *marcato*, and complete silence in the rests in measures 24, 26, and 28. These features give Grieg's *Funeral March* its awesome solemnity (see Ex. 4.8) and effectively prepare the way for the beautiful melody that appears in unison octaves in measure 29. The accompaniment should be short enough that it dies away before the *legato* line in the right and left hands moves forward (see Ex. 4.9).

Ex. 4.8

Ex. 4.9

At measure 33, the character changes to that of a straightforward, homophonic work. Play it pliantly, sensitively, velvety, *dolce*, perhaps with a gentle emphasis on the lower voice to imitate the sound of an organ (see Exx. 4.10a and b).

Ex. 4.10a

The repetition of the beginning, starting with measure 37, is identical except for the last measure, where the tremolo continues until it dies away. At this point there are two esthetic possibilities (as is also the case in *Wedding Day at Troldhaugen*—which in other respects is very different musically—as well as in *March of the Dwarfs* [Op. 54, No. 3], *Halling from the Fairy Hill* [Op. 72,

Ex. 4.10b

No. 4], and *Røtnams-Knut* [Op. 72, No. 7]): you may play the repeat exactly like the first iteration—to give the architectonic impression of a perfectly symmetrical archway—or you can opt for a subjective expression the second time. If you choose the latter course, make sure that measure 12 is only *ffz* and reserve the *fffz* for measure 48. Since Grieg notated the dynamics this way do you suppose that he intended the repeat to be more intense? Whatever he may have had in mind, *Funeral March for Rikard Nordraak* is great music.

CHAPTER

5

Piano Sonata in E Minor, Op. 7

This youthful work is marked by *joie de vivre*—indeed, by the giddy joy of a young man who has just gotten engaged to be married. Pianists planning to perform it should be in a positive frame of mind and should approach it with enthusiasm in their hearts as well as in their fingers. There are many beautiful lyrical passages in addition to the brilliant ones, so one cannot get very far with this piece without a sensitive spirit and a subtle touch. That is always true of Grieg's music.

An extant wax recording made by Grieg himself requires us to undertake some thorough technical preliminary work. Grieg was at his best in this piece, playing the last movement in a truly virtuosic manner—a rousing, rhythmic performance! The most technically demanding parts are the *finale* of the first movement and the middle section of the last. I recommend that you spend considerable time each day practicing these passages so that you don't falter during the performance.

In the *Allegro molto* section of the first movement it might be advisable to use the left hand for some of the notes. It depends on the size of your hands and whether one hand gets in the way of the other (see Ex. 5.1). There are also a couple of places in the fourth movement where the right hand can come to the assistance of the left (see Ex. 5.2).

The double stops in thirds in measures 146–47 of the fourth movement

Ex. 5.1

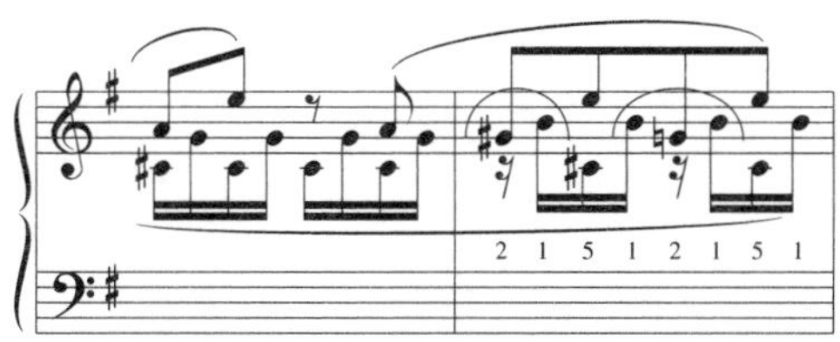

Ex. 5.2

work best with a bit of arm support, i.e., a slight movement of the arm (see Ex. 5.3). In measures 154–55, try to achieve independence between the hands. Be sure to produce a good *legato* in the left hand (see Ex. 5.4). In the

Ex. 5.3

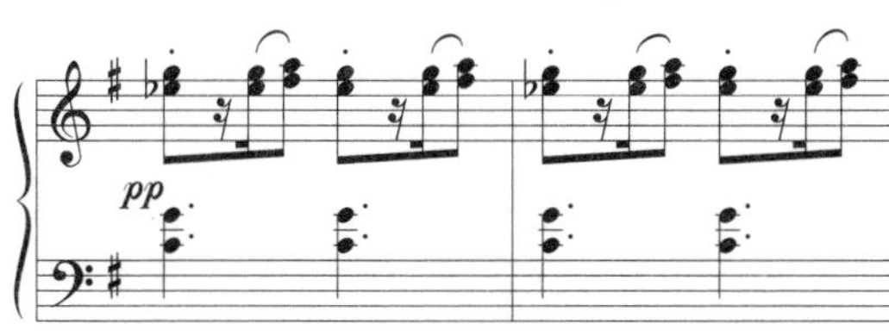

Ex. 5.4

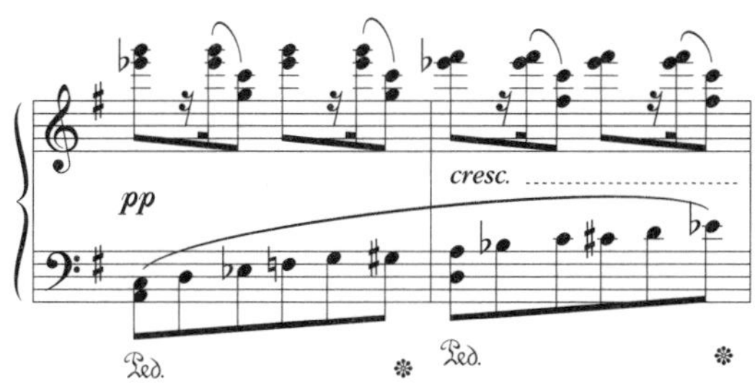

left-hand trills in measures 162 and 163 it is a good idea to move the wrist slightly to keep it loose (see Ex. 5.5). The figure in the right hand in measure 166 easily becomes indistinct; to avoid that, lift the fourth finger after playing the first note of the figure (see Ex. 5.6).

In the most difficult passage (measures 182–85) it is a good idea to have a little wrist action relative to the keyboard. Relax after each chord! In the left hand in measure 182 I recommend the fingering indicated in Ex. 5.7.

Very often one hears the sonata played quite well except for technical deficiencies in these two places. Plan to practice them in such a way that they are progressively mastered.

First Movement, Allegro moderato

The beginning of the first movement (measures 1–4) calls for a singing *legato*. Let it sound dreamy and romantic. Make the first three measures lead to the B in measure 4 (see Ex. 5.8). Be careful to keep the volume of the lowest bass notes in balance with the sound of the whole: the responsibility for this rests entirely with the fifth finger (see Ex. 5.9).

Maintain rhythmic precision and full-sounding chords. All the notes of each chord should be of the same volume (see Ex. 5.10).

Note that Grieg sometimes calls for an accent on the last part of the measure (see Ex. 5.11a), sometimes on the last part of the phrase (see Ex.

5.11b). It is important to observe these accent markings in order to achieve a plastic phrasing—lest you start to sound like a hurdy-gurdy.

Ex. 5.8

Ex. 5.9

Ex. 5.10

Exx. 5.11a and b

The second theme, which enters in measure 50, is like a lullaby. Its last two measures may be played more softly than the preceding ones. The long, sustained D in the left hand must come out clearly, however—like a horn sounding in the distance (see Ex. 5.12).

Ex. 5.12

The passage marked *piano dolce* in measures 66–73 should be played lightly and with as smooth a *legato* as possible. Once again, be careful to keep the notes played by the fifth finger in the left hand in balance with the rest (see Ex. 5.13).

Ex. 5.13

One is reminded of the words of Danish composer Carl Nielsen: "The accompaniment should be like the water in relation to the boat. It is always softer than the melody, but it carries it and follows along as the melody rises and falls." It must not be too loud, but neither should there be a great difference between the volume of the melody and that of the accompaniment.

The tender, beautiful opening theme is restated in major, grandly and majestically. It is extremely important to maintain precise rhythm in the accompaniment, with as exact a relationship as possible between sixteenth notes and triplets, so the music does not become episodic.

The rhythm in measures 94–114 can be a bit more flexible, however. Establish a *parlando* between the melodies in the two hands (see Ex. 5.14).

The playing in measures 118–26 must be as crystal clear and transparent as possible. Both the six notes of each group in the right hand and the tremolo in the left hand should be heard. At times the parallel sixths can almost sound like the wind howling around the wall of the house. Isn't that a nice goal toward which to work? (See Ex. 5.15.)

Note the *subito piano* in measure 130, before the first theme returns in 6/8.

Ex. 5.14

Ex. 5.15

This time it can be as tender as you please—the chord is a Neapolitan subdominant—as you approach the capricious *leggiero* passage that follows (see Ex. 5.16).

Ex. 5.16

The reappearance of the "lullaby" theme in measure 175 poses a new pianistic challenge, namely, to present the melody in a clear and carefree manner without burying the *bourdon* notes. And it adds to the excitement of the piece if the *Allegro Molto* in the Coda (measures 191–229) really is faster than the rest of the movement. It is a buzzing, fast-moving little *finale*, and it is wise to plan the whole movement so that the ending can be faster than what preceded it. The beginning of the movement is marked *Allegro moderato*. The contrast between the beginning and the end appears to be deliberate.

Second Movement: Andante molto

Can you imagine a more beautiful melody than the folk tune that appears at the beginning of the second movement? It calls for a strict *legato* in the right hand, with smooth motion in the arm, a loose wrist, a feeling of caressing the keys.

Listen to the accompaniment in measures 5–8 in order to get the rest of the section to hang together. It should be even but soft. To attune your ears to this evenness, practice it a little louder than it ought to be at first (see Ex. 5.17).

Ex. 5.17

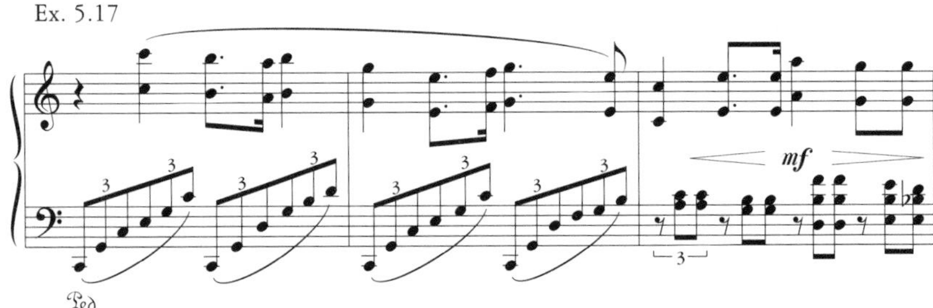

In measures 9–17, marked *L'istesso tempo* in 12/8, it seems natural to use a bit of *crescendo* in the sequences—even though Grieg has indicated *fortissimo* throughout. At times he was generous in his use of *fortissimo* markings. Perhaps he was thinking more of inner intensity than outward bravado. Be that as it may, the attack here should not be percussive.

Paint the phrases in the right hand in measures 17–20 in response to the changing harmonies. The left hand, meanwhile, can imitate a horn (see Ex. 5.18). An exquisitely charming little dance appears in measures 21–23. A bit of arm support here will help to keep the double stops precise (see Ex. 5.19). Play the descending arpeggio figure in measure 25 with both hands in order to keep it completely even (see Ex. 5.20).

Ex. 5.18

Ex. 5.19

Ex. 5.20

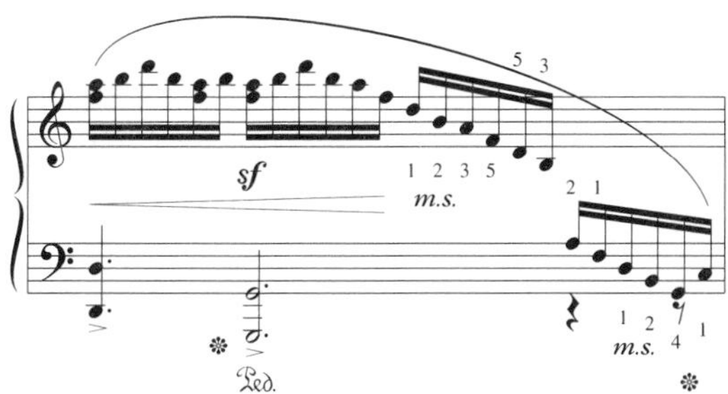

Measures 26–30, marked *fortissimo*, must not be *too* loud. You may want to preserve a *cantabile* sound. Measure 30, *a tempo*, is marked *pianissimo*, but you may wish to move into it gradually. In the first edition of the sonata Grieg had written *fff* at this point. Then he changed it to *pianissimo*, presumably because that would create equally great—perhaps even greater—excitement. In any case, the *pianissimo* occurs very suddenly, and we need a little time (see Ex. 5.21).

Ex. 5.21

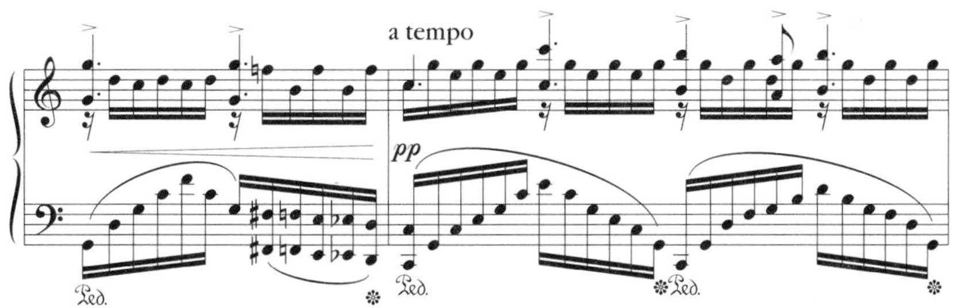

We also need time for the shift to the upper mediant key of E♭ major in measure 31. Play the sixteenth-note descending chromatic passages orchestrally. Their importance derives primarily from their effect as part of a larger whole (see Ex. 5.22).

Ex. 5.22

In the transition to the Coda in measures 38–39, try to create an even *crescendo* and *diminuendo*. Many performers think of the rising and setting sun as a visual picture of what they are trying to achieve. Others say that *crescendo*

is talent and *diminuendo* is art. However you manage it, be sure to pay a lot of attention to the *diminuendo*.

I recommend that the bass notes in the Coda (starting in measure 40) be played firmly. They are few in number and of relatively long note values, and they must be loud enough to support the rest of the notes. In measures 41–42, try to achieve the correct rhythmic relationship between four notes in the right hand versus six in the left (see Ex. 5.23). From measure 40—marked *a tempo*—to the end of the movement, the eighth notes should be played as evenly as possible.

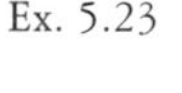

The eight chords in measures 49–52—marked *sempre diminuendo*—are a pianistic challenge. They create breathless excitement and a marvelous effect if each of them is given a unique sonority within the context of a steady diminuendo. It is important, therefore, that the first chord in the series not be too soft. An old rule of interpretation states that *diminuendo* means loud and *crescendo* means soft. "Not too much, not too little" is another rule of thumb. So: start out loud, but not too loud. The concluding arpeggio can be divided up in such a way as to maximize the contrast between the bass and the upper voices (see Ex. 5.24).

Ex. 5.24

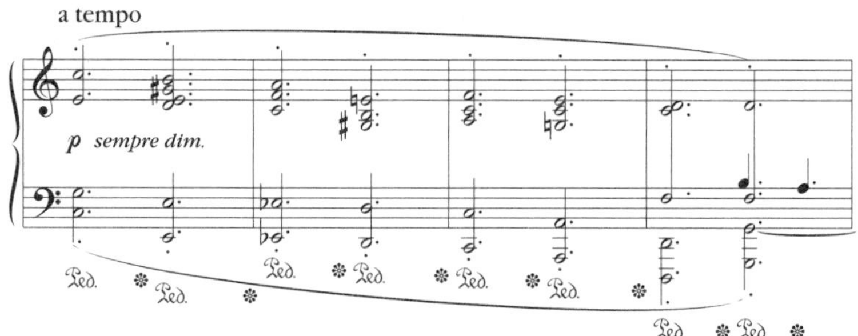

Third Movement: Alla menuetto ma poco lento

This movement has an "Old Norse" character, as if Grieg wanted to give us a little glimpse of an ancient drama, to pull it out of the past, recreate it in his own time, and unite it with a slow dance. The blending of moods is surpassingly beautiful. The movement should be played *piano* with precise chords, completely even triplets, and with as steady a *crescendo* as possible (see Ex. 5.25), and then an equally steady *diminuendo* (see Ex. 5.26). To produce this *diminuendo*, the fingertips have to be somewhat firm. Let the accompaniment lead the way, evenly but softly. Gradually it comes to the fore and more or less dominates the sound picture. The evenness of the accompaniment creates the line.

Ex. 5.25

Ex. 5.26

Measures 40–48, in E major, are brightened by the high notes, and the rests help to define the mood. The result can be absolutely charming (see Ex. 5.27).

Ex. 5.27

The quadruplet figure in G♯ minor (measure 56) may be phrased as an upbeat.

To get a completely organic *ritardando* in measures 90–91, think triplets all the way through, including the final rest. The decelerating triplets take us directly into the *finale* (see Ex. 5.28).

Fourth Movement: Finale. Molto allegro

The last movement is technically challenging, and it must be practiced thoroughly and for a long time if it is to match the level of the other movements. Only through complete mastery of the technical difficulties can the musical dimension shine through. A fast tempo, rhythmic vitality, and an exuberant forward thrust are the keys to its success.

Ex. 5.28

The rhythm of the first theme is extremely important (see Ex. 5.29). Be sure to get it right from the very beginning. The same pattern returns again and again throughout the movement. It is one of the principal ingredients of its rhythmic bounce—and one rarely hears it played well. Younger players should grasp the opportunity to learn it right!

Ex. 5.29

The use of the pedal in measures 1–7 is largely a matter of taste. I personally prefer to use the damper pedal only on the chord in measure 6 (see Ex. 5.30).

Ex. 5.30

When playing the dotted figure in measure 7 and elsewhere, take advantage of the rests to relax the wrist. The trill in the left hand in measures 23–26 easily becomes cramped; it is a good idea to move the wrist a bit while playing it in order to maintain some degree of looseness. Think of six notes, not twelve.

The last movement is a brilliant pianistic crowning of the entire work, one that gives the performer an opportunity to inflame the audience's enthusiasm in a most exciting way. The movement is not uniformly dazzling, however: the second theme is like a faint memory or reminder of something distant and all but forgotten (see Ex. 5.31). This soft *legato pianissimo* gives the movement an extra perspective. Some of the intervals in the left hand may be difficult if your hand is small; in that case, play the circled notes in Ex. 5.32 with the right hand.

Ex. 5.31

Ex. 5.32

Note the rhythm in the *pesante* theme in measures 106–108 (see Ex. 5.33). It contrasts with measures 305–307, where the rhythm is duple (see Ex. 5.34).

Ex. 5.33

Ex. 5.34

Let us look once more at a simple accompaniment figure. A fine percussive effect results if all the notes really can be heard (see Ex. 5.35).

Ex. 5.35

The development of this movement is extremely difficult. It is the acid test of a performer's ability and requires extra careful preparation.

One can achieve some variation in sonority by coloring the second theme somewhat with the right hand when it is in C major (Ex. 5.31) and with the left hand when it is in E major (see Ex. 5.36).

Ex. 5.36

To make a successful approach to the Coda, it is best to listen carefully to the accompaniment, letting it slow down gradually (see Ex. 5.37). In the Coda think in terms of eighth notes throughout in order to maintain an inner feeling, an internal resistance to racing into harmonies that are filled with suspense.

Ex. 5.37

When we come to the last ten measures, onstage it is easy to think, "Fortunately, it is over!" But suddenly the three-note figures in the left hand disappear (see Ex. 5.38). So practice those three-note figures extra solidly and powerfully, extra clearly and precisely—and don't relax the tension until the sound of the last chord has died away (see Ex. 5.39).

Ex. 5.38

Ex. 5.39

CHAPTER

6

Piano Concerto in A Minor, Op. 16

Now we come to the flagship, the composition in the armada of Norwegian music that is in a class by itself. Grieg's A-minor Concerto is one of the most frequently played piano concertos in the world. In Norway it has been played constantly ever since it was written. All pianists who aspire to professional careers must have it in their repertoires, and Norwegian pianists are not taken seriously until they can deliver a virtuosic performance of this great work. It has drawn attention to the piano tradition and has had an extremely positive effect on the level of piano playing in Grieg's homeland.

The Grieg Concerto occupies a natural place among the great Romantic concertos, such as those by Schumann and Tchaikovsky, but Norwegians feel that it is rather special. Its lyricism and uniquely Nordic flavor make it different from the heavier Romanticism of central Europe. Of course it is warm, brilliant, and majestic—but it is also folkish. All these elements must be present if the Concerto is to come to life in all its glory.

The Lyrical Dimension

To get acquainted with the lyrical strain that permeates the Concerto, first work with the middle section of the third movement (see Ex. 6.1). This section is in many ways the very backbone of the entire concerto, the lyrical high point. The melody sounds like a beautiful folk tune, but that is not what

Ex. 6.1

it is. Grieg composed it in the *style* of a folk tune. He once said that his only true accomplishment was to turn his back on German Romanticism, to distance himself from what he had learned in Leipzig in order to focus on something distinctively Norwegian. The middle of the third movement of the concerto is a particularly successful example of what he was talking about.

Lyrical means "full of feeling," but with light sonority and gentle phrasing. Do not make the phrases heavy, but let them soar. Use the high points to expand the breadth rather than simply to play loudly. The music should reflect something of the Nordic summer sky, which is seldom leaden; it is more pastel than the sky at more southerly latitudes. And very often the Norwegian landscape, dominated as it is by countless fjords and inland lakes, is reflected in water. Sky, landscape, water—these are some of the elements that you can depict musically through appropriate use of pedal and overtone effects. They are surely what Grieg had in mind near the end of the middle section of the third movement (see Ex. 6.2).

Ex. 6.2

Lyricism also dominates the scene in the opening of the second movement, as if something is enticing us to follow along. The music is not that of a true *kulokk*, a traditional Norwegian cattle call, but to Norwegian ears it sounds very much like one.

Technical Aspects

The concerto also has many passages of technical brilliance. Grieg was a great admirer of Franz Liszt, and in both sonority and structure his Concerto has more in common with Liszt than with Chopin. The A-minor Concerto must never be played in a Chopinesque manner, or it will fall apart and begin to sound like salon music. Try instead to feel that it is based on Norwegian folklore and Norwegian lyricism, perhaps with a subtle allusion to Liszt.

The Concerto is a bravura piece. Some passages are easy to play, others quite demanding. Obviously, one must spend a good deal of time working on the technical aspects of the piece before performing it. Much could be said about how and in what manner the intricate passages ought to be practiced. I will limit myself to saying that everything must be practiced thoroughly, everything must be completely and securely in hand. Countless passages must be practiced note by note, measure by measure, rhythmically, one hand at a time. Some things must be practiced for many years before one begins to achieve the brilliant sound that the piece deserves.

Young people who plan to become pianists would do well to start working on the Concerto at an early age. That makes sense, for Grieg was a young man himself—just 25 years old—when he wrote it. He was madly in love with his beloved Nina, giddily happy—and he was a young genius. Young aspiring pianists should tackle Grieg's Concerto even if it seems a bit difficult. It is a concerto that should begin and end with infectious joy, and it is a great advantage if these passages can "grow in the hand" while the hand is still developing.

Assuming that the playing is technically correct—and that it is both rhythmically and dynamically in order—there are still a few pointers that one might give. My advice presupposes a player who has already mastered the notes, the dynamics, and the rhythm. If it is not played rhythmically and with confidence, the result will be amateurish and a disappointment to both listeners and performer.

Rather than review the concerto movement by movement, I will discuss a few of the difficult passages wherever they may occur.

Look first at the little cadenza in measure 348 of the third movement. You need octaves of hardened steel in this part, octaves in which every note is like every other note, octaves in which there is no upper voice or lower voice but in which lower voice = middle voice = upper voice. Use primarily the first and fifth fingers, with the other fingers tucked up under the palm of your hand. Keep your arm flexible: that is the way to get a brilliant sound. There is something Peer Gyntish about this hazardous passage. It does not work to play it with the motto "safety first." You have to take chances, pull out all the stops, throw caution to the winds. If you have practiced sufficiently, you will do all right. If you master this cadenza, you will conjure up some of the shimmering beauty of the majestic landscape of Norway—and from a technical/pianistic point of view you will remind your audience of Liszt. The same might be said of the opening cadenza in measures 5–8 of the third movement (see Ex. 6.3) and the big avalanche of octaves in the cadenza in the first movement (see Ex. 6.4). It really pays to practice these passages up, down, and sideways—as well as measure by measure—until you have them down pat.

Ex. 6.3

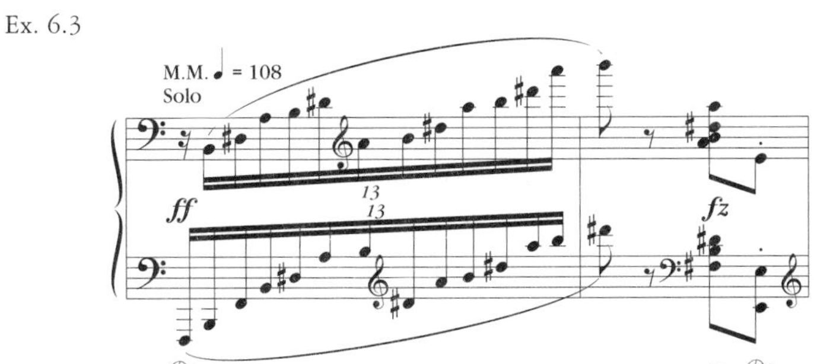

Ex. 6.4

The first measure of the virtuoso opening cadenza of the third movement (measure 5) may be done in three beats. We know that Grieg considered this an acceptable way to play this passage. The tempo indication is *Allegro moderato molto e marcato.* If the conductor and the orchestra maintain this tempo, the pianist should be able to play it in two beats. That would give a nice boost to the rhythm, but this introduction is rarely taken so slowly. If it is too fast, the pianist has no alternative but to play it in three beats. In this case I recommend subdividing the run into groups of 4 + 4 + 5, using the fingering indicated in Ex. 6.5.

The descending scale in Ex. 6.6 may also be done in three beats; the run in parallel octaves in Ex. 6.7 may be taken in two beats if you can play that fast.

The opening of the first movement is also somewhat risky. You must prepare for your next hand position in order to play correctly, yet you must continue to play without a break in order to maintain the rhythm. The only solution is to work at coordinating your thoughts and your hand movements until the hand knows the route by heart—in short, until you can move directly from one hand position to the next without missing a note. It is especially important to be able to do this in the opening flourish (measures 2–3). Here is the situation: you come onstage, the audience applauds, you take your seat at the piano, and before you have time to gather your thoughts the drumroll begins and *boom*, you are on!

Ex. 6.5

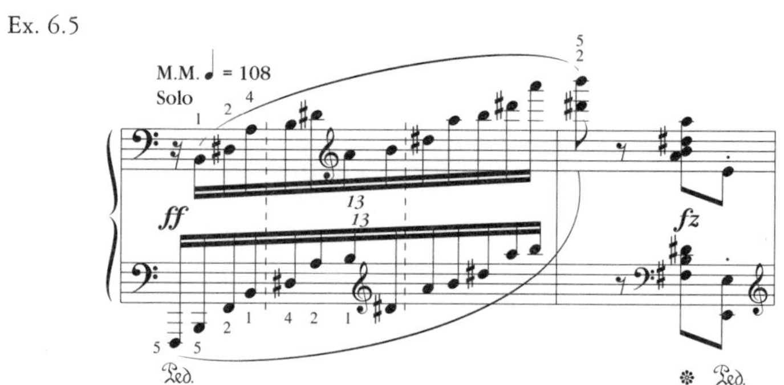

Ex. 6.6

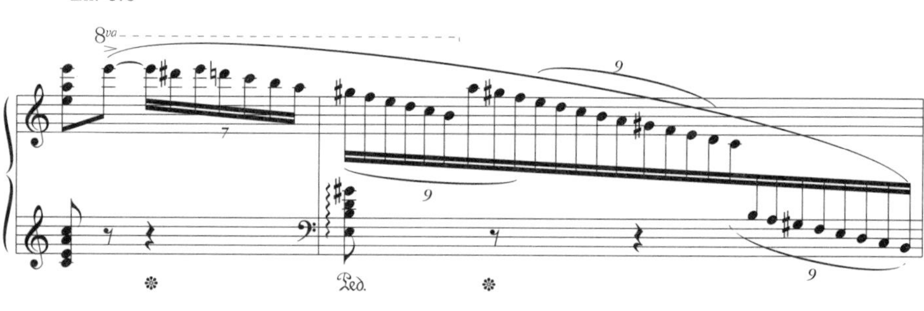

Ex. 6.7

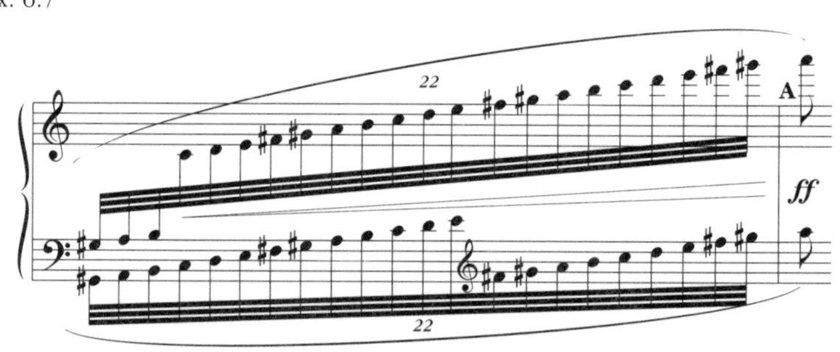

Therefore you must be able to play the opening especially well. Many pianists have stumbled at this point—muffed the opening—and have never been able to get the performance back under control. The opening drumroll and piano cadenza are the very hallmark of this concerto. That cadenza is one of the most important things in the entire performance, and it must be done flawlessly. You will be forgiven if you miss a note or two later on, but not in the opening cadenza. Pay tribute to Liszt as well!

The octaves in measures 67–68 of the first movement must also be played as brilliantly as possible. Grieg's tempo indication here is *stretto*, so it's all right to go faster and faster. Let it run until the music gushes at this point—your audience will love it. Whether you wish to use your fifth finger always on these octaves is a matter of personal preference. I like to use the fourth finger on the black keys in the ascending *crescendo* passage in measure 67 but the fifth finger going back down. Using the fifth finger is the surest way to achieve a true *fortissimo* throughout the descending line.

Think of the octaves in the left hand in Ex. 6.8 in groups. It is especially difficult to keep one's orientation in this passage because all the notes are played on white keys. It is easy to lose one's bearings. Practice backwards to increase the probability that you will manage it correctly onstage (see Ex. 6.9).

Ex. 6.8

Ex. 6.9

The brilliant run in measure 101 can be played with one hand if your hand is big enough and strong enough to manage it. If not, use both hands, as indicated in Ex. 6.10.

Ex. 6.10

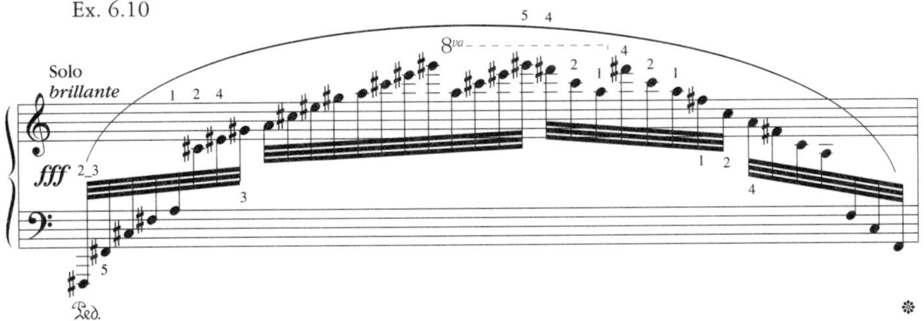

You can add a nice touch to the big *fortissimo* run in measure 108 if you play both F♯'s on beat 3 with your right hand. The octaves in measures 110 and 112 must once again be of the "hardened steel" variety. Because you are echoing triplets played by the trumpets, you should not use much *rubato* the first time through. You can take a few more liberties with the tempo in the sixteenth-note octaves that follow, however.

The *presto* run in the cadenza in measure 176 is also somewhat Lisztian in character. You may decide how many times you want to repeat the four-note figure (see Ex. 6.11). Some editions recommend fourteen repetitions, others

Ex. 6.11

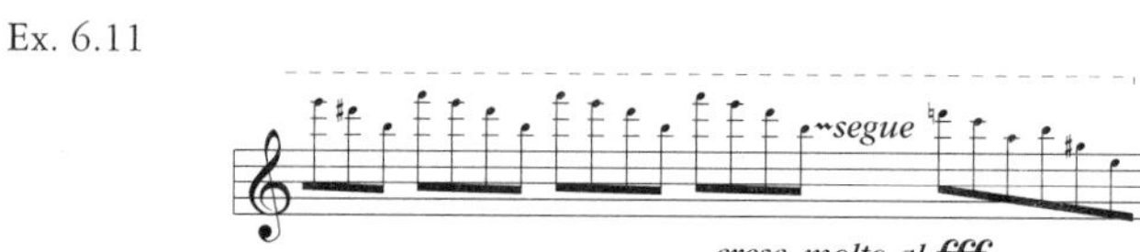

as many as 22. You do not have to decide in advance how many to use: the number can vary from pianist to pianist and even from performance to performance. It is wise, however, to practice a certain number in order to have something definite in mind. Fourteen repetitions feels about right to me, but if I sometimes use only twelve or thirteen it really doesn't matter.

The main part of the cadenza, starting in measure 177, is a technical challenge for any pianist. Your goal should be to get the left hand playing evenly and clearly without losing any of the notes. Begin by practicing one hand at a time. Although it is important to have a good flow from note to note, think of the left-hand arpeggios as chords in groups in order to keep your orientation in performance. Practice with a clear mind, for it is easy to lose one's concentration at this point when one is onstage (see Ex. 6.12).

Ex. 6.12

Measures 187–90 should be played with all the grandeur you can muster. Make the anacruses as short as possible (see Ex. 6.13).

Try to maintain approximately a 4/4 rhythm (see Ex. 6.14), for it is of great importance in producing a *maestoso* effect. The tempo need not be as fast as in the rest of the first movement, however. On the contrary, think in terms of an augmented tempo—as if the music were written in half notes instead of quarters.

Ex. 6.13

Ex. 6.14

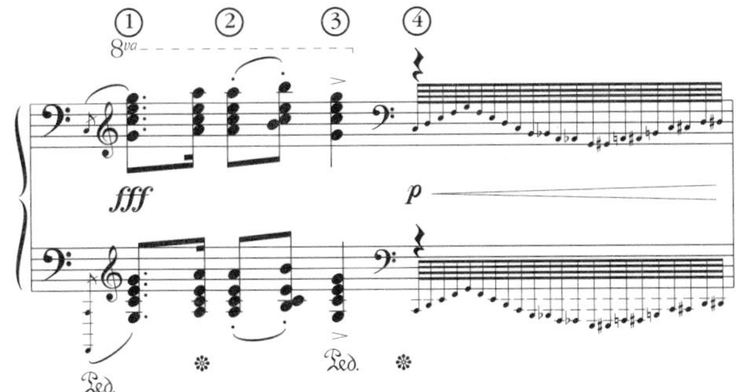

The same recommendation applies to the section that follows, measures 191ff. It is very difficult to achieve clarity in the thirty-second notes. One possible fingering is suggested in Percy Grainger's edition of the concerto (see Ex. 6.15). Other performance traditions recommend a quite different distri-

Ex. 6.15

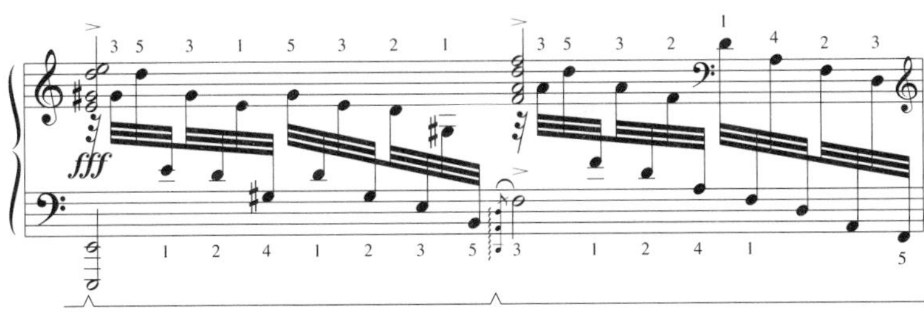

bution of the hands—Ex. 6.16 shows the one given in the Peters edition. Many pianists prefer the distribution indicated in the original score. Each performer must choose the method that works best for him or her.

Ex. 6.16

It is a tremendous challenge to play the last six measures of the first movement cleanly and clearly; achieving that is a great pianistic triumph.

A similarly bravura passage occurs in the little cadenza in measures 103–107 of the third movement. The sixteenth-note octaves in measure 104 must be absolutely uniform in volume and rhythm; if possible do not hesitate between them. The descending chords must also project an air of confidence. Do not think in terms of upper voice and lower voice: think of all the notes as being equally loud, equally important.

It is essential that the *prestissimo* run in measure 107 be played as lucidly as possible. Let it rise like a rocket on the Fourth of July. Some performers use pedal during the run, shifting when they get to the top. On a modern grand piano it is possible to use the third pedal, as indicated in Ex. 6.17.

Ex. 6.17

Another set of "hardened steel" chords in measure 107 is followed by a big scalar run. Play as evenly and as brilliantly as possible. The lowest G♯ can be played with the left hand. Some performers stop briefly after the last note in order to get in perfect sync with the orchestra. This is acceptable as an emergency solution, though we all have a preference for jumping right into *a tempo*—but only with a conductor and an orchestra that are on top of the situation.

Measures 108–29 of the third movement constitute an enormous physical challenge. The music is brilliant in all its awesome majesty. It incorporates, among other things, a *halling*[*] dance of Grieg's own invention. This section

[*]See footnote, p. 13.

should be played a bit more broadly than the rest of the movement so as to draw attention to the *halling*. To give yourself an opportunity to *crescendo* during each iteration of the *halling*, reduce the volume slightly at the beginning of this part (see Ex. 6.18).

Ex. 6.18

So much for the Lisztian aspect of the concerto. Needless to say, it comes to the fore once again in the concluding measures of the Concerto, and if adequately expressed, there will be a festive atmosphere in the concert hall. But the Concerto is much more than a compliment to Liszt.

Echoes of Norwegian Folk Music

I mentioned the lyrical element of the Concerto before discussing its technical dimension, for if the lyrical element is not present, the Piano Concerto loses its essence. It also has an undeniable folk-music quality. The main theme of the third movement, for example, is a genuine, spirited *halling* dance, and it is not sufficient just to play it clearly and fast. Pay close attention to Grieg's dynamic markings. The accents and slurs are also placed in a quite decorative—almost explosive—manner (see Ex. 6.19).

Ex. 6.19

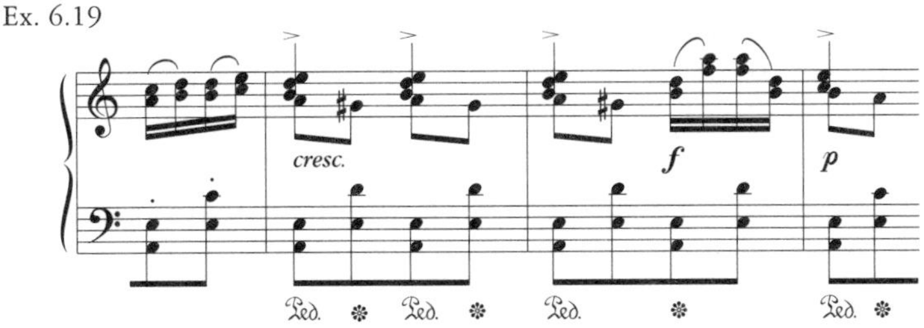

The *halling* twist is clearly evident in the left-hand accompaniment in measures 46–58 (see Ex. 6.20), where Grieg calls for accents on the weak beats. The unusual accents continue in the solo passage starting in measure 59. Although the runs in the right hand are fast, they must be clean and clear.

Ex. 6.20

But mere clarity in the runs is not enough—nor will it be fully achieved unless the accents are played just as Grieg specified, i.e., on weak beats. Measures 46–48 also have syncopated accents. The same pattern should be carried over into the *a tempo* section, starting in measure 75. This *halling* dance is quite subdued, but be sure to retain some of its dancelike character.

The *quasi presto* section, starting in measure 353, is a *springdans*.* The left hand must be *staccato* at all times, and the third beat should have a little hint of staccato in the right hand. Also try to articulate the slurred thirds (see Ex. 6.21), and bring out the hemiola in measures 370–71 (see Ex. 6.22).

Ex. 6.21

Ex. 6.22

These suggestions will make the coda bouncy and interesting rather than merely fast. At measure 402 Grieg has written *sempre più forte e stretto*. Most performances are somewhat lacking in the latter: there usually is no *stretto* because the performer was already playing at maximum speed. Obviously the coda should be fast throughout, but hold the tempo down a little so that a

*A folk-dance tune in 3/4 time; also called *springar*.

stretto is possible. Use these amusing folkish means to control the tempo and keep you from just racing along.

The main theme of the first movement is also folkish. The anacrusis in the left hand at the beginning of measure 19 is important: it helps avoid sugary sweetness (see Ex. 6.23). Do not play it as an eighth note; be very clear about the fact that it is an anacrusis in contrast to the eighth note at the end of the measure.

Ex. 6.23

In measures 19–22, note the performance instructions: *staccato*, *tenuto*, and *portamento*. Often all we hear is *portamento*, which makes the theme too saccharine and Chopinesque. On the other hand, if the entire theme is played *staccato* it becomes too angular. The intended articulation is very subtle and includes all three modes of attack, thereby varying the tone color (see Ex. 6.23).

At measure 31 Grieg has written *animato e molto leggiero*. This section is unbelievably virile and spirited! Of course it is difficult, of course it must have a certain tempo—but no amount of technical brilliance will be sufficient unless you pay attention to the accents. Grieg knew exactly where he wanted them—namely, primarily, on the weak beats (see Ex. 6.24). Even in measure 39 it is the dancelike accents that add spice to the whole (see Ex. 6.25).

Ex. 6.24

The beautiful theme played in a duet with the oboe in measures 43–47 also calls for an accent that is rarely observed. Pay attention to it and your performance will more closely approach the Norwegian taste. These measures are not really folkish, but they do contain slurs that alter the rhythmic pattern. Try to observe them so that your performance will not sound careless.

Ex. 6.25

Folk music is evoked once in the second movement as well, though obviously in a different way. The orchestral introduction is surpassingly beautiful and sounds best when played in a true *adagio* tempo, but that is an enormous challenge for the strings. Only the best orchestras are capable of a really slow tempo. Ideally the conductor will coax forth a tonal picture of a quiet mountain lake, but with elements of passion and pathos—all within a framework that is both grand and peaceful. When this can be achieved, the introduction becomes a worthy preparation for the piano solo at measure 29. As mentioned earlier, this melody was inspired by a *kulokk*, a cow-call. Try playing measures 29–30 in an "extroverted" manner and the next two measures more "introspectively" (see Ex. 6.26). Don't overdo the *ffz* markings, but increase their intensity as you proceed (see Ex. 6.27).

Ex. 6.26

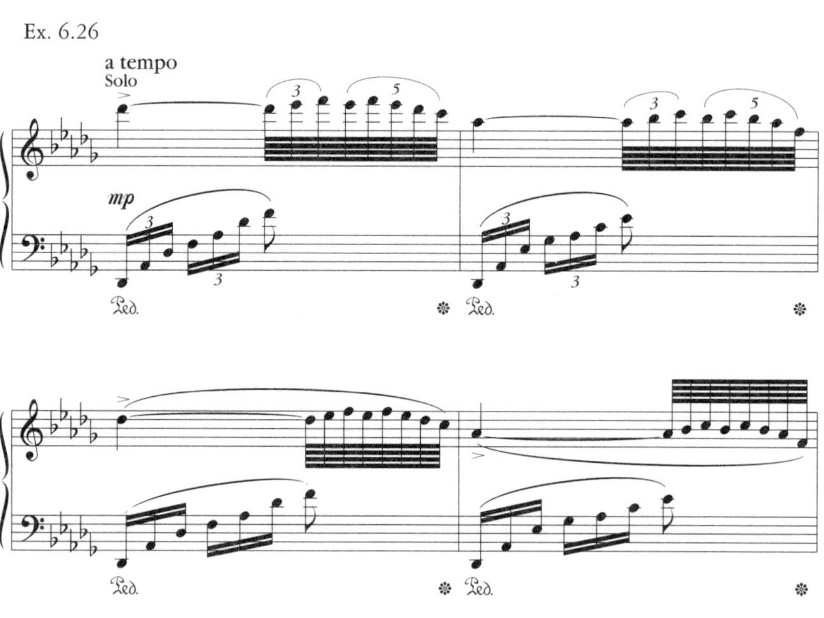

The B♭ in measure 36 can be very effective if you change the pedal several times without releasing the note. The result approaches a vibrato effect. Grieg used this device a number of times. It reminds one of the sound of a *lur*, an indigenous Norwegian instrument that resembles an alpenhorn.

Ex. 6.27

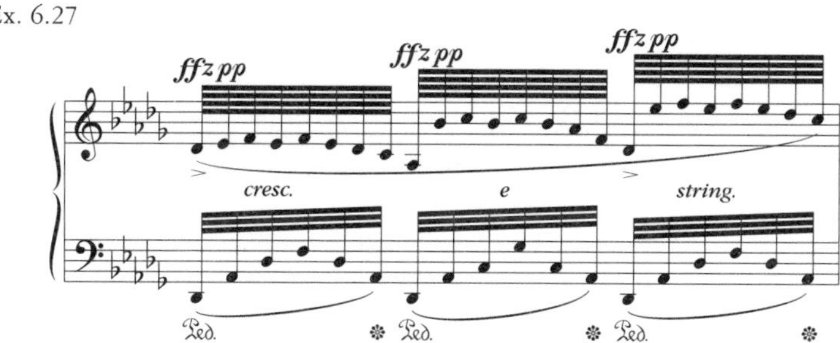

The long *pesante* section of the second movement (see Ex. 6.28) displays an entirely new dimension of the folk song: it becomes grandiloquent and majestic, like a national anthem. To bring out these qualities, pay special attention to the anacruses in the left hand. It is difficult to make them short enough, but if they are too heavy the music will not soar. Most performers place the anacruses midway between the chords, thereby allowing time to get ready to play the next chord. This is obviously the safest procedure, but the result is far from what Grieg intended. (This passage is similar in some respects to *I Wander Deep in Thought*, Op. 66, No. 18.) If you can play this section broadly—*pesante*—with a big, melodic sonority and short, majestic anacruses in the left hand, you will create a high point in the second movement that will enhance the whole Concerto.

Ex. 6.28

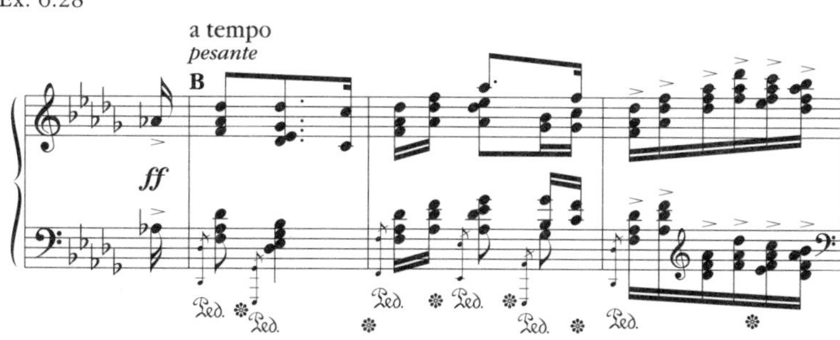

The two last trills in the second movement—in measures 81–82, where the piano follows the French horn—are also folkish. The heterophonic adaptation of the horn theme works best if the piano trills are perfectly parallel. It takes a lot of work to achieve that, but the result is worth the effort. Many pianists of earlier generations have made this passage extra captivating by playing it *pianissimo*, with fast, parallel trills. Try to carry on this tradition.

The Romantic Element

This Concerto could be described as lyric-Romantic: it is Romantic with a difference. The warm, sentimental, melodious dimension first appears in the *cantabile* section in measures 23–29 of the first movement (see Ex. 6.29). Play the melody broadly, and create a duet between the hands. The accompaniment should be as full-bodied and as even as possible, taking its cue dynamically from the melody—never overpowering, but always in support.

Ex. 6.29

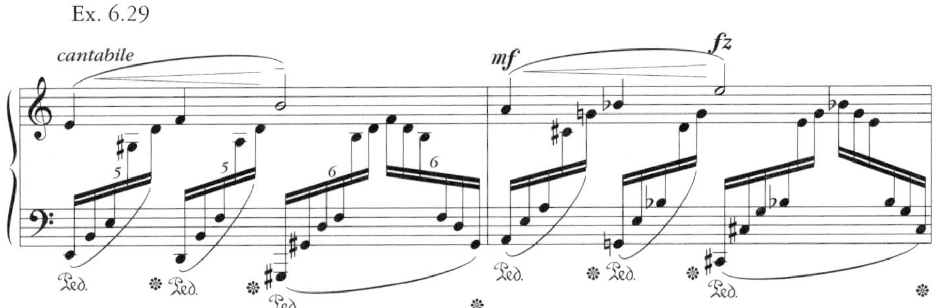

The transition to the *animato* section in measure 30 (see Ex. 6.30) sounds best if the rhythm is as reserved and the sonority as precise as possible. The *animato* section itself also calls for warmth and expressiveness (see Ex. 6.31).

Ex. 6.30

Ex. 6.31

In the second movement, in measures 64–70, summon all the warmth and lyricism you can muster. Let the chords sound forth gently at first, growing step by step to *fortissimo*—the first time *piano dolce*, the second time louder, and the third time with all the notes of the chord equally loud. Your goal should be to "coax out of"—not just to "press down," for then the attack becomes too hard.

In measures 75–76, try to achieve something of a bell-like attack, i.e., abbreviated, but with pedal. The conclusion should be played very *legato*, with a subtle *diminuendo*. Be mindful of the duet between the hands in measures 79–80 (see Ex. 6.32).

Ex. 6.32

In the Percy Grainger edition, measure 80 is marked *piano subito*, allowing the E♭ in the upper voice to sound forth more prominently (see Ex. 6.33).

The sonority of the concluding measure, marked *lento*, should also be as warm as possible. Play a good, solid bass note, but still give the greatest emphasis to the fifth. Note that the score calls for *crescendo* all the way to the fifth (see Ex. 6.34), which is a formula for warmth, but it also has something of a folk-tune feeling.

Exx. 6.33 and 6.34

For another beautiful passage in the third movement, Grieg has written *cantabile* the first time this melody appears (see Ex. 6.35) and *marcato* when it reappears (see Ex. 6.36). Play more aggressively when you come to the *marcato* version; the orchestra should support this to some extent. Another warm and lush passage is the *agitato* section in the third movement (see Ex. 6.37).

The grandiloquent, majestic qualities that characterize the middle section of the second movement return in the coda of the third. Here again we need short anacruses in order to keep the tempo moving; play them at the last possible moment (see Ex. 6.38).

Ex. 6.35

Ex. 6.36

Ex. 6.37

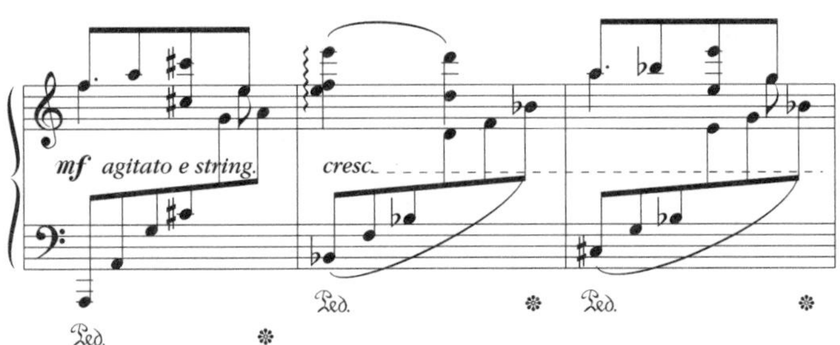

Ex. 6.38

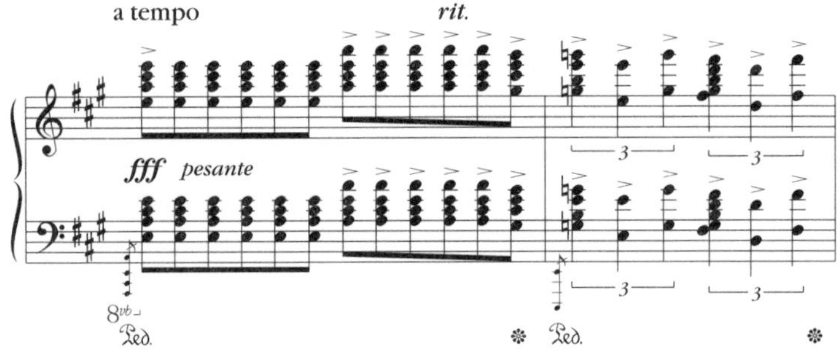

A hidden harp runs through all three movements of the A-minor Concerto: note the accompaniment figures in measures 23–29 of the first movement and the concluding chords of the long *andante* coda of the second movement, measures 79–80. These harplike figures should be supple, not obtrusive, and if you make them very even the result will be wonderful. The runs in measures 302ff. of the third movement should also be even. Make a smooth transition from the top note of one figure to the first note of the next (see Ex. 6.39). It is altogether too easy here to leave a tiny space between contiguous figures. The use of the pedal in these passages can vary; you might use a little to begin with and then increase it as you go along. That way you can achieve an effect like that of a murmuring brook.

Ex. 6.39

Miscellaneous Comments

These final comments are a collection of tips and hints, some of which may be helpful to you. Your temperament and your personality will bring all the elements together in a natural unity.

First Movement

The broken chords in measure 4 can be divided between the hands as indicated in Ex. 6.40.

Ex. 6.40

Some pianists play the chord in measure 6 less forcefully than that in measure 5 (see Ex. 6.41). To some extent this is a matter of personal preference, but Grieg does not specifically call for it.

Ex. 6.41

Even the main theme can be given a more plaintive sound when it returns in the recapitulation. Note that Grieg marked it *mezzo piano* the first time it appears but *piano* in the recapitulation (see Ex. 6.42).

Ex. 6.42

It is easy for the lyric-Romantic middle section—dominated as it is by the second theme—to become overly episodic and to use too much *rubato.* You can avoid that by letting the left hand lead the way, controlling the *rubato,* then it will never get excessive. The left hand gives time and takes it back, and the right hand follows along. Listen to the hidden harp (see Ex. 6.43).

Try to distribute the sixteenth notes in measure 26 as evenly as possible. Let the *rubato* be "like a rubber band" (see Ex. 6.44).

In the right-hand run in measures 31–32 practice each hand separately and also as tied exercises, as indicated in Ex. 6.45.

Ex. 6.43

Ex. 6.44

Ex. 6.45

Measures 33–34 work best if you make a little upward movement preceding each accent (see Ex. 6.46), then a downward movement on the last one (see Ex. 6.47).

Ex. 6.46

Ex. 6.47

Pay close attention to the short rests notated in measures 39–40. Make the rhythm a little "swingy" at that point; it lends a playful, amusing touch to the music. Outward and inward arm movements are helpful from a technical point of view (see Ex. 6.48).

Ex. 6.48

Various fingerings are possible for the chromatic runs at an interval of a third in measures 41–42 and 139–40. I recommend the pattern indicated in Ex. 6.49.

Ex. 6.49

Try to produce even thirty-second notes at the conclusion of the *tutti* section in measure 47 (see Ex. 6.50).

The chords in both the right and the left hand in measures 65–66 and 163–64 sound great if they are played with convincing sonority and compactness (see Ex. 6.51).

The arpeggio interlude starting in measure 89 should be as even as possible. Listen especially to the transition between the two hands. Some pianists play the top notes with the left hand (see Ex. 6.52).

Ex. 6.50

Ex. 6.51

Ex. 6.52

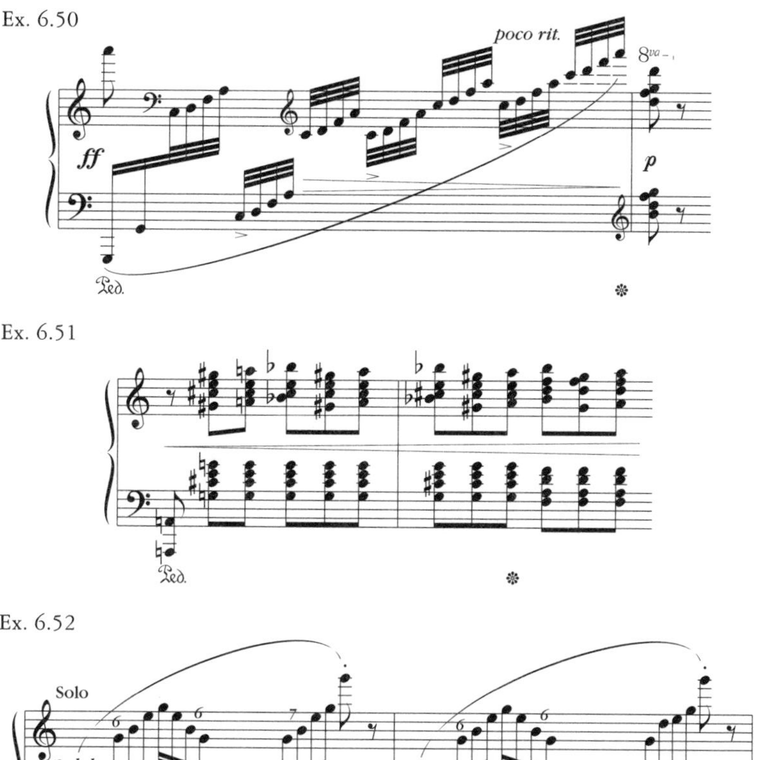

In measure 95, which is in F minor, perhaps you can create a slightly darker coloring by giving a slight emphasis to the left hand (see Ex. 6.53).

Ex. 6.53

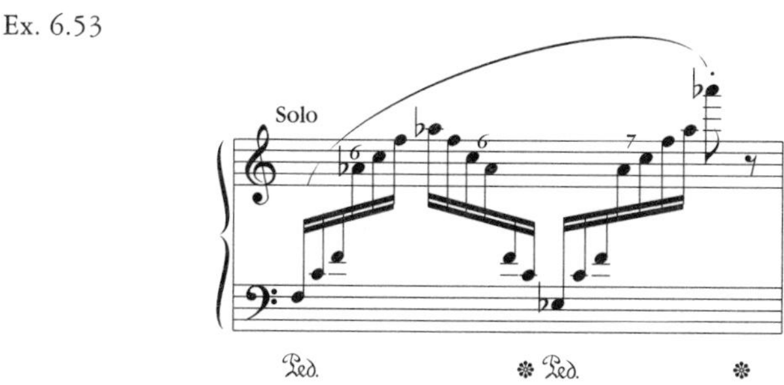

If your hand is not big enough to handle the music as written in measures 103–107, try playing some notes of the troublesome chords with the left hand, as indicated in Ex. 6.54.

Ex. 6.54

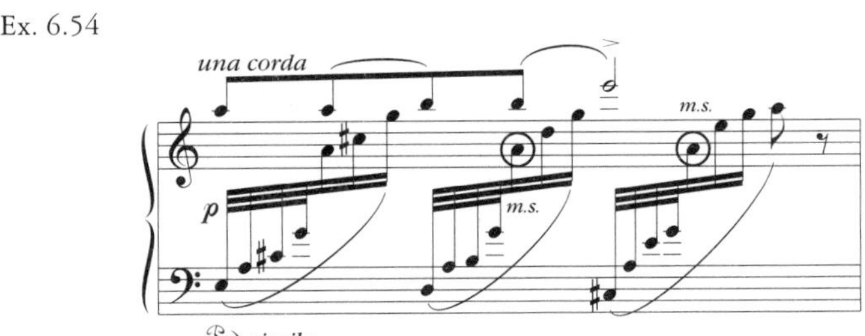

Note that the sprightly little passage in measure 137 (see Ex. 6.55) is marked *pianissimo* in contrast to its first occurrence (in measure 39), where it is marked *piano*.

Ex. 6.55

When the second theme is repeated in A major, in measures 151–52 (see Ex. 6.56), try to produce a little warmer sound—more of a mid-register sound—than in measures 53–54, where it is in C major. You can achieve this effect by giving a slight emphasis to selected notes in the left hand.

Ex. 6.56

The chords in measures 167–68 can be handled as suggested in Ex. 6.57.

Ex. 6.57

Make the *ritardando* in measure 170 quite broad (see Ex. 6.58).

Ex. 6.58

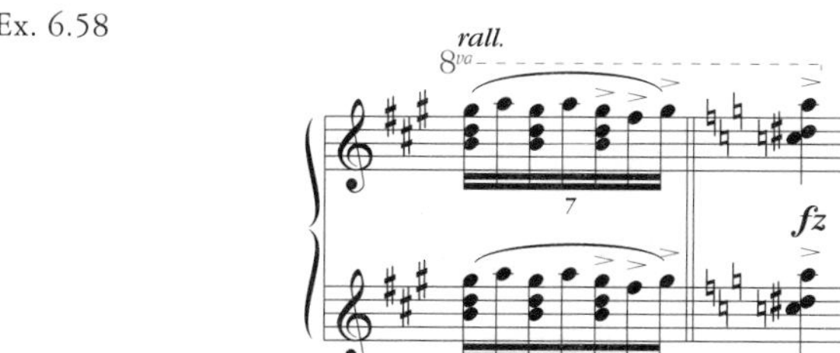

The beginning of the cadenza in measure 176 can be colored in various ways—for example, with an immanent polyphony in the broken chords (see Ex. 6.59). Note that the three sequences near the end of the measure do not start out fast: the marking is *meno presto*. Each iteration is slower than the preceding one; that is the idea behind this whole section. The last six notes of measure 176 can be really slow—they are marked *Lento*—and you can create a powerful effect by maintaining that tempo all the way to the rest and counting two slow beats (see Ex. 6.60).

Ex. 6.59

Ex. 6.60

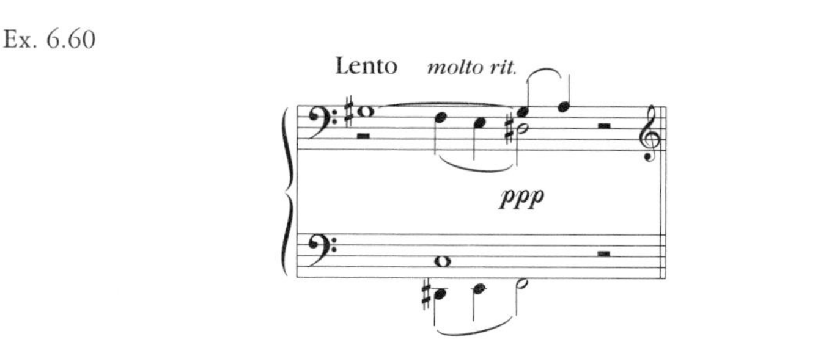

It is essential that the melody come to the fore in measures 177–85 of the cadenza. The trills and the rest of the accompaniment should of course be clear, but preferably as soft as possible. In any case they must not be allowed to obscure the melody (see Ex. 6.61).

The descent via fifths and fourths in the second half of measure 200 need not be exceedingly fast, but it should be very clear. Try to evoke the sound of a brook. Practice this passage as finger *staccato* and as tied exercises, i.e., hold down one interval and strike the other.

Ex. 6.61

The trill between the left and right hands in measures 204–205 (also called a Liszt trill) should be as even and fast as possible—until it dies away (see Ex. 6.62).

Ex. 6.62

The opening of the solo at the end of the movement has a sophisticated *halling** character. It is quite a challenge to get the sixteenth notes truly *staccato* and separated from the contiguous notes. Do this in combination with accents on beats 2 and 4 and the result will be stunning (see Ex. 6.63).

Ex. 6.63

Second Movement

In measures 49–54, try to feel a steady eight-beat rhythm. Don't accent these beats, but be aware of exactly where they occur. Both the orchestra and the conductor will be grateful to you.

---

*See footnote, p. 13.

Third Movement

In measures 7–8, think of the runs as clusters of notes and practice them that way so that you can keep your bearings in the midst of a fast tempo (see Ex. 6.64).

Ex. 6.64

In measures 65–66 it is very easy to "steal" time inadvertently. To avoid that, try to feel a definite beat right at the sixteenth-note rest. Let it be a weighty silence! (see Ex. 6.65.)

Ex. 6.65

Recommended fingering for measures 67–68 is shown in Ex. 6.66.

Ex. 6.66

The lyrical passage in measures 162ff. depends on a smoothly gliding left hand. Play *legato*: evenly, connecting each note with the next one, and making the notes as equal as you can. The left hand controls the *rubato*. After the various *rubato* passages that Grieg has indicated, note that the final section in F major (measures 218–29) is marked *a tempo*. Thus there should not be any further *ritardando* toward the end. In that way the sound is left "standing" in the air—like the air on a sunny summer day (see Ex. 6.67).

Ex. 6.67

The figure in measures 294–95 can be fingered as indicated in Ex. 6.68.

Ex. 6.68

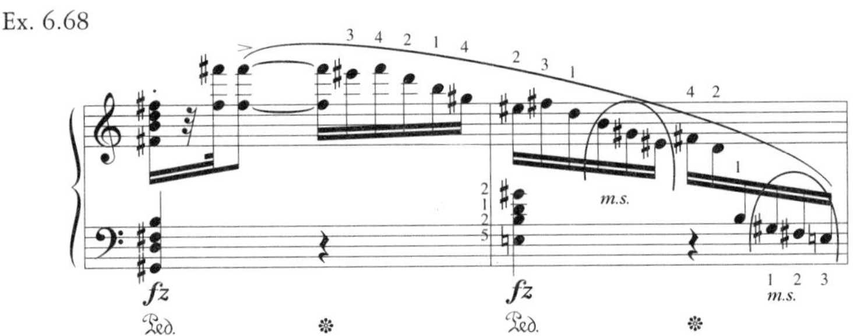

The octave runs in measures 318–25, marked *Meno Allegro*, should be built on a completely even left hand. Cooperation with the orchestra is important. To that end, do not play too fast and be sure to keep something in reserve so you can build up the sequences. The best way to play the descending octaves is to use the fifth finger throughout (see Ex. 6.69).

The thirds in the coda—measures 365ff.—are troublesome for many performers. Try using the following fingering throughout: $\frac{3\ 4}{1\ 2}\Big|\frac{3\ 4}{1\ 2}$. If your hand is big you might use the fingering indicated in Ex. 6.70. In measure 371, I recommend the fingering shown in Ex. 6.71.

In the transition from measure 375 to measure 376, note that the marking is *f*, *fz*, *p*, i.e., suddenly soft. Do not hold the pedal all the way, but let the last note be short. From here on it is just a matter of playing clean chords, clear *staccatos*, and entrancing rhythms. In this way the music develops its own forward motion.

Ex. 6.69

Ex. 6.70

Ex. 6.71

Grieg's Piano Concerto provides an opportunity for you to hone every facet of your pianistic skill. It stands in all its glory as one of the finest products not only of Norwegian art but of the Romantic period in general. There will always be orchestras that wish to perform the Concerto as well as audiences who wish to hear it—and there will always be pianists who dream of playing it. If you are one of those pianists, go for it! Your dream can become a reality! By playing the A-minor Concerto animatedly, majestically, beautifully, proudly, you will create a magical world of sound, starting with the opening chords (see Ex. 6.72)!

Ex. 6.72

CHAPTER

7

Pictures from Folk Life, Op. 19

The first edition of this work, published by the Danish firm Horneman & Erslev, carried the subtitle "Humoresques for Piano." This subtitle gives us an important clue as to how the pieces should be performed. The first edition also contained an invaluable Preface:

> It should be noted that familiarity with the first two pieces is a prerequisite to understanding the last one, for in *From the Carnival*, in the midst of the surging crowd one glimpses in the distance a Norwegian bridal procession, which is then followed by gigantic figures that leap into the air in the manner of a dancer of the *halling** (motives from *In the Mountains*) as if to clear the stage. Finally comes the wild ride, which is signaled by the fifth in A major that enters after the *stretto*. The situation at this point in the carnival has become one of complete wildness. The shouting and screaming of the crowd, plus the horses, whose snorting constantly pierces the air—everything comes together in a picture of the most abandoned revelry. The ideas arose in part during the Carnival period in Rome, though there is no claim to be depicting anything in detail; and to some extent they emerged from the memory of folk life in general, which later—in order to clarify the recollection—the composer thought he ought to elucidate.

*See footnote, p. 13.

Op. 19 is one of Grieg's great solo works for piano. It is a major challenge, a complex work with many pianistic and interpretational aspects. Grieg had scored a great success with his piano concerto, and once again he is striking out with Lisztian bravura. All three pieces—*In the Mountains*, *Bridal Procession*, and *From the Carnival*—are demanding. A highly developed technique, firm and pungent chord playing, and sparkling passages are not enough. The pieces also require a pronounced rhythmic vitality, a good deal of imagination, an enthusiastic will to work, and a positive attitude. If you can combine all of this with a bit of tenderness here and there, then the table is properly set for something of a piano celebration. These pieces are always appreciated when they are well played, so it is worth investing the considerable practice time required to get them in your repertory.

The key to the spirited rhythm is Grieg's accenting of weak beats, a pattern that appears in all three pieces. To give the pieces a suitable form it is important to plan out the tempos in *In the Mountains* and *From the Carnival*. In both of them there is a tendency to rush, leaving nothing in reserve for the *finale*.

No. 1, In the Mountains

It is not enough to just play rhythmically in *In the Mountains.* The rhythm must be accentuated and then made to swing! Consider the three tempos in this piece: *Un poco Allegro*, *tranquillo*, and *Presto*. It might be wise to continue the *tranquillo* character all the way to the recapitulation. Be sure that *Un poco Allegro* is allowed to become just a *little* allegro. Do not let it start out too fast, for that would decrease the effectiveness of the *Presto* coda.

To set the mood—or, more correctly, to tune your instrument the way fiddlers do—the piece starts with a ringing but soft open-fifth chord. If you hold the pedal down and then strike the chord with an upward movement, you can create the illusion of someone tuning a fiddle (see Ex. 7.1).

Ex. 7.1

In the Mountains begins with a "staccato show." It is marked *pianissimo e sempre staccato*, and it should be practiced as evenly as possible. Bring it to life with lopsided, swinging, syncopated rhythms—but *pianissimo* (see Ex. 7.2).

When the theme returns in octaves we need a little wrist movement. If your hand is big enough, use the fourth finger on the G♯; if not, use the fifth

Ex. 7.2

finger (see Ex. 7.3). When this passage repeats in measures 43–45, the chords in the left hand should be cut off as shortly and tersely as possible, and the movement in the eighth notes can be a little wilder than before.

Ex. 7.3

Note the accompaniment in *fortissimo* and the phrasing with a slight accent on the second beat (see Ex. 7.4).

Ex. 7.4

Measures 59–64, with the tremolo figure in the left hand, are quite intricate: 3 + 2 notes, not 4 + 1. Musically, try to combine periods of 2 + 2 measures; i.e., play the long line rather than focussing on one or two measures at a time (see Ex. 7.5).

Ex. 7.5

It is nearly impossible to make the accompaniment perfectly accurate with an ordinary tremolo movement: one's fingers tend to become almost paralyzed and one slips into a pattern of 4 + 1 notes (see Ex. 7.6). I recommend practicing this passage with tied exercises (see Ex. 7.7).

Exx. 7.6 and 7.7

In measures 67–70 bring out the accents that alternate between the hands so that the imitations are obvious (see Ex. 7.8).

Ex. 7.8

The conclusion is marked *sostenuto molto*. Let it slow gradually, and think of it as continuing organically right into the rest, which serves as a transition to the *tranquillo* section (see Ex. 7.9). This section is marked *sostenuto molto*, but

Ex. 7.9

it should not be as sustained as the recapitulation, where Grieg has indicated *molto ritardando* all the way down to *lento*. Save something for that! The *tranquillo* section comes across as a musical depiction of the Norwegian landscape, with a majestic mountain reflected in the surface of a sparkling lake. Play gently, *dolce legato*, and keep the eighth-note pattern in the left hand—later divided between the two hands—even. The top voice predominates, and in the dotted middle voice it is good to use a bit of lower arm support (see Ex. 7.10).

Ex. 7.10

In the second part (measures 77–86) we have two voices to emphasize. There is also the possibility of an echo effect as well as a *sostenuto* in the second half. The last figure has the character of a refrain, such as we find in some folk songs. Measures 87–94 constitute a kind of canon (see Ex. 7.11).

Ex. 7.11

Ex. 7.12

In measures 103–108 the two themes are combined (see Ex. 7.12). This passage is quite interesting contrapuntally. As mentioned earlier, it probably is desirable so far as the form of the piece is concerned to maintain the same *tranquillo* tempo here. That gives it an almost *maestoso* character, but it also gives one a better opportunity to clarify things that need to be clarified.

The dreaded octave skips on all white keys can also be managed at this tempo. Try to play all of them *fff* (see Ex. 7.13).

Ex. 7.13

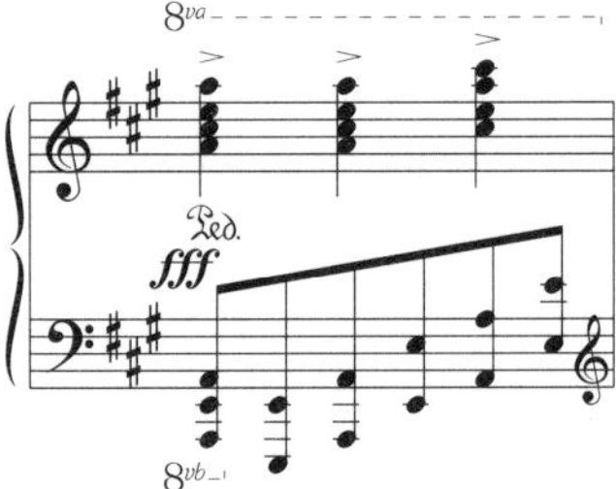

It was mentioned earlier that the transitions should continue organically right into the rest. Think in terms of eighth notes all the way to the recapitulation (see Ex. 14).

Ex. 7.14

The transition to the Coda is broader than the first conclusion. The rest is at a retarded tempo. Think of it as indicated in Ex. 7.15. You will then have produced rests of different durations at each of the three conclusions/ transitions.

Ex. 7.15

In the *Presto* section, starting in measure 200, there should be a slight accent on the second quarter note in the accompaniment to bring out the slur. Let your arm do part of the work. It is not easy to produce the accents in the furiously fast descending passage at the end of this section (measures 217–28). Here, too, the arm must help out, for finger motion alone will not produce enough of an accent. Moreover, there are accents on the first beat in the right hand and the second beat in the left hand. Some performers use an upward movement in the right hand, others prefer a downward impulse. Do whichever works best for you, but don't shy away from the friction inherent in the passage. Remember: accent on the first beat in the right hand, the second in the left. That, together with absolute clarity in the playing of the eighth notes, is more effective than just racing through the run—at worst, with too much pedal. Play clearly and lustily (see Ex. 7.16)!

Ex. 7.16

No. 2, Bridal Procession

This piece became popular as soon as it was published, and within a year or two it was published separately. Today it is still one of the most frequently played piano pieces by a Norwegian composer. The title could have been "The bridal procession is heard in the distance, comes closer, passes by, and disappears again." This is the idea the performer should have in mind while playing the piece. It must be one long line from the first ringing E major in the distance until it dies away far off on the horizon. Grieg is supposed to have said that a country bridal procession is not made up of well-trained soldiers, but of young and old people—everyone in the community. Therefore it is not necessary to maintain a strict march tempo. This remark might be interpreted as a license to introduce a little unevenness here and there. But not too much! Overdoing this aspect can make the performance sound amateurish. The piece is marked *alla marcia* but it exhibits a swinging rhythm with a slight accent on the second beat (see Ex. 7.17), and, later in the piece, on other weak beats.

Ex. 7.17

The grace notes in measures 5–7—i.e., the trills following the upbeat in the right hand—should not be taken for granted, for they are not easy to play clearly. I recommend the fingering indicated in Ex. 7.18.

Ex. 7.18

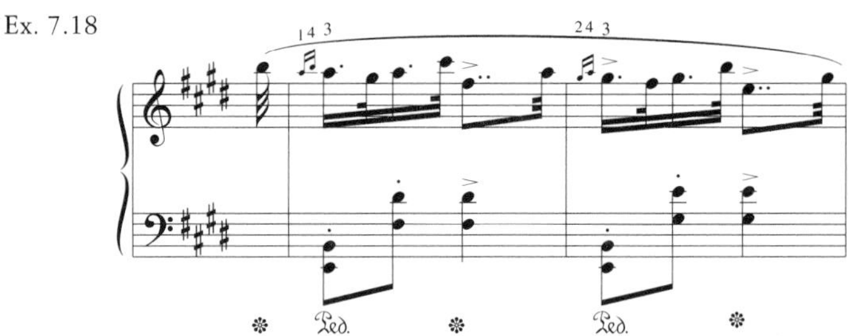

Starting at measure 13, the accompaniment leads the way. It is best to practice the piece in rhythm at all times. Later you may find room for latitude here and there, but always in moderation. For this piece to be successful you must master the figure in the left hand at a constant low dynamic level and at a uniform speed, always maintaining a slightly reserved sensitivity.

Note the figure in the right hand that regularly accents a weak beat. It is an interesting folkish feature that you can make much of in performance (see Ex. 7.19).

Ex. 7.19

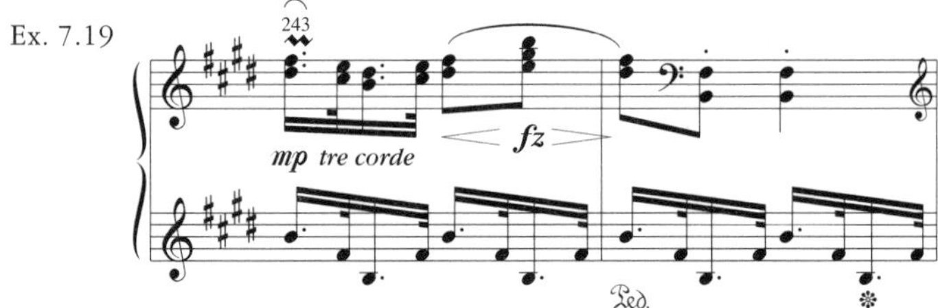

The embellishment in measures 33 and 34 is difficult to play clearly. Just as in the introduction, it works best if the upbeat is not treated as part of the trill—for then it sounds like a trill from the auxiliary note. The best effect is achieved if the trill is a little faster than the upbeat (see Ex. 7.20).

Ex. 7.20

The use of the pedal in *Bridal Procession* is a matter of some controversy.

Many think that Grieg calls for more pedal than is appropriate, and with the clear and precise dampers on modern pianos that may in fact be the case. I think there is a little room for variation here; indeed, the use of pedal in this piece can vary from concert hall to concert hall, from instrument to instrument. Here and there, however, one should create a little pedal effect in the *pianissimo* passages—inspired by Grieg's pedal indications, even if one does not follow them slavishly (see Ex. 7.21).

Ex. 7.21

In measures 43–44, at the modulation from C to C♯ and the decrease from *piano* to *ppp*, take a little time, linger just a bit (see Ex. 7.22).

Ex. 7.22

The recapitulation in *fortissimo marcato* (measures 58–59) is quite syncopated, with many accents on weak beats (see Ex. 7.23).

In measures 62–63, be careful that the triplet rhythm in the right hand does not influence the very different rhythmic pattern in the left. Keep them apart (see Ex. 7.24).

In measures 68 and 72, where the melody is in the left hand, it is important to use the pedal on the lowest note of the anacrusis. Plan carefully, and get it down without delay (see Ex. 7.25). The open fifths in measures 70–71 can be a little softer than the main melody. The grace notes that follow are extremely difficult and can perhaps be handled best with the fingering indicated in Ex. 7.26.

In measures 78–81, try to feel the downbeat on each measure, despite the ties (see Ex. 7.27). Compare this passage with the Lyric Piece *Once Upon a Time*

(Op. 71, No. 1). Staccato phrasing as indicated in Ex. 7.28 contributes to the heightening of tension.

The entire concluding section (starting in measure 82) calls for a slight

emphasis of the two motives reproduced in Ex. 7.29. The accents and the overall dynamic level decrease gradually as the bridal procession recedes slowly in the distance. As was stated earlier, *crescendo* is talent, *diminuendo* is art. The artistic effect is stunning if you can achieve a gradual *diminuendo* stretching all the way from measure 90 to the very last chord in *ppp* (see Ex. 7.30).

No. 3, From the Carnival

From the Carnival is a grandly conceived picture. Grieg said that from his hotel room in Rome he had once witnessed the clamor of an Italian carnival. He had enjoyed it, but at the same time he had experienced an intense homesickness for his beloved Norway. I think the longing for home is the inspiration for several parts of the piece.

Both Agathe Backer Grøndahl and Percy Grainger suggested that if *From the Carnival* is played by itself, one might consider cutting from measure 151 through the first beat of measure 170 and treating the E-major chord in measure 170 as an upbeat to the *Prestissimo* section (see Ex. 7.31). The strains

Ex. 7.31

in the *Poco Andante* section are reminiscences of *Bridal Procession*, and the allusion loses some of its meaning if the latter has not been played. The best solution is to play the entire opus, so that the allusion creates a nice cyclic effect: first a gentle hint *ppp*, then—after a brief return to the *Carnival* theme *pp*—an affectionate little quotation from *Bridal Procession*.

It is important to plan one's tempos carefully. The *Allegro alla burla* must not be so fast that the *Prestissimo* loses its effect (see Ex. 7.32). Often this piece is played in what sounds like a wonderful tempo at the start, but the *finale* falls flat because the tempo remains the same. Don't let that happen.

Ex. 7.32

The accompaniment figures set the pace for the entire piece. Practice them separately (see Ex. 7.33). The left hand controls the pace, and the right hand follows along. Practice the left hand alone until your ear is able to follow the pattern even when you are playing with both hands—and even when you are

Ex. 7.33

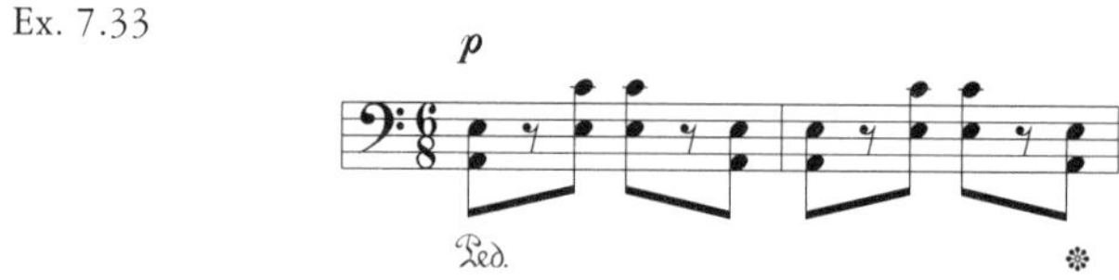

playing softly. Technically, we need a certain tremolo swing in the right arm—not too much when the intervals are small, however, for then the sound tends to get muddy. I personally like to use tremolo with intervals of a fifth or greater, but this is a matter of the size of one's hand. The fingering of the trill in measures 15–16 can be handled in the same manner as in *Bridal Procession* (see Ex. 7.34).

Ex. 7.34

The *pianissimo* in measures 36–38 is another shimmering, impressionistic passage so typical of Grieg. It calls for a bit of pedal, but the real challenge is to play it softly enough (see Ex. 7.35).

Ex. 7.35

The ascending arpeggio in the left hand gradually becomes more and more important musically. In this respect it is somewhat similar to the broken chord in the cadenza of the A-minor Concerto (see Exx. 6.61 and 7.36). In

Ex. 7.36

From the Carnival, too, the broken chord in the left hand is effective if it gradually becomes louder and louder. Mentally place a slur over the whole cadenza. To keep the attack clean in that long passage, it is good to have lower arm support. That is true also for the three-note figures in measures 49–52 (see Ex. 7.37).

Ex. 7.37

According to the score, the section in A major (measures 63–94) is supposed to continue in the same tempo. However, its *legato* character may suggest that Grieg was longing for home, so perhaps it is permissible to make it somewhat reflective and melancholy. The melody in octaves can be varied slightly with each iteration, i.e., sometimes it can be "cheered up" by emphasizing the right hand, at other times made more somber by leading with the left. *Mezzo piano* in the right hand, *pianissimo* in the left—or vice versa.

The beautiful bass line in measures 71–78 deserves to be emphasized. It is every bit as interesting as the repeated sixteenth-note figure in the right hand (see Ex. 7.38).

Ex. 7.38

In the *fortissimo* passage in measures 79–86, it is possible to use different tone coloring for each harmonization. In the first one, emphasize the dominant seventh; in the second, a diminished chord—which is to say, turn up the suspense even more. The third harmonization is a Neapolitan subdominant, so it can be either still more suspenseful or a little more rounded off. The last one is indeed another dominant seventh, but it resolves to the tonic and can be played a little more softly (see Ex. 7.39). The recapitulation of this theme is marked *piano*, but it should in fact be softer than in the original statement (see Ex. 7.40).

In the recapitulation of the principal theme in A minor, it is possible to allow a slight pedal effect to remain in order to return gradually to the atmosphere of the principal theme (see Ex. 7.41).

Ex. 7.39

Ex. 7.40

Ex. 7.41

The recapitulation also presents new modulations: this time the middle theme starts on A (i.e., in D minor) instead of on B (in E minor), as in the exposition. The passage should be colored differently in each key—presumably a little darker in D minor than in the E-minor version (see Ex. 7.42).

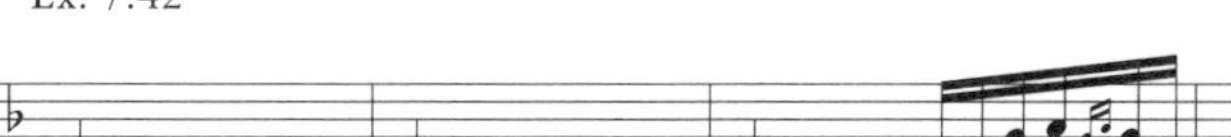

Ex. 7.42

The problems, then, are pretty much the same in the balance of the piece. We have already discussed measures 151–70, the reminiscence, marked *Poco andante*. All that then remains is to craft a good *finale*. The *Prestissimo* must be significantly faster than what has preceded it. No way out! Before the long sequence begins, insert a couple measures of *piano* so that you have something to go on dynamically in the *finale* (see Ex. 7.43).

Ex. 7.43

It is very important to play the broken chords in measures 193–200 cleanly. Decide how you are going to finger them, and practice them over and over again (see Ex. 7.44). Maintain an absolutely steady rhythm and a steely sound in the fanfare (measures 201–12; see Ex. 7.45).

Ex. 7.44

Ex. 7.45

The long ascending passage in measures 213–19 is difficult to do cleanly, but it must be as brilliant as you can make it. Here again, prepare your fingering carefully—but articulate with active fingers and an open hand. The last four notes of the passage (measure 219) can be given a somewhat accented effect with impulses from the arm, but without the slightest hint of *ritardando*.

Brilliant, crisp chords bring us to the end (see Ex. 7.46). Guaranteed

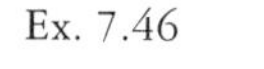
Ex. 7.46

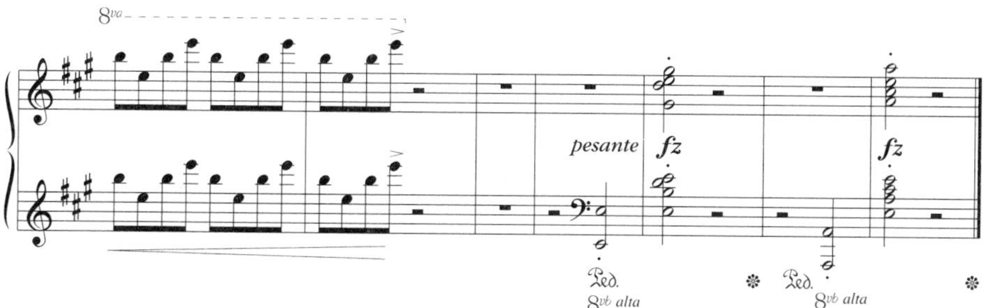

success! The piece is always well received if it is played with élan. *Pictures from Folk Life* is worthy of the time, hard work, and desire that are required to play it well. It is and always will be one of the most illustrious opuses in the entire corpus of Norwegian piano music.

CHAPTER

8

Ballade in G Minor, Op. 24

The point of departure for this piece is the folk ballad *The Northland Peasantry*, which is very well known in Norway:

I know so many a lovely song
Of beautiful lands elsewhere,
But ne'er have I heard a single song
of my home in the north so fair.
So now I'm going to try my skill
To write a song so that people will
See that life up north can be happy and gay—
No matter what folks down south might say.

The melody is the product of a long development, spanning several centuries and several countries. It eventually found a home on Norwegian soil and in 1875 became the basis for Grieg's greatest composition for solo piano.

The *Ballade* is the very heart of Norwegian piano literature and is significant in countless ways. It is Romantic, profound, tender, and introspective, and its form is grandly conceived. Its substantial pianistic and architectonic demands are a challenge for the performer. We cannot thank Grieg enough. The *Ballade* has had and always will have enormous importance for Norwegian pianists and for the overall level of the art of piano playing in Norway. All

Norwegian pianists must play the Piano Concerto and the *Ballade* if they expect to be taken seriously. These majestic works inspire each new generation of pianists and give us a goal to reach for. We must, therefore, solve the numerous problems posed by these two pieces.

The theme of the *Ballade* is a most beautiful melody. The opening section, beginning with the very first note, is marked with a long slur, indicating that the passage is to be played with the smoothest possible *legato*. Note Grieg's genius as a harmonist: the bass voice descends in an almost perfect chromatic line through the entire eight-measure passage (see Ex. 8.1).

Ex. 8.1

The theme must sound as if it is coming from another world. To achieve this try to feel the upward movement of the key as you release it. Obviously it must be struck downward, but caress it as it comes up again: you will find that it changes the character of the sound in a very special way. Even if you manage to produce an ethereal and delicate sound, however, the theme will not achieve its full potential unless at the same time you are aware of the descending bass line, which warns of gloom, of despair, of the possibility of drama. Grieg made good use of the expertise he had acquired as a harmonist during his student days in Leipzig. He remolded it and used it as a principle of cohesion that gives the piece a feeling of great maturity. This aspect of the bass line must be given suitable prominence in the total picture.

Grieg struggled with this composition. In his early sketches he tried a variety of things. Even the title varied: sometimes he called it *Capriccio*, sometimes *Ballade*. He wrote a number of different versions of the variations before he settled on their final form. The sequence of the variations, too, was helter-skelter at first, showing that he struggled for a long time before finding the final order. For the performer this means that the piece is *not* a *capriccio*—the title that Grieg abandoned—but something more substantial, which should be held together and presented as a single story. The progression from one variation to the next should also exhibit logical development, as indicated by Grieg's early sketches.

The middle part of the theme is a little less somber in character, and the section marked *poco animato* (starting in measure 8) is reminiscent of a dance. It is not really a dance, of course, just a gentle memory of one. In measure 9, emphasize the tied F in the left hand. That will give a certain dominant character to the harmony—a folkish detail that is worth bringing out. Give a little emphasis to the chromatically descending octaves in the left hand in measures 13–16, and use the fifth finger to bring out the darker color (see Ex. 8.2).

Ex. 8.2

The *Ballade* challenges one's musicality, technique, and endurance. Like an athlete—a long-distance runner—the performer must keep something in reserve for the ending. Practice the *finale* much more than the rest of the piece! Obviously one improves as one performs the piece again and again, but even in your first performance you should have the ending in mind from the very beginning. It is easy to lose the relationship between one variation and the next. Think in terms of contrasts, but let each one follow from the preceding one. Group them in such a way that you experience the work as a unified, natural whole.

First plan the so-called funeral march. Play it, and experience it as the deepest point in the entire composition (see Ex. 8.3). It is marked *Lento*, but the tempo has something breathless about it by virtue of the *tenuto* indications on the chords and the stereotyped, steady accompaniment, which is almost like a death knell. Consciously experience this part as the somberest passage in the piece. Emphasize the bells a bit with a dark color to begin with, lightening up somewhat at measure 146. It is almost impossible to produce the differences that Grieg calls for between *pianissimo dolcissimo* and *ppp*—but

Ex. 8.3

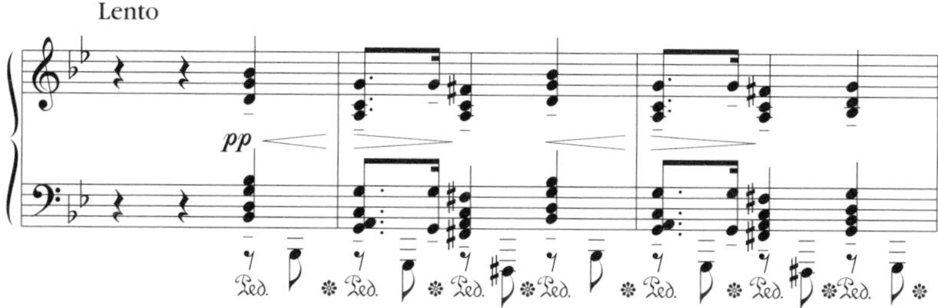

do your best. When interpreting a piece, it often happens that if you wholeheartedly attempt the impossible, it may not come out exactly as you had hoped, but at least there is a hint of transcendence.

When the theme returns in measures 154–58, you can vary the sonority: the first time emphasize the tenor voice, the second time perhaps the bass, i.e., stress the notes played by the thumb and fifth finger respectively. That may be somewhat difficult, but it can be done.

Next, the third variation, go to *Adagio* (measure 49). Try to make it smooth. If the *Adagio* is too slow, the forward motion stops. Something that is coming later is anticipated. Things come to a halt prematurely.

Despite such tempo markings as *Adagio* and *Lento*, the *Adagio* is replete with flowing sixteenth notes. Some performers like to emphasize the upper voice at the beginning of the variation, then the lower voice in measures 57–58. I find it a little tedious to emphasize the same melody over and over again, so I treat the upper third as a melody, although that is a matter of personal preference. Another challenge is to achieve differences in tone color between the various tonal planes: G minor, B♭ minor, and, not least, the beautiful transition from B♭ minor to B♭ major (see Ex. 8.4).

Ex. 8.4

In the section marked *agitato e stretto* it helps to use a little arm movement (see Ex. 8.5). A shimmering conclusion following the B♭ and G, but using the pedal throughout as Grieg prescribed, creates a fine shadowlike effect (see Ex. 8.6).

Ex. 8.5

Ex. 8.6

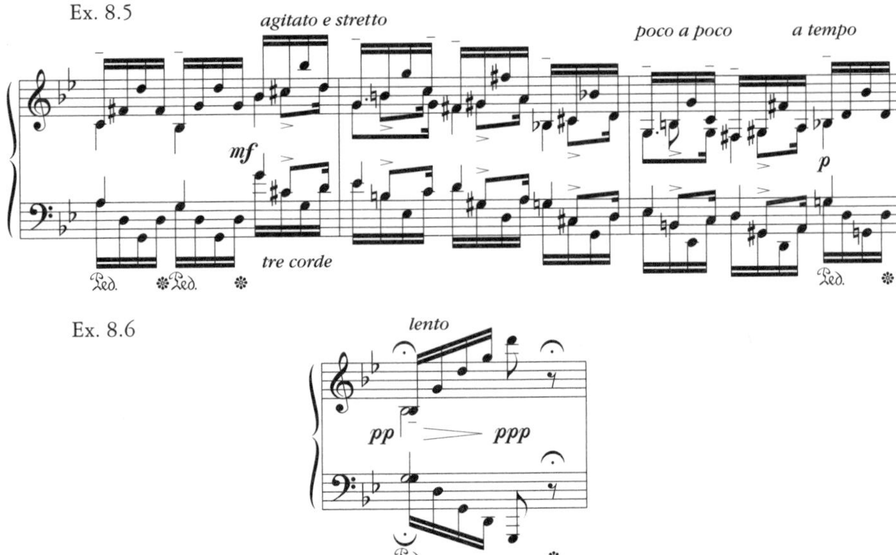

Now go to the variation that follows the funeral march (starting in measure 159). It can be played freely and pliably, as a contrast to the firmness that precedes it. Give free rein to your imagination and enjoy this *ad lib*. The portamentos with pedal in measure 164 provide a nice opportunity for coloration (see Ex. 8.7). They give you several dimensions in the different

Ex. 8.7

layers of sound. Build a bit of dramatic tension at this point by starting a kind of dialogue between the two layers (see Ex. 8.8). The portamento effects recur and become all-inclusive, giving the sound an ethereal tinge (see Ex. 8.9).

These introductory thoughts may be of some help in "getting a grip on" the *Ballade*. After the relatively straightforward opening theme comes the first variation, an impressionistic improvisation that is as wispy as a mirage. This infinitely delicate sound runs like a golden thread through the entire *Ballade*, alongside the dramatic element. Treat the keys gently in the *dolce* passages; they are the pianist's closest friends. Keep your fingers on them not

Ex. 8.8

Ex. 8.9

only on the way down but also as they come back up. Use just a little *ritardando* and a brief fermata at the end of the first variation. The fermata is placed over an eighth note, so it should not be longer than two eighth notes (see Ex. 8.10).

Ex. 8.10

Try to achieve an organic relationship between the variations, preferably all the way to the funeral march. Be careful with the transitions between variations.

With consummate skill, Grieg used his memories of Norway's abundant mountain streams to enrich the second variation. In addition to mastering the technique, try to phrase the right hand dynamically-harmonically (see Ex. 8.11). The figure in the left hand can provide support. It is the simpler one, so let it establish the rhythm for the right hand to follow. The left hand helps to play the most difficult chords, the ones involving leaps (see Ex. 8.12).

Ex. 8.11

Practice and prepare until it is no longer necessary. Do not play and prepare, but *practice* and prepare the positions until you no longer need to do so, until your hand naturally finds the position by itself. This is not a platitude, for it is at this place in the *Ballade* that the performance often begins to fall apart.

The passionate Norwegianness—the union of the melancholy and the ethereal—which is omnipresent in the *Ballade* makes the *Allegro Capriccioso* incredibly charming. Let yourself go—but do not forget the *staccato* on the first beat and the accent on the third (see Ex. 8.13). It provides a mischievous element that is difficult to achieve but fun to listen to!

Ex. 8.13

In measure 68 use a wrist *staccato* in the right hand and a springy lower-arm *staccato* in the left. Measures 72, 73, 79, and 80 are difficult, so it would be wise to prepare the reaches. The *p* in measure 78 has to be done with strong arm support, possibly with an upward movement in order to be ready to come down again on the third beat. And you must play the *staccatos* with a lot of movement if all the notes are to be heard. The D's should explode all over the place (see Ex. 8.14)!

Ex. 8.14

Più lento does not mean slow; it just means slower than what preceded it. It is an artistic challenge to vary the *recitando* figures (see Ex. 8.15). Practice

Ex. 8.15

them by themselves, without the intervening passages, and make them into your own personal statement. Keep the *a tempo* passages simple—*semplice*, as Grieg has indicated. Practice them by themselves, one after another. You can vary the tonal color to some extent according to the pitch: *legato* in the first octave, a more open style and a lighter sound in the second. Measures 99–102, marked *pianissimo*, have a subtle bass progression that enriches the variation and adds to the feeling of depth. The beautiful twittering passage can be fingered as indicated in Ex. 8.16, with the circled notes played by the left hand.

Ex. 8.16

Measures 107–108 (the second ending) are marked *ritardando* and *lento*, as a result of which the two bars that follow must also be a little different. The first ending should be without *ritardando*, the second with increasing *ritardando* and *lento*. Then it starts to sound the way it should!

Practice the two infamous variations marked *allegro scherzando* (starting in measures 108 and 125 respectively) in many different ways: top voice alone, bottom voice alone, middle voice alone; also as trills in rhythmic patterns, and as tied-finger exercises (see Exx. 8.17 and 8.18). Such exercises are the most productive for my hand, after I have gotten all I can out of other methods. The conclusion of the first pair requires a good, solid fifth finger in the left hand.

Ex. 8.17

Ex. 8.18

The second of these two variations has much in common with Mendelssohn's *Variations Serieuses*, Var. 4 (see Ex. 8.19). To bring this variation to life pianis-

Ex. 8.19

tically, you must practice it every day over a considerable period of time. Practice it both slow and fast in every possible way, paying attention to appoggiaturas, rhythmic patterns, etc. Do not shy away from the *sforzandos* in measures 132–33. Granted, they occur in the "craziest" places, but if you observe them convincingly they create surprising twists. One effective way of practicing is to mentally reverse the *legato* and *staccato* markings. By playing *legato* in the *staccato* passage you will learn what your arm movements and hand position ought to be, and the *staccato* exercises will help make the *legato* passages clearer. This variation need not be very fast. Feel the resistance of the harmonies, but let it bubble and sparkle with sixteenth notes.

The Finale, *Un poco Allegro e alla burla* (starting in measure 187), is the most difficult part of the *Ballade*, and many a fine performer is overwhelmed at this point. So tackle the Finale without delay.

Grieg's tempo indications make it very clear how the Finale should be developed: *Più Animato*, *Meno Allegro e maestoso*, *Allegro furioso*, *Prestissimo.* Start with the last section, and let the *Prestissimo* be your *prestissimo*, one you can handle with confidence, strength, and clarity. It must be the high point, so play the *Allegro furioso* just a shade slower than the *Prestissimo.*

Go next to the *Più animato* section. Notwithstanding the tempo marking, the tempo is slower than the *Allegro furioso*. But it should be faster than the opening *Un poco allegro e alla burla*—and this is where the performance often falls short. Start it more slowly, and emphasize the rhythm. Be careful with the figures in Ex. 8.20; many performers mistakenly play them as if they were in 2/8 time with a grace note in between. Pay attention to the pedal markings here; this usage lends charm and a swinging accent on the weak beats.

Try to play the rolled chords in measures 213–14 in such a way that each is fully arpeggiated, one after the other. They are often incorrectly played with an arpeggio in the left hand followed by an awkward chord in the right (see Ex. 8.21).

Ex. 8.20

Ex. 8.21

In measure 215ff., marked *Più animato*, maintaining good coordination between the hands adds to the feeling of conflict (see Ex. 8.22).

Ex. 8.22

In the G-major section (measures 224ff.), try to give the right hand and the afterbeat figures different tone colors, i.e., let the chords sound through. In the left hand, when playing the upper D with the thumb, raise the fourth finger (see Ex. 8.23).

The big *Meno allegro e maestoso* starting at measure 235 is the part we have been waiting for, the part we have dreamt of hearing and getting to play. Proceeding on the basis of the decisions made up to this point, let it really be a *meno allegro*—i.e., slower—and then let the *maestoso* call to mind the majestic, soaring mountains of Norway or the joy that accompanies a great personal victory!

Concentrate on getting the chords perfectly solid, i.e., making sure that all the notes are equally loud. Then the sound will not be hard, but as sharply hewn as mountains and fjords on a clear summer day. The rhythm should be

Ex. 8.23

maintained throughout—and it is in triple, not duple, time. Give the chords a bit of additional support with the back (see Ex. 8.24).

Ex. 8.24

At the recapitulation (measure 259), Grieg has written *più ff*. Many players reduce the dynamics a bit at this point in order to have something to draw on later, and that is a matter to decide yourself.

In the *Allegro furioso*, try to create a clear dialogue between the upper and lower voices. The contrary motions require steel-firm fifth fingers (see Ex. 8.25).

Ex. 8.25

Grieg has been criticized for the long series of F-major chords in measures 302–305 (see Ex. 8.26), but I think one should play all six chords with as much of a *crescendo* as one can muster, as one last display of strength.

It goes without saying that the trill in measure 330 (see Ex. 8.27a) is almost

Ex. 8.26

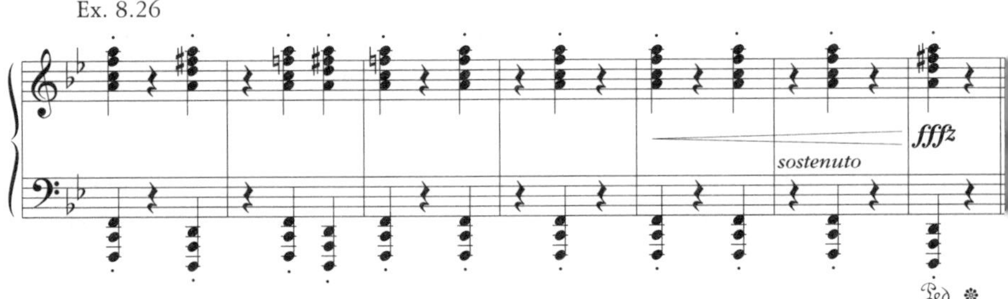

impossible to play as written. Most performers modify it in the direction of the so-called Liszt trill in order to achieve the desired forcefulness (see Ex. 8.27b).

Exx. 8.27a and b

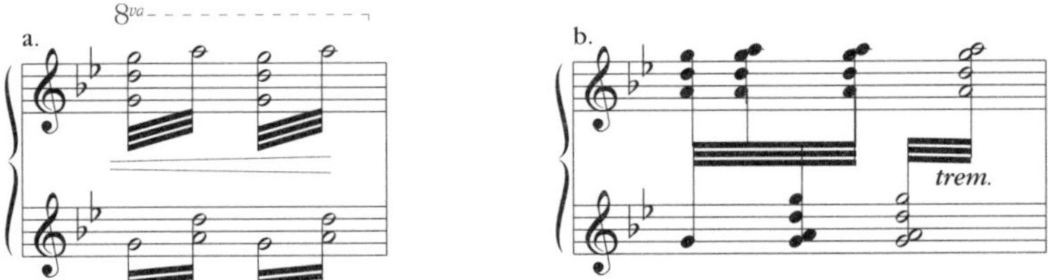

Be sure to maintain the rhythm in measures 331–34. Count it out precisely—three beats with no *ritardando*—and continue thus until you reach the fermata in measure 334 (see Ex. 8.28). There is a tendency to lapse into an *ad lib* rhythm at this point, with an unfortunate loss of intensity.

Ex. 8.28

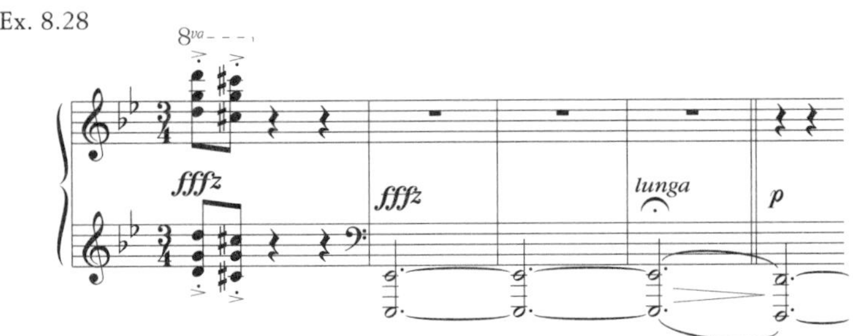

The *fffz* on the low E♭ beckons one to look down into a deep, deep chasm—in nature, in one's own soul, especially the latter. D'Albert played this octave with clenched fists. You may not wish to do that, but at a minimum use both hands, perhaps using the second and third fingers of each.

Try to make the *Ballade* into a personal triumph. Keep it unified, a single organic whole from the first statement of the theme to the last chord of the final restatement. What is the meaning of this beautiful melody, and how are you going to play it at the end after all that has gone before? Perhaps as a recollection of what you understood the first time, a reminder of the melody and the harmonies that were the foundation of the entire composition.

Play the *Ballade* as a whole with breadth and depth. Allow your listeners to sense some of the difficulties that Grieg was experiencing at the time (though we know that he never performed it in public). Feel the conflict between the harmonies, for example, between the many dominants and their turns that Grieg inserts at various points. Then the piece can stand as both a gripping confession and a great, brilliant work for piano. Many have loved this composition. Many have played it splendidly, and in so doing have created a noble tradition.

CHAPTER

9

Album Leaves: Four Piano Pieces, Op. 28

The title *Album Leaf* occurs a number of times in Grieg's works, especially in the *Lyric Pieces*, but in Op. 28 this title applies to a whole collection. The first piece was written in 1864, the second in 1874, the third in 1876, and the last one in 1878. It is interesting to follow in a single opus the development of Grieg's compositional style over such a long period of time. The *Album Leaves* are not at all intense in character, nor are they particularly demanding. In Op. 66 and other of Grieg's later works one often finds suggestions of Expressionism—vivid contrasts, oil paint, and the like. But these four *Album Leaves* appear to be painted with watercolors. Play them like aquarelles, as transparent, airy impressions, and they will be irresistible. Don't smother them with heavy attacks and big dynamic effects. The secret is just to hint at what these pieces are trying to express rather than to blurt it out.

No. 1, Allegro con moto

This piece begins with a recitative-like passage that immediately suggests a positive and rhapsodic mood (see Ex. 9.1). Play with melodic and harmonic contrast. By this I mean that the melodic line must always be more prominent than the harmonic background. A gently articulated, almost quiet motive takes over in measure 7. It is not easy to play the triplets in measures 7 and 8 clearly. Lift the first and second fingers before striking B and D (see Ex. 9.2).

Grieg gave detailed instructions regarding the articulation: slurs (some

Ex. 9.1

Ex. 9.2

short, some long), little syncopations, *tenuto* signs (see Ex. 9.3). The articulation indications are asymmetric, thus enlivening the music.

Ex. 9.3

Grieg is very meticulous about the placement of such indications as *ritardando*, *a tempo*, *stretto*, *poco ritardando*. Practice these transitions exactly as he specified them. Seldom in his music does one find changes in tempo indicated as in these pieces. Op. 28 serves as a guide to Grieg's thinking with respect to the use of *rubato* (see Ex. 9.4).

Do not subdivide the long lines of the middle section, but emphasize the top voice especially prominently at the beginning. In the repeat you might bring out the tenor voice to provide a bit of contrast

Ex. 9.4

The conclusion has an ethereal character. Technically it is by no means easy. If it works for you, use the left hand to help out on the chords as indicated in Ex. 9.5. Whatever fingering you use, it is important to play the end of the piece pliably—with what the French call *souplesse*—with no sharp corners or jerkiness. Using the third finger on the final A♭ achieves an elegant conclusion.

Ex. 9.5

The first theme can be varied a little each time it is played. You might wish to give it a special intimacy at its last occurrence, and possibly let the left hand dominate the coloration toward the end.

The numerous instances of *rubatos* and the butterfly-like triplets in this *Album Leaf* inspire youthful feelings and an excitable frame of mind—the first spring of one's youth, the tenderest elegance.

No. 2, Allegretto espressivo

The second piece in the set is flowing and lovely, with a "question and answer" relationship between the hands. The overall character of the sound is unique, almost like humming instead of singing (see Ex. 9.6).

The most Norwegian aspect of No. 1 is undoubtedly the introduction, the recitative. In No. 2, it is the middle section that has the national flavor; the single-voice recitative passages and the trill sound especially Norwegian. The ninth chord with the melisma at the top in measure 25, for example, is reminiscent of a *stev*, an old traditional folk tune (see Ex. 9.7).

The many rolled chords contribute much to the character of this piece. Work them out carefully so that all the notes are sounded clearly, one after the other. Anticipate the rolled chords in order to keep the melody flowing in an unbroken stream. Pay particular attention to the pedal so that the lowest note is not lost. Always be sure that the bottom note of the chord is included so the harmony will sound logical (see Ex. 9.6).

Play as if you didn't have any fingers! By this I mean play with suppleness and flexibility in all the joints so that the fingers slither over the keys. Your arm and hand should function as one unified whole, with no joint exerting its own will. The sound will be so convincing that it will make us forget that it is being produced by the mechanical process of hammers hitting strings. The joints in one's arms and hands perform almost like a caterpillar tractor: the tracks crawl over and around the bumps and even them out, and one's inner feeling is that the arm is open and free. The result is a captivating sound, the product of a devoted mind and ear.

Have you noticed the different ways that the piano reacts at the various octave levels? Richly colored playing begins with an awareness of these differences. The traditional melodic *legato* is especially well suited to the octave below middle C and the octave and a half above it. From that point upward an intense *legato* becomes less and less necessary and xylophone-like attacks produce an attractive sound. This technique can be employed in the present piece. The middle section is sequential and should be played *poco più agitato*, that is, each motivic element should be presented with greater intensity than the preceding one as the pitch rises—and the reverse as it falls.

Bring out the sequences in measures 24–31: first you are in D♭, then A, then E♭, then G, finally leading to C.

The *portamento* notation in the last sixteenth-note passage is charming (see Ex. 9.8). Play it with steady support of the right thumb on the B♭, and use a

Ex. 9.8

kind of "waving" technique, with the motion originating in the lower arm or wrist, to make each note separate from its neighbors. The result will be Chopinesque. Finally, try to produce a sound that simulates humming, and phrase the whole in a slow, swinging character.

No. 3, Vivace

The third leaf in this album is a charming, saucy waltz. Like the waltzes in the *Lyric Pieces*, it is hardly suitable for ordinary people to dance to. One is inclined to think instead of a pair of professional dancers, perhaps even ballet dancers (see Ex. 9.9). Keep that in mind if you wish to elevate Grieg's waltzes to a high

Ex. 9.9

artistic level. If you play too sluggishly, too ponderously—with too dense a sound—and if the rhythm is a metronomic 3/4, the piece won't come alive. Indeed, many of Grieg's pieces can be ruined this way. Ballet and professional dance of any kind must be light and precise, with the dancers' feet striking the floor so softly they can scarcely be heard. Applying the same concept to piano playing means that one's arm should be floating over the keys rather than weighing down on them. The finger work must be very well developed and elaborate. Use more finger activity than downward pressure. However, the arm should in no way be isolated or stiff; on the contrary, it must be free and flexible and very light.

Grieg has played it very safe in this piece with respect to volume levels: they mostly alternate between *piano* and *pianissimo*. The *forte* passages are quite short and should be treated in accordance with the dancelike character of the piece. Don't make them too loud—*poco forte*, perhaps, rather than an outright *forte*.

Try varying the rhythmic pulse a bit from time to time. This can be accomplished in many different ways. According to Béla Bartók, the third quarter note is the most important in 3/4 time because it gives new life to—and is an upbeat to—the next phrase. He also said that the second beat is sometimes the most interesting, dynamically or agogically. Although we are discussing Grieg and Norwegian music, Bartók's remark can inspire us to introduce a bit of a swing, a subtle rhythmic adjustment here and there, to help avoid the monotonous accenting of first beats that puts audiences to sleep. Moreover, it is a good idea to create "long measures" here and there. At the beginning there are two one-measure periods followed by a two-measure period, so it makes sense to think of measures 3–4 as constituting one six-beat measure (see Ex. 9.10).

Ex. 9.10

This point relates to the indication *poco stretto* for this passage. Grieg was very explicit about the *rubato* he wanted, writing such things as *stretto*, *a tempo*, *poco ritardando*, etc., at various places. So far as *rubato* is concerned, you will get plenty of ideas if you just follow Grieg's copious instructions (see Ex. 9.11).

Ex. 9.11

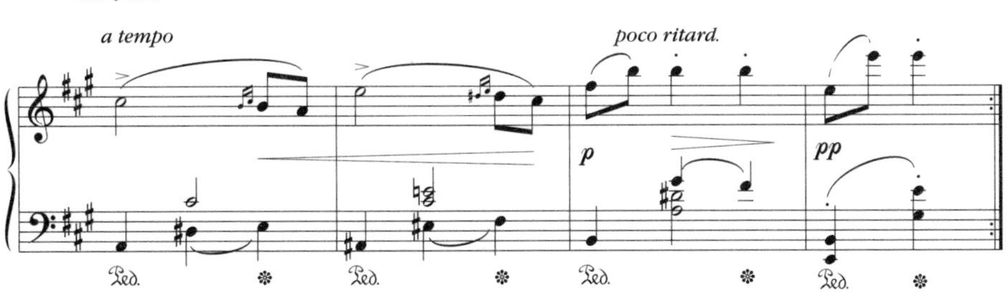

Rhythmic emphasis within a measure is another matter. In measures 1–2 it is possible to prolong the second beat slightly so as to bring out the slur in the left hand. To keep from getting too episodic it is wise to follow Grieg's pedal indications in measures 9–12: the pedal is to be held down for four whole measures (see Ex. 9.12).

Ex. 9.12

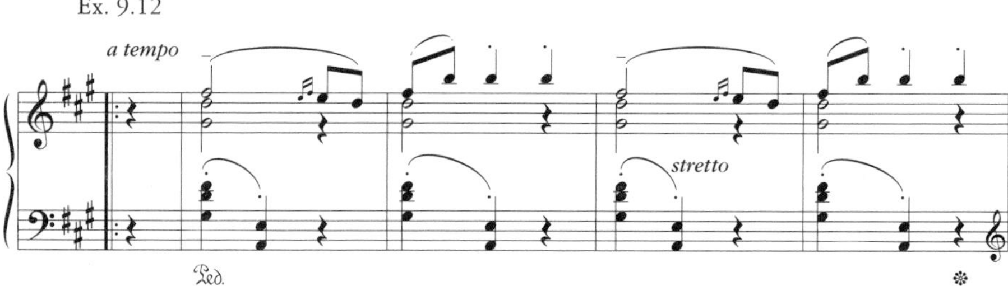

The result is a shimmering effect, a leveling out that is refreshing in contrast to the short units of the first part. Measures 13ff. constitute a sequence, part of a long sentence encompassing eight measures that provide a counterbalance to the rapid-fire outbursts of the first part.

The middle section is in A minor. Because one tends to think of minor as an aspect of the corresponding major, this section is somewhat melancholy. Measures 29–36 reflect the first several measures of the piece. The coloration, therefore, should be somewhat different from that in the opening: delicate fingertip activity to achieve a legato in the top voice, all the while being careful to maintain the alto voice in the right hand. The left hand, meanwhile, should maintain a swinging rhythm, not overly articulated. This passage is interrupted in a humorous way by a measure marked *fp*, with slurs and staccatos (see Ex. 9.13).

Ex. 9.13

The subsequent development of the middle section is also humorous. Grieg's Norwegian roots are abundantly evident here as he serves up a coquettish mixture of waltz and *springar* in measures 31–32 (see Ex. 9.14). The tonality has made a strong shift to the left on the circle of fifths; that is why the sound seems so distant from what preceded it (see Ex. 9.15).

Sometimes the principal motive can be colored with the right hand, sometimes with the left, i.e., with either the light or the dark octave. I tend to prefer the dark coloring, emphasizing the left hand so it stands in sharper contrast to the bright soprano part. Repetitions follow: the game with the third beat, the second beat, periods of varying length.

Ex. 9.14

Ex. 9.15

Starting at measure 9, however, it is the first beat that calls for the greatest emphasis—as Grieg himself has indicated. *Tenuto* appears in every other measure, and the left hand has a *portamento* on both chords, but connected with a slur (see Ex. 9.14). For that reason it is a good idea to use a connecting movement in the left hand, mainly downward on the first quarter note and a little more upward on the second. In this way you may conjure up a picture of a charming nineteenth-century salon.

No. 4, Andantino serioso

The last piece of the set elevates the entire collection. Its main section consists of a beautiful folklike melody. The middle section is a delightful little *halling* that sounds as if it came straight out of a bridal procession in a mountain community where fiddle music still flourishes. It was the last of the four pieces to be composed, and it was written a good fourteen years later than No. 1. Now the master is in full control as he skillfully arranges material based on his experience with Norwegian folk music.

The first theme, in C♯ minor, starts on the subdominant. The magnificent melody, which is both soaring and serious, nonetheless ends with a hint of a swinging rhythm (see Ex. 9.16). The accent on the first beat in measure 4 means that you must depart slightly from the established rhythm, i.e., delay the second beat slightly so as to give the music a dancelike character (see Ex. 9.17).

Measures 5–8 are related sequentially to measures 1–4 and may be colored a shade darker. The continuation in E major is even softer than the passages

Ex. 9.16

Ex. 9.17

preceding it, marked *p* and *mf* respectively. The swinging rhythm returns. The quarter note on the first beat can be prolonged slightly by lifting the wrist. Measures 13–16 again constitute a sequence of what precedes them, but this time in the inspired key of G♯ major. Be careful here: Grieg has written *dolcissimo* (see Ex. 9.18).

Ex. 9.18

Then follows a dramatization, first with a Neapolitan subdominant chord—in this case a D-major chord with F♯ in the bass. A steady *crescendo* leads to a heavy and significant harmonic shaping of the melody (see Ex. 9.19). You can emphasize this shaping by giving the passage a dark coloring, following the progress of the bass all the way down to the lowest C♯.

In measure 2 and elsewhere in this piece, the grace note is notated in such a way that it becomes a descending arpeggio. The same thing occurs in one of the *Lyric Pieces*, the *Notturno* (Op. 54, No. 4). It is interesting to compare the two instances (see Ex. 9.20).

Ex. 9.19

Ex. 9.20

Play as smooth a *legato* as possible in the opening section. A lowered, gliding hand with pressure far forward on the fingertips is best. It is as if the blood flows out to the ends of your fingers, and from there onto the piano keys. As for phrasing, emphasize the upbeat. Try not to feel that you are starting slowly, but that you have a long, long phrase that extends all the way to measure 4. It is not easy to achieve this emphasis on the upbeat, which requires a downward arm movement. It is equally important that you do not inadvertently accent the downbeats in the first section. Try to strike the note as your hand is moving upward—*sneak into* the chord at the beginning.

It has been said that a pianist who wishes to master the technique of a songlike *legato* should observe a vocalist or a wind player. The performance of a truly good singer is characterized above all by resonating head tones, by the gentle placement of the sound in the head. You can indirectly apply this technique to the piano by means of upward-oriented playing. Concentrate especially on the intervals: diatonic lines are easier to make *legato* than nondiatonic ones. In the beginning this means *legato*, especially on the descending triads G♯–E–C♯ and D♯–B♯–G♯ (see Ex. 9.21). The same advice applies to other similar passages in the piece.

After this impressive beginning, Grieg paints a picture, a tableau, that in its purity and richness of color and national character is worthy of the great Norwegian painters Adolf Tidemand and Hans Gude. The dance tune becomes a picture of a Norwegian landscape, and the landscape is reflected in a fjord or a lake.

Ex. 9.21

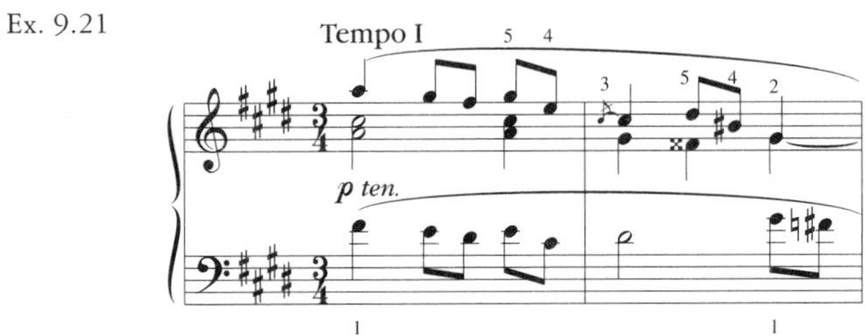

Measures 25ff., marked *Allegro giocoso*, acquire a magical depth by virtue of the low D♭ that functions as a pedal point, or *bourdon* (see Ex. 9.22). The illusion of a reflection is achieved by keeping the pedal down throughout the entire passage. It works if you play so softly that you can scarcely be heard.

Ex. 9.22

A surprising little change occurs in measure 28, with accents on the second and fourth eighth notes preceded by an upward jump from the first and third. This pattern is repeated in measure 32. This is by no means easy to do *pianissimo*. First practice it with a full-bodied tone and with exaggerated accents until you have it down pat both mentally and physically. Then decrease the volume little by little, down to the softest of softs, perhaps with a little left pedal if the instrument you are using allows it and is not too dull.

The first section had accents mainly on the first beat, the second section mainly on the second beat. Keep your left hand independent—without accents, but with a light, tripping staccato (see Ex. 9.23). Grieg has written

Ex. 9.23

senza pedale. Let that be your guide. Use a damper pedal in the preceding section, no pedal at all here. Do not use pedal throughout: it gets too monotonous. In measure 36 it would be a good idea to delay the second beat briefly (see Ex. 9.24).

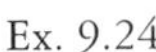
Ex. 9.24

The pedaled fifths in measures 41–50 are reminiscent of music for the Hardanger fiddle, an instrument indigenous to Norway. The melody must come to the fore here, but the rhythm must be emphasized as well. The merry afterbeat in the left hand imitates the Norwegian *langeleik*, a type of zither. The somewhat dark undertone of the preceding section has disappeared. The *staccato* markings in measure 33 should be precisely and painstakingly observed, perhaps with a bit of wrist action. The *fp* on the second beat in measure 46 is cleverly placed. The effect of the last sixteenth-note groups (measure 47)—which are not *staccato*, but in groups of two—is subtle. It evolves gradually into the next two measures, with an afterbeat on the fifth in a lower register. Be careful to make them light: strike the keys with an upward motion so the attacks are not heavy.

The recapitulation is identical to the opening. The performer must decide whether to play it the same or whether it feels a little different now that it follows the middle section. Both views are worthy of consideration, but presumably it is most natural to recreate the slow folk tune in a slightly different way after all that has gone before. The trills can precede the beat and can be light and supple, in most instances—for example, in measure 73 (see Ex. 9.25).

Ex. 9.25

That was not the case in measure 41, in the *Allegro giocoso*, where Grieg wrote them out and subtracted their value from the note to which they were attached. Various fingerings are possible here. One option is 5–4–1 on the first chord and 2–4–3 on the trill. If you do the trill with 2–3–2 watch out for the second finger. Be careful that the action does not get locked so that the second E♭ fails to sound (see Ex. 9.26).

Ex. 9.26

No obstacle is too great for one who will use the piano to create beautiful watercolors. This collection provides an opportunity for you to paint four lovely, luminous, dainty aquarelles, real album leaves.

CHAPTER

10

Improvisata on Two Norwegian Folk Songs, Op. 29

In 1878 Grieg got actively involved in the project to create a monument in Bergen to honor the playwright Ludvig Holberg, who was born in that city in 1684. Grieg contributed his honorarium for the publication of Op. 29 to the Holberg fund and later wrote two works specifically for the Holberg jubilee, the *Holberg Suite*, Op. 40, and the *Holberg Cantata*, EG 171.

Apart from the fact that the royalty was given to the Holberg fund, the *Improvisata* have little to do with the great dramatist. They are, in fact, much more reminiscent of Liszt than of Holberg. One gets the impression that these *Improvisata* are Grieg's attempt to write a Norwegian counterpart to Liszt's *Hungarian Rhapsodies*. The Lisztian formula is evident in the basic concept of the composition, namely, to create a virtuosic arrangement of material drawn from the folk music of the composer's native land. The form is slow–fast; in the *Hungarian Rhapsodies* the sections are called *Lassú* and *Friss.* Grieg's *Improvisata* are also divided into slow and fast sections, and musically, too, they have much in common with Liszt's compositions. Brilliant runs and crackling accents high in the upper register remind one of the Hungarian master. Grieg was familiar with Liszt's *Tarantella* from *Venezia e Napoli* (see Exx. 10.1a and b). Despite certain similarities to Liszt in concept and pianistic style, however, the musical substance and overall spirit of Op. 29 are thoroughly Norwegian.

No. 1, Allegretto con moto

The first improvisation opens with a flourish in a recitativic arpeggio. To Norwegian ears this arpeggio—ascending, lingering on a plateau, then descending again—recalls the unmistakable pattern of a *stev*, one of the oldest strata in our folk music. The first theme is a *stev* from Hallingdal entitled *The Boy and the Girl in the Hayloft*. In this very earthy song, the boy and the girl take turns singing to each other. He sings, "Hi there, my Mari! Here I am, and thanks for the last time we were in the hay. Thanks for all the fun we had from evening until dawn of day." She replies, "Ola, why didn't you come earlier in the evening? Long have I lain here waiting for you under the blanket. Ugh, you are so cold! Get away from me! And while you are lying there, tell me: do you know that boy who came dashing by last year—who, when I let the bull out, followed me to the house and went to bed in the loft, and then hurried away before morning?"

The first melody, which initially appears in the tenor voice, has a rocking, yearning rhythm. The girl, a frivolous milkmaid, answers in the middle section, marked *Allegro*. The rhythm used here appears in several of Grieg's works, not least in the last half of *Ballade*, Op. 24. Maintain this rhythm exactly as written, observing the *staccatos*, the note values, and the sixteenth rest. Do not slip into a pattern that sounds like two eighth notes with an anacrusis preceding the second one (see Ex. 10.2).

Ex. 10.2

Keep the tempo slow enough that you can make this rhythmic pattern come through. Use an animated, short attack for all dynamics—*p*, *pp*, *f*, or *ff*—to portray this frisky lass the boy has met in the hayloft!

The gentle slur from the quarter note to the eighth in the bass in measures 31–34 provides a fine contrast to the *staccatos* in the soprano voice. Use some downward wrist motion on the first beat and upward motion on the last. Note the *legato* voice in the middle, which is very effective (see Ex. 10.3).

Ex. 10.3

In measures 35–37 the melody is in the middle voice in the right hand. Practice Cortot's accent studies to learn how to bring it out without losing the outer voices. The sixteenth-note run in measure 38 should be practiced with fast, active fingering.

Measures 39–41 consist of a tremolo passage with a clear upper voice. Everything is controlled by the eighth notes in the left hand, which must be rigorously in time.

The girl is impudent, and now she refers to boyfriend No. 2 even as she is lying under the blanket with No. 1. In the *Molto vivace* the contrary rhythm is spiced with articulated, dotted rhythms (see Ex. 10.4). It leads to a lively little dance tune—a *springar*—with amusing accents on the third beat (see Ex. 10.5).

Most of all, the rhythm is marked by triplets in the Liszt manner. They clash with the hidden rhythm of the melody and tend to accelerate. If you think too much about emphasizing the melody, you may inadvertently quicken

Ex. 10.4

Ex. 10.5

the tempo. The melody should be emphasized dynamically, but it is important to keep the passage under control. Try to feel the rhythmic placement of the triplets (see Ex. 10.1a). In measures 64–65, pay attention to the accents and to the hemiola effect (see Ex. 10.6).

Ex. 10.6

Prepare the accompaniment of the *Molto vivace* section carefully. Put a little emphasis on the fifth finger on the first beat to keep a good grip on it, and to maintain precision in the afterbeats. The pattern of emphasis in this section in 3/4 time is strong, weaker, weakest.

The form has some symmetry in that the piece ends in a kind of recapitulation, now recast with thick *pesante* chords. This section calls for a rich, almost compact sound, in which all the notes in the chord are made to count. The bass is very important: the pedal point is the foundation of the entire passage. After seven measures on A it descends chromatically via A♭–G–F♯–F–E, and this line should be brought out.

There is an unmistakably Griegian touch in the sudden rest in measure 84, where we seem to have reached an important point, where the music seems to continue into the rest. The arpeggio at the end is not as big and elaborate as the opening one, but it provides an architectonic counterbalance to it.

No. 2, Andante

Grieg got his material for the second improvisation from Valdres, a particularly scenic area of Norway about a hundred miles northwest of Oslo. The words of the song are as follows: "There once was a king, from England he came, and he had a princess so lovely and fair. And there was a sailor courageous and bold, he asked the fair princess: will you have me to wed?"

The melody depicting the princess is almost in the style of the great pianist Sigismund Thalberg. This lovely thumb melody alternates between the hands to an accompaniment of chords on the afterbeats. The pattern is similar to Op. 17, No. 16, *I Know a Little Maiden* (see Exx. 10.7 and 10.8).

Ex. 10.7

Ex. 10.8

Elsewhere Grieg varies the rhythmic pattern—for example, in measure 9, we find a half note, eighth notes, a dotted eighth followed by a sixteenth, and finally a triplet (see Ex. 10.9). Get these rhythmic niceties down as accurately

Ex. 10.9

as possible so that you can differentiate the various patterns, i.e., so that the sixteenth note does not sound like the last note of the triplet and the eighth note is properly placed between the second and third notes of the triplet. Grieg's music has many such rhythmic peculiarities, and one should play them as written rather than to take liberties. There is room for *rubato*, but only after you have mastered the score.

No. 2 also exhibits some characteristically Griegian harmonizations—a dominant thirteenth (see Ex. 10.10) and some altered dominants (see Exx. 10.11a and b). "Feel" this expressive music, especially as the dissonances are being resolved.

Ex. 10.10

Exx. 10.11a and b

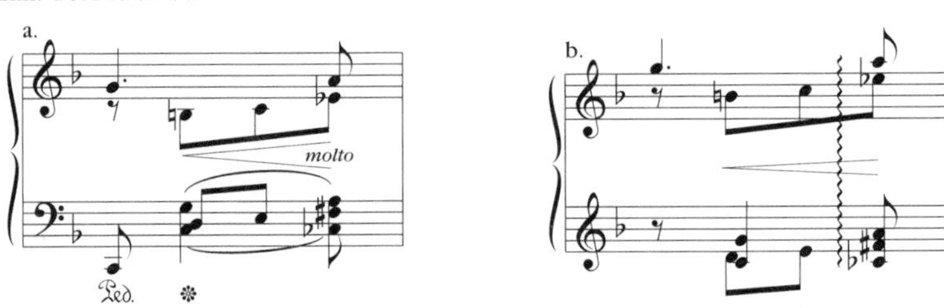

The leftward shift in tonality—in this case to E♭ minor—can be very effective. Emphasize the shift with a *subito piano* (see Ex. 10.12).

When the melody is repeated an octave higher, use an extra light and clear tone, almost as if a soprano were singing in falsetto (see Ex. 10.13).

Ex. 10.12

Ex. 10.13

Rolled chords have a unique expressiveness if they are crystal clear (see Ex. 10.14).

Ex. 10.14

The melody ends in a full-measure rest. Count it! (see Ex. 10.15).

Ex. 10.15

The middle section, marked *Presto*, is cut from the same pattern as Liszt's *lassú* and *friss*. It portrays the sailor who has caught the princess's eye. The theme that enters in the left hand in measure 48 is an imitation of a Hardanger-fiddle dance melody (a *springar*). The time signature is 3/4, and the first two measures are what one would expect, i.e., a half note and a quarter note, but measures 46 and 47 have a hemiola effect (see Ex. 10.16).

Ex. 10.16

The hemiola reappears as a rhythmic variation throughout the piece, sometimes against a duple division of six beats, sometimes simultaneously in both hands. The latter effect is especially electrifying. First practice the rhythmic pattern in plain quarter notes. Then beat the quarter-note rhythm with your foot while the right hand stresses the accent pattern (omit the triplets!) and the left emphasizes the accents that create the hemiola effect, i.e., those that contradict the underlying beat. Getting this rhythm "in your bones" is more important here than mere technical skill. This middle section is constantly in danger of getting out of control—like a runaway horse—because of our preoccupation with the technical dimension. The difficult execution of the triplets tends to overshadow everything else. But the rhythmic pulse and the rhythmically varied accents must be in the foreground and control the progress of the whole. The triplets are merely part of that larger rhythmic pattern. The hand with the quarter notes must lead. This Presto is a demanding piece of pianistic pyrotechnics.

The triplets in this *Improvisata* are reminiscent of those in *Dance from Jølster*, Op. 17, and in the middle section of *From the Carnival*, Op. 19 (see Ex. 10.17a, b, and c). The triplets in all three passages consist of stepwise

Exx. 10.17a, b, and c

ascending figures. Give support from the elbow. There is a need for a little pull of the lower arm on each group of triplets, starting with the first note.

Use the same fingering throughout, with the left hand always beginning with the third finger, the right hand always with the first.

The diminished chords in the upper register are of special interest (see Ex. 10.18).

Ex. 10.18

Readers familiar with the first movement of Grieg's *Violin Sonata No. 2* may recognize the virtuosic little intermezzo in measures 73–76 of the present piece (see Ex. 10.19).

Ex. 10.19

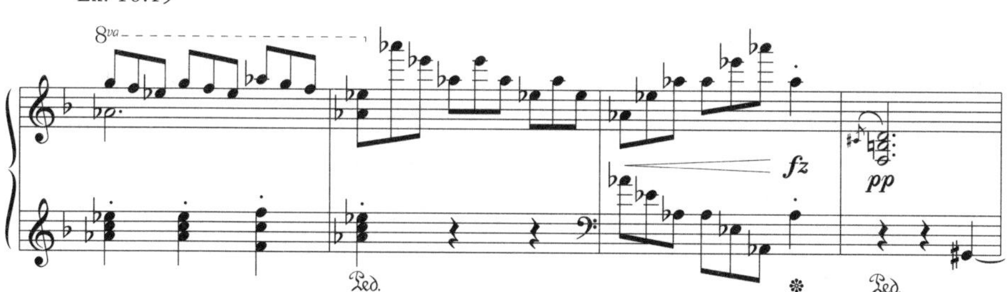

Technique is important, and so is the precise fingering of each figure, but most important of all are rhythm and temperament. Temperament is based on rhythm, so without rhythm there is no temperament. Sudden outbursts and cascades come off best when you hold back rhythmically in the moment of performance, in the same way that one might control a wild horse by holding back firmly on the reins. To put the same point negatively, without holding back there can be no truly convincing high point and no outbursts. Do not just get louder in the *ff* passages; rather, broaden out a little (see Ex. 10.20).

Ex. 10.20

The *Presto* section concludes in a fervent and supple manner. In measure

115 the accent is on the third beat. Then, after an eloquent measure-long rest, there follows another figure with the accent on the first beat and another eloquent and even longer rest. Clearly the princess had to fall for *such* a sailor!

The recapitulation is almost identical to the opening of the piece. Play it with great passion and with a supple and ingratiating shading of the sound. Note the alternation between the left and right sides of the circle of fifths in measures 137 and 138. Emphasize this contrast with a humming *pianissimo* (see Ex. 10.21).

Ex. 10.21

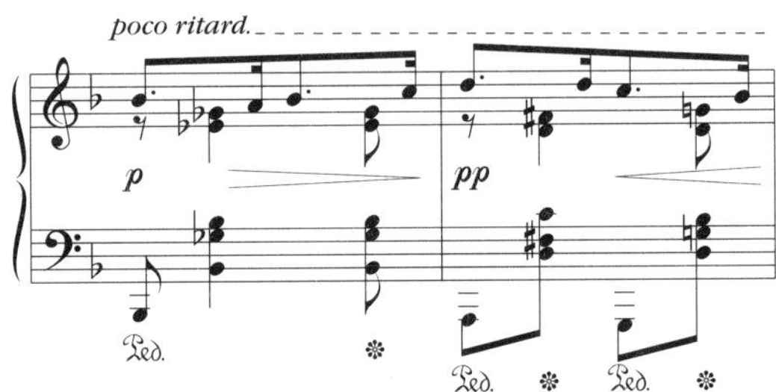

In the coda, rolled chords that remind one of the sparkling waters of a mountain stream are moved to the middle register and then resolved in a simple and tuneful way. Pay attention to the pedal here, for the lowest notes tend to get lost, and they are important for the overall sound. The sound spectrum is formed consistent with the proportions of the overtones, with considerable accenting of the root of the chord, less of the fifth, and least of the third. Let this principle be your guide for the proper sonority, especially in chords covering a long range (see Ex. 10.22).

Ex. 10.22

CHAPTER 11

Holberg Suite, Op. 40

Shortly after completing this composition, Grieg referred to it in a letter to his Dutch friend Julius Röntgen by the title *From Holberg's Time* and characterized it as his "suite in the old style." It was written for the Norwegian pianist Erika Lie Nissen and is a pianistic jewel. We denizens of the keyboard are proud of the fact that Grieg wrote the piano version first, not—as many mistakenly believe—the string version. Thus the piano version is not an arrangement but an original piece that Grieg himself premiered in Bergen before the string version was arranged and published. It was only with an eye to sales in Germany that Peters published the string version first—in the hope that it would gain entry into the literature for chamber orchestra as an original work rather than as an arrangement of a piano work.

The first and last movements are virtuoso pieces for the piano. It is as if a *Waldstein Sonata* had been written on Norwegian soil. Add to that a generous portion of Holbergian wittiness and cheeky humor, perhaps with a dash of irony, and you will begin to sense the brilliance of Grieg's *Holberg Suite*. Give it plenty of practice time! *Preludium* and *Rigaudon* realize their potential only if we master their technical challenges. If they are not practiced sufficiently they can be a disaster onstage.

First Movement: Preludium

This movement, marked *Allegro vivace*, must be effervescent, unbridled, Romantic. Imagine a slur over the whole movement and create one long, uninterrupted line, a single irresistible wave that continues from the first note to the final chord.

This virtuoso piece also has something hymnlike about it. Practice it chordally, as indicated in Ex. 11.1, and bring out the melody slightly without losing the overall rhythm (see Ex. 11.2).

Ex. 11.1

Ex. 11.2

Phrase the whole movement chordally on the basis of these progressions. Listen carefully to the balance between bass and treble. Despite the fact that you are thinking chordally, the sixteenth notes must sound crystal clear and even. With music like this you must first practice it with a good, solid attack on each note before you can hope to play those notes softly, lightly, and still evenly. When the melody begins in the right hand in measure 9, it is advisable to view the *piano* indication as applying to the whole, i.e., a differentiated *piano* in which the right hand must be especially soft—a *mezzoforte* in the left hand, let us say, and a *pianissimo* in the right. The sum of the two will be a *piano* in which the sixteenth notes neither dominate nor recede.

The middle section (measure 19ff.) is somewhat cadential in character. The two *sforzandos* in succession in measures 29–30 call for a little breadth (see Ex. 11.3).

The treble passage marked *piano* immediately following must be very soft but still clear, like a bit of side lighting—a contrasting color, a pastel, a soft fragrance—that is added to the mix. It requires a lot of solid technical practice to get this right (see Ex. 11.4).

The broken chords leading up to the long run in measure 41 can be notated

Ex. 11.3

Ex. 11.4

in various ways. Ex. 11.5 is one version. The chord on the first beat of measure 41 can be divided in two, as a violinist might play it. The descending run itself calls for all the brilliance and razzle-dazzle you can muster. The passage can be handled in any number of ways, but for practice purposes it might be subdivided into groups of 7 + 7 + 7 + 6. During performance it is best to think of it as one long line, without subdivision (see Ex. 11.6).

Ex. 11.5

Ex. 11.6

Try to bring out the beautiful countermelody in the left hand in measure 54 (see Ex. 11.7). Resolve the inherent polyphony in the figures in measure 54 as you make the transition to *piano*, *a tempo* in the next measure (see Ex.

11.8). The theme in the left hand is to be played somewhat more calmly than the first time. In measure 9 Grieg wrote *cantabile*, but here the indication is *tranquillo cantabile*, i.e., a little more reflective than before. The contrast makes a good impression in performance (see Ex. 11.9).

In order to provide a solid foundation in the *crescendo*, follow the progress of the bass from G through F to E (see Ex. 11.10).

Second Movement: Sarabande

The excitement increases for the performer with the Sarabande. Marked *Andante espressivo*, it incorporates the spirit of ancient tragedy. At the same time, it is highly melodic and is for the most part in a four-voice homophonic style.

A fine, caressing, stringlike *legato* is needed in the individual voices in order to bring out their separate lines. The most exciting aspect for the performer is the phrasing, which must be gentle to the point of subtlety. One's imagination is put to the test. There are relatively few notes, so one can easily introduce too many emphases—and suddenly the forward movement

Ex. 11.10

comes to a halt. Seek out elements that make for lightness and play them in a manner that points upward (see Ex. 11.11). The repeat of measures 1–8 should perhaps be played very softly.

Ex. 11.11

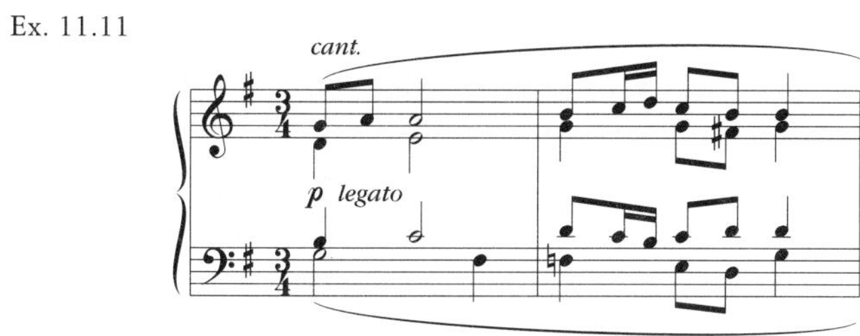

The second section, which begins at measure 9, is a challenge to one's imagination. The repeat sign should, of course, be observed, but therein lies the challenge, because you have an opportunity to create some truly long lines. One possibility is to play it very softly the first time and increase the dynamics in the repeat. If you choose this option, you should not create a feeling of conclusion at the repeat sign; rather think of the music as continuing through the repeat, as if there were a tie between measure 32 and measure 9. Other phrasing details can also be changed in the repeat—for example, measure 30 might be played with a *crescendo* the first time and a *diminuendo* the second (see Ex. 11.12).

In bel canto singing, soloists often sing an ascending line with a subtle *diminuendo* in place of the expected *crescendo*, resulting in an especially effective

Ex. 11.12

espressivo. You can achieve something of the same exciting effect as a lyric soprano ascending into her upper register with a beautiful, controlled *diminuendo*.

Measures 18–20 give a hint of a dance rhythm. Vary the expression as the music sequences downward in measures 21–22 so that it does not become monotonous.

The *Sarabande* can be a successful piece if you can keep it moving and prevent it from becoming too episodic. There should be a slight emphasis on the second beat, not a heavy one. A subtle stress here and there helps to give the *Sarabande* its special character (see Ex. 11.13).

Ex. 11.13

Third Movement: Gavotte

In this movement the spirit of Ludvig Holberg really comes to the fore. With archaic elegance it conjures up a picture of men in formal evening dress politely bowing to perfumed ladies in elegant gowns, who curtsy in return. It is satirical, perhaps with a note of sarcasm: maybe Grieg is poking fun at the superficial elegance of the seventeenth century. In the middle of the movement the ladies and gentlemen seem to interrupt their chatting and allow themselves to be entertained with a charming little Musette—with a folkish cast, as is to be expected. Grieg gives many instructions for playing the *Gavotte*. The time is *alla breve*, and the numerous ties and slurs should be carefully observed (see Ex. 11.14).

Ex. 11.14

Nonetheless, you must not lose sight of the longer lines. At the beginning, for example, you should mentally add a slur extending from the first note all the way to the half-note E in measure 2.

Play the *Gavotte* clearly with a consistent firmness in the fingertips. Obviously the principal theme is sounded again and again, but note that Grieg varies the dynamics. It is *piano* in measures 1–2 and *forte* in measures 4–6 (see Ex. 11.14), *pianissimo* in measures 15–17 (which repeat the opening) and *forte pesante* with a crescendo to *fortissimo* in measures 36–38 (see Ex. 11.15).

Ex. 11.15

The execution of the trill in measure 40 can be a problem. I recommend the solution indicated in Ex. 11.16.

Ex. 11.16

In the Musette the left hand leads. It gives the piece the hint of a Hardanger fiddle—or *bourdon*. This allusion to folk music is faint but deliberate. Syncopation adds excitement. In measures 52–56 use the left hand for the quarter notes, thereby freeing the right hand to concentrate on phrasing the melody line (see Ex. 11.17).

Ex. 11.17

The resounding half notes in the soprano voice in measures 43–44 and 59–60 are like sleigh bells (see Ex. 11.18).

Ex. 11.18

The *Gavotte* is a catchy little piece!

Fourth Movement: Air

There is a singular depth and gravity in the melodic lines, the harmonic coloring, the introspective mood, and the essential singability of this movement. It can be a dismal failure if it is not played with great musical sensitivity. One must approach it with an open mind and a keen ear. It is essential to create long melodic lines. You must decide whether to observe the repeat signs, but if you meet the challenges posed by the repeats, the picture you paint can be even bigger and richer. You will be taking a chance, but the reward can be great. The form of the suite as a whole is enhanced if the repeats in the *Air* are observed, for they put a little more distance between two virtuoso movements, thereby giving the listener a bit of a breather before plunging into the last movement.

As in the *Sarabande*, it is advisable to vary the dynamics from one iteration to the next. One possibility is to play the repeat of the first section (measures 1–15) with greater intensity as a continuation of the emotion suggested in measures 14–15. The repeat of the second section (measures 16–57) should in general be very soft and delicate, but the loud parts should be even louder than in the first iteration. Try various possibilities until you find what works best for you.

The *Air* is marked *Andante religioso*. The left hand will largely determine whether you will realize Grieg's intentions. Play soft chords. Play them tightly, evenly, in as controlled a manner as you can. Think of them as the inexorable march of time and destiny. For the most part the chords play an accompanying role, but occasionally they contribute a snatch of melody (see Exx. 11.19a and b).

Exx. 11.19a and b

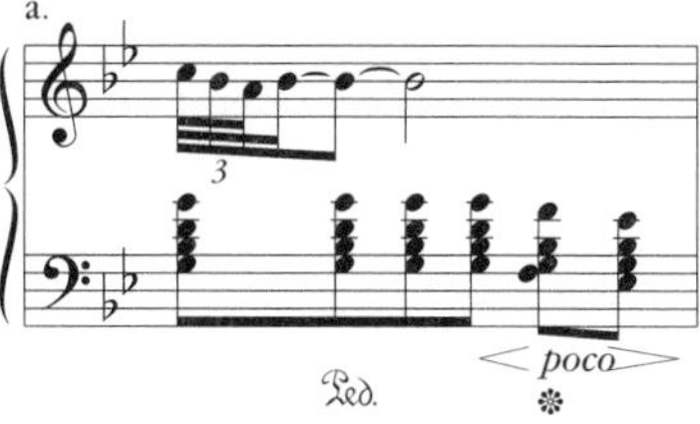

The beautiful melody hovers delicately over the relentless accompaniment. Be flexible in phrasing, touch, and rhythm. Keep your arm relaxed. The left hand must be firmer in the tight chords, but the right hand must be loose and relaxed.

In the second section you can lighten up a bit; play the middle voices softly and let the soprano voice come out clearly. The lightening is just a matter of changing the coloration, not the dynamics. Grieg was very preoccupied with subtle coloration nuances. When he performed in Paris during his prime it was said that he was a master of subtle shading.

There are many small slurs in the second section. Measure 20 is typical (see Ex. 11.20). These slurs are important, but they must be incorporated into the longer melodic lines of which they are a part. Thus you must think at the same time of a long slur that encompasses an entire phrase.

I play the E♭ chord at the beginning of measure 26 as indicated in Ex. 11.21.

The resolution of the section must be polyphonic, i.e., the various voices

Ex. 11.20

Ex. 11.21

must all reach their goals. Planning a *diminuendo* is not an easy task, but as mentioned previously, the art is in the *diminuendo*. There is much evidence in his music—especially in the *Ballade*, Op. 24, and in his arrangements for piano of *Nineteen Norwegian Folk Songs*, Op. 66—that Grieg was very fond of the descending scale in the bass. In measures 35–38 of the Air emphasize the descending scalar line in the left hand, first in quarter notes, then in eighths.

Measures 38–39 can be played with a *diminuendo* the first time, a *crescendo* the second time (see Ex. 11.22). This is just one possibility for the handling of these measures. There are other interpretations; choose your own.

Ex. 11.22

The passage with the melody in the tenor voice in measures 40–43 is difficult to play smoothly. I recommend using the right hand for some of the notes, as indicated in Ex. 11.23.

Try to achieve an even *crescendo* in the coda (measures 48–56) during the repeat. Listen carefully, and let the left hand lead (see Ex. 11.24).

Fifth Movement: Rigaudon

The concluding movement of the *Holberg Suite* is sheer fun. If there was ever a case of musical satire, this is it! It is a jovial rigadoon, but a bit caustic and impudent in its observations. After all, it was inspired by the memory of the lusty Ludvig Holberg.

The *Rigaudon* requires a lot of practice so that the eighth notes will come out clearly. We need not assign a specific metronome number for this fast *Allegro con brio*, but it must shimmer with wit and irony. The *staccato* quarter notes, for example, should be spicy. Everything depends on keeping the playing light and precise in the runs as well as in the *staccatos*. Be meticulous in handling the imitations, which are numerous. Try to make the piece sound like an uninhibited conversation *sotto voce*: "Hush, now—but hurry!" (see Ex. 11.25).

Ex. 11.25

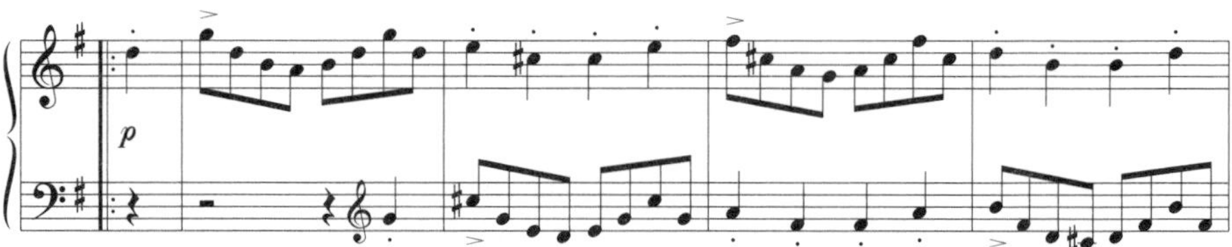

The coloring in measures 26–28 should be different from that in measures 22–24 (see Exx. 11.26a and b). The same suggestion applies to measures 30–31 and 35–36 (see Exx. 11.27a and b).

Exx. 11.26a and b

Exx. 11.27a and b

The quarter notes control the tempo, the eighth notes must follow along. First practice with good support at the bottom of the key. Later you can work at achieving a light finger movement with straight fingers, i.e., with no bend at the knuckles. A little arm support is helpful in keeping the *Allegro* section under control. The old counsel to "practice loud in order to be able to play soft" is good advice for playing *Rigaudon*.

The Trio is typically Griegian in that the same theme is repeated a number of times. This repetition creates yet another challenge to the performer: vary the statement slightly each time to avoid monotony. Varying a motive each time it appears can be very charming. Play a little passage several times, but differently each time. Vary the phrasing, the attack, the mood, the idea. In this way you will create a ready stock of options that you can draw upon in performance when you must play the theme several times in succession.

The sighing slurs in measures 45–47 of the Trio are lovely. Just as in the *Air*, however, the slurs should not be so prominent that the melody line is lost (see Ex. 11.28).

Ex. 11.28

The basic approach to the Trio should be the opposite of that of the first section: as relaxed a hand as possible and as smooth a transition from note to note as you are capable of producing. The *fortissimo* near the end of the Trio may seem a little overstated. Fridtjof Backer-Grøndahl, a Norwegian pianist who studied with Grieg, understood from the composer's verbal instructions that *fortissimo* indicated greater volume than Grieg really wanted. Can you interpret *fortissimo* more as an inner strength conveyed through the entire instrument than an instruction to press harder on the keys? Perhaps in that way you will achieve a more rounded and restrained *fortissimo*, powerfully expressive without being extremely loud.

The final repeat—all the way back to the beginning of the movement—calls for brilliance and good humor. The *Holberg Suite* seems to be smiling mischievously at the performer and saying, "If you can master *me* you will bring down the house."

CHAPTER

12

Twenty-five Norwegian Folk Songs and Dances, Op. 17

The arrangements of folk songs, Opp. 17 and 66, require a good deal of preparatory work before sitting down at the piano, for they are not piano pieces in the usual sense of the word. We must capture the magical moods and images that inspired them, and see and feel what Grieg saw and felt. Listen first to Norwegian folk dances and folk songs of various types. Study L. M. Lindeman's *Older and Newer Mountain Melodies*, the source from which Grieg drew most of his material for these two opuses. Get acquainted with the Hardanger fiddle, the fairy flute, the *lur*, the ram's horn, the *langeleik*.* Listen to the distinctive sound of these instruments, observe some Norwegian folk dancing, and do a little dancing yourself. If you have never seen dark, narrow valleys, open meadows, soaring mountains, rushing waterfalls, or the magnificent fjords of western Norway, you really cannot play these pieces. Travel around, or look at pictures of this wild land. Both opuses were born out of love for Norwegian scenery and the Norwegian temperament, and they must be played accordingly. Any musicological critique of these pieces is totally irrelevant. Cast aside all academic reservations, open your mind, and enter the rich world of which these pieces are a part.

*For a discussion of these and other folk instruments used in Norway see N. Grinde, *A History of Norwegian Music* (Lincoln: University of Nebraska Press, 1991), pp. 87–96.

Op. 17 is for the most part light and congenial in character. It sparkles with simplicity and *joie de vivre*. Op. 66, on the other hand, is somber, chromatic, and harmonically developed in considerable detail. Every note is weighty and can be interpreted in several ways. It is more important here than in any of Grieg's other works that one have a mental picture, an association, for each piece in the set. You can get some help from the text associated with each melody. The original texts are in Lindeman's book.

Opp. 17 and 66 were conceived as cycles. Individual pieces can be played by themselves—and some have become very popular—but there is a special challenge in playing the entire opus and finding appropriate colors for each piece. In playing the whole set, we become aware of new and previously unnoticed subtleties. Rhythm, dynamics, pedal, attack, light vs. dark in your sound spectrum—these are some of the means available to you.

Grieg dedicated Op. 17 to Ole Bull, the virtuoso violinist who did so much to acquaint concert audiences all over the world with Norwegian folk music. Even the dedication says something about the manner in which these pieces are to be played.

No. 1, Springar

Try to produce a single, unbroken line from the first open fifth in the left hand to the final chord; think of the final quarter-note rest as the goal toward which the whole piece is leading. There is a jovial swing to the rhythm. The accompaniment consistently accents the first beat, whereas the right hand sometimes stresses the first beat, sometimes the second (see Ex. 12.1).

Ex. 12.1

An interesting polyrhythmic effect is created by the long descending line in duple time in the left hand. It is like a persistent hemiola in contrast to the triple time in the right hand (see Ex. 12.2).

Measures 25–35, marked *pianissimo*, may be played with a touch of pedal to imitate the sound of a *langeleik* (see Ex. 12.3).

The conclusion, beginning in measure 36 with *subito fortissimo*, contains many harsh accents. Nonetheless, keep everything together in a single, uninterrupted line (see Ex. 12.4).

No. 2, The Swain

The text of this song from Våge is as follows: "The young swain asked his girl, his very dearest friend, if he could have permission to go away, and soon come back again." There is room for freedom and flexible declamation in this piece—as if it were marked *parlando*. Maintain a rocking rhythm and an open sonority. Try to create a dialogue in which the second phrase sounds like an answer to the first (see Ex. 12.5).

Make the last phrase grave and calm. The most advanced harmonies occur here and should be emphasized. Play broadly here.

No. 3, Springar

This *springar* is a little pearl. Some arm support is needed, but for the most part this piece is played with fingertips tripping lightly over the keys. The accompaniment is varied and incredibly interesting (see Exx. 12.6a, b, and c).

Ex. 12.5

Exx. 12.6a, b, and c

The different *staccato* types make this virtuoso music festive. After broadening out a bit in measures 29–31, marked *poco ritardando*, the concluding measures sparkle with energy and enthusiasm (see Ex. 12.7).

Ex. 12.7

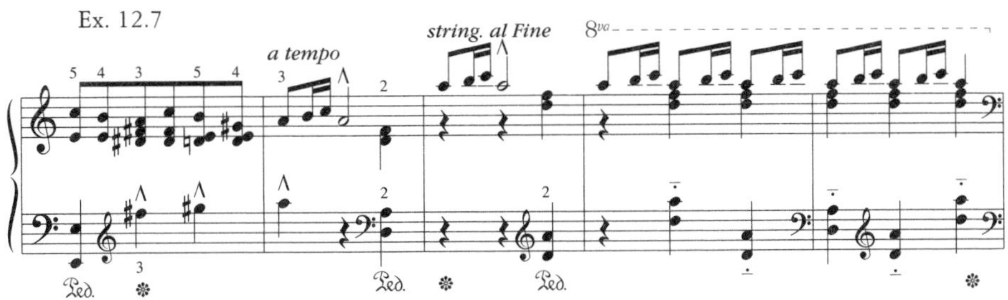

No. 4, Niels Tallefjorden

This song is from Hjerdal and has the following text: "Niels Tallefjorden, that strapping fellow, went a-courting to the Håkstul farm, and the courting went very well: it was Madam Tulde he was after." This beautiful piece has meticulous voice leading and restrained but effective harmony. The lovely melody has a distinctively Norwegian cast. You can enhance its depth with a little darker color in the middle section and a sparkling light one in the coda (see Exx. 12.8a and b).

Exx. 12.8a and b

No. 5, Dance from Jølster

This piece is one of the most popular and most often played in Op. 17. It begins with a jovial echo effect, *fortissimo/pianissimo*. On the first A with a fermata, add a little pedal, and perhaps release the key. Picture yourself hiking in the mountains, giving a shout, and hearing the echo (see Ex. 12.9).

Ex. 12.9

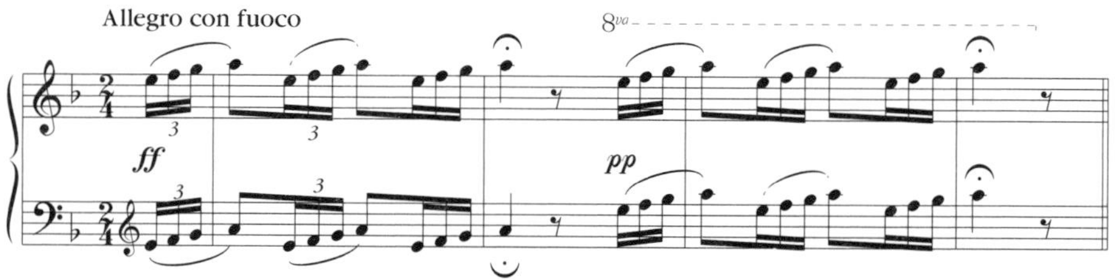

The remainder of the piece should be played *piano*, like an echo reverberating across the valley. In the section marked *Moderato e marcato*, however, nothing should be unclear or inexact. Play with an insistent rhythm and a pronounced *sforzando* on all the afterbeats. Keep the hands independent of each other. From measure 8 onward, calculate a steady increase in the intensity of the *sforzando* as well as a steady increase in volume and, therefore, of the arm weight being applied (see Ex. 12.10).

Ex. 12.10

The section following the repeat, marked *piano*, calls for different accents in the right and left hands and requires independent movements. When one hand goes down, the other goes up. Tread softly if you want to follow the tradition. *Dance from Jølster*, as the name implies, is a *dance*—a toe dance! (see Ex. 12.11.)

Ex. 12.11

The middle section, measures 27–44, resembles a Norwegian *lokk*, a folk tune associated with the calling of farm animals. Play it with a light, delicate sound. The part marked *Piú mosso* imitates a round dance: "and then we join our hands and we dance in a ring!" (see Ex. 12.12.)

The coda includes some intricate finger work in measures 49–52. Practice them as trills and as tied exercises (see Exx. 12.13a–d).

The two 2/8 measures are in a fairly fast tempo, with the eighth notes having the same values as in 3/8. In other words, do *not* spread these two beats over the same amount of time allocated to three beats in the preceding measures. That sounds like stale beer. It is exciting, but also difficult, to strike

Ex. 12.12

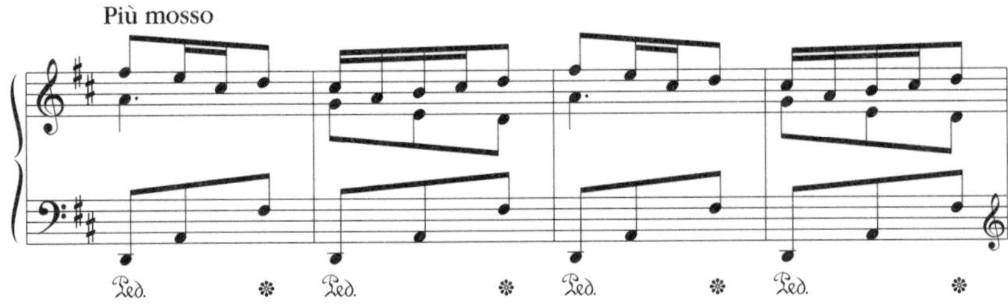

Exx. 12.13a, b, c, and d

the high chord at the end of measure 58 and then, immediately, the low chord in measure 59. But it is worth the effort to get it right, for it brings the piece to an exciting conclusion (see Ex. 12.14).

Ex. 12.14

No. 6, Wedding Tune

This tune is from Gol, in Hallingdal, and according to L. M. Lindeman it is "a wedding tune that they played in the hall right after they have eaten." The imitations that occur as the various voices enter call for a rather transparent type of playing. Many performers find it best to play with a slightly lowered wrist (see Ex. 12.15).

Ex. 12.15

The form resembles the refrain of a folk ballad, which is usually simpler than the rest of the text. Similarly, the conclusion of this piece should be played in a light and unaffected manner (see Ex. 12.16).

Ex. 12.16

No. 7, Halling

This piece is best known as Johan Halvorsen's *Norwegian Dance* for violin and piano, but Grieg's arrangement for piano is on a par with Halvorsen's in charm and subtlety. You can make much of the accompaniment starting *pianissimo* in measure 11 and changing to *forte* in measure 25 (see Exx. 12.17a and b).

Ex. 12.17a

Ex. 12.17b

No. 8, The Pig

The text of this song from Hjerdal is, to say the least, rather silly: "And the pig had a snout that went fifteen miles out, O you dirty pig." Is it a joking song or a *vals dolce?* I take it to be the former, so I try to create something of the sound of a pig grunting. But remember: pigs are not always so rhythmical! I play the middle voice in the accompaniment in measure 9 *staccato* and sometimes exaggerate the slurs in the opening measures. Do not let the piece sound overly Romantic. When you play Op. 17 in its entirety, No. 8 can be one of the most exciting challenges in the entire set. It's really filthy! (see Ex. 12.18.)

Ex. 12.18

No. 9, Religious Song

This song comes from Hitterdal in the county of Telemark, and the text is quite a contrast from No. 8:

> When my eyes, amidst all of life's woe,
> Have wept till they can weep no more,
> They look with longing from this prison
> Up toward Salem's blessed shore.
> How my woe then disappears!
> How it calms my spirit's fears!

Grieg found this piece in Catharinus Elling's collection of religious songs, and it is said that he played it at Ole Bull's funeral. It is similar to an organ chorale. The first four measures may be thought of as a short prelude, in which case the soprano voice should be colored as a melody starting in measure 5. Measures 7 and 8 are again accompaniment, with the solo voice continuing in measure 9 (see Ex. 12.19).

Ex. 12.19

No. 10, The Wooer's Song

In the first edition of Op. 17 the first line of the text of this song was listed as the title of the piece. The text reads: "Ole once got it into his head to court Rev. Mikkel's daughter, the prettiest girl in the community. But do you think she had any interest in him? She has money, a bed already made, she can have no need of suitors, no she can't."

If *The Pig* is a joking song, then this one must be a boasting song. Part of the secret of interpreting it is *not* to play it as an ordinary waltz but to convey the flavor of the boasting. How? Perhaps by showing off the rolled chords; play them with a flourish!

The dotted rhythms can be varied slightly. Note that Grieg sometimes notates them with dots, sometimes with rests (see Ex. 12.20). Lift the wrist slightly when there is a rest but not when there is a dot, and the difference will be apparent.

Ex. 12.20

The coda is subtle. Play the *pianissimo* chord in measure 22 while the preceding one is still sounding. The ascending broken chord in A minor in the last measure begins calmly, becomes more insistent, and then concludes calmly. Calculate it carefully. Think about the proportions of the overtone series and pay attention to the relationship between root, fifth, and third (see Ex. 12.21).

Ex. 12.21

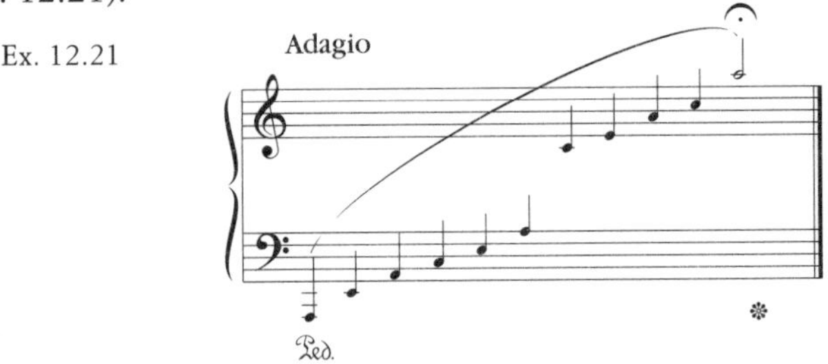

In the first edition, a note at the fermata in measure 10 read: "You don't know what's going to happen, Ole, but don't be shy, you can't do any worse than get a turn-down." And under the last measure appeared the words, "I'm not discouraged; besides, I'm as good a fellow as she is a girl." That's the spirit in which the piece should be played!

No. 11, Heroic Ballad

In the first edition this piece was called "In Norway's Dovre mountains." The text, which comes from Peder Syv's collection of heroic ballads, is as follows: "In the Dovre Mountains of Norway lay heroes without sorrow, but who shall lead our rites when we ourselves cannot do so?" In Norse mythology the Dovre Mountains are the legendary home of the gods, so the opening chords should thunder like a mighty Thor. Don't play too fast, and create a terrace effect dynamically as you move from *piano* to *mezzoforte* to *forte* to *fortissimo*. Pull out all the stops on the *fortissimo*, especially on the repeat; then the *pianissimo* echo at the very end will be all the more effective (see Ex. 12.22).

Ex. 12.22

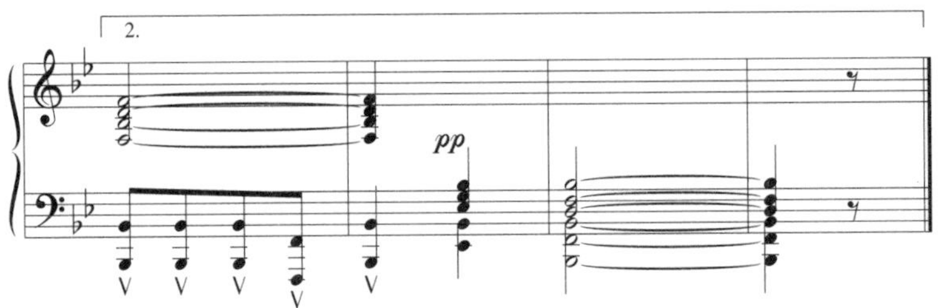

No. 12, Solfager and the Snake King

This is yet another pearl from the rich store of Norwegian folk music. The melody is exceptionally beautiful, and Grieg's simple harmonization is just right. Play it lovingly, giving equal attention to the sonority and the phrasing. To vary the expression you might think of phrases 1 and 3 as text and phrases 2 and 4 as a refrain. The words are: "And the snake king came riding to the farm, and the woman was so young. Solfager stood outside sunning her hair, I feel like riding into the woods." Note that lines 2 and 4 of the text underscore the situation in an indirect way. Try to bring this out in the phrasing of the music, making it austere and simple in contrast to the expressiveness of lines 1 and 3 (see Ex. 12.23).

Ex. 12.23

The first verse should be played relatively *legato* because of the low tessitura. After a very soft *pianissimo* accompaniment in the transition, perhaps you can lighten up a little in the higher range that follows (see Ex. 12.24).

Ex. 12.24

The "lightening up" is achieved by stressing the top voice, concentrating a bit on the fourth and fifth fingers. Imagine that you are playing the top notes on a piccolo. Then the contrast will be all the greater in the *piano* passage that follows with an almost baritone timbre. There you can play with flat fingers and good arm support to produce a broad sound (see Ex. 12.25).

Ex. 12.25

Solfager and the Snake King is the kind of melody that could become a "hit" if people had a chance to hear it. Play it as if you expected it to win first prize at the Grand Prix!

No. 13, Wedding March

The tone in this piece is light and friendly. According to Lindeman, this march is played "as the bridal procession emerges from the church." Like No. 6, it is from Gol, in Hallingdal. To make the chords precise, use some arm movement, with impulses for the most part from the elbow. The accompaniment is especially effective in measures 13–15, where it consists of soft eighth notes on the afterbeats (see Ex. 12.26).

Ex. 12.26

Don't let the rhythm get away from you. Accent a note here and there in the right hand (see Ex. 12.27).

Ex. 12.27

No. 14, I Sing with a Sorrowful Heart

This remarkable piece comes from Valdres. If it is played thoughtlessly, mechanically, it doesn't amount to anything. But if it is played with feeling—as a lament, and with imaginative tonal coloring—it has a beauty all its own. The introduction is indeed marked *pianissimo*, but try to make the three iterations different, e.g., make each one softer than the preceding one, or change the coloring each time (see Ex. 12.28).

The softer those cries of sorrow are at the beginning, the more dramatic will be the *forte* accents in measure 10 (see Ex. 12.29).

Ex. 12.28

Ex. 12.29

Like most people, you have your own sad story to tell. Tell it in this piece (see Ex. 12.30).

Ex. 12.30

No. 15, Last Saturday Evening

The text reads: "Last Saturday evening I wandered about, headstrong and free, and I didn't go home when the clock showed ten, for on the way home we came upon a party—and they played and danced all night long until the sun came up again." In this piece about an all-night party, try to combine a smooth, flowing line in the top voice with a precise, guitarlike accompaniment. That is difficult, so practice each component by itself. (Some say it should be practiced at night—*all* night.) (See Ex. 12.31.)

No. 16, I Know a Little Maiden

Here, as in No. 14, there are rich possibilities for tonal coloring. Play the introduction as softly as you can—as if from afar. Imagine that you are hearing a sound in the distance (or behind the curtain in the concert hall). (See Ex. 12.32.)

Ex. 12.31

Ex. 12.32

The thumb melody in measures 15ff. is especially effective. It has a really dark color, like a baritone or a cello. There are many ways of playing with one's thumb—even striking the key way up by the joint (see Ex. 12.33).

Ex. 12.33

No. 17, The Gadfly and the Fly

The text of this song from Kvikne is very odd and contains many nonsense syllables: "The gadfly said to his fly: pirium. You will surely become my dearest darling: piri again in parium, diriduri darium, pirium." The melody might sound a little confusing at first—a bit disordered and incurably episodic—but once you understand the form it makes sense. It consists of a principal melody (see Ex. 12.34) interrupted by two refrains (see Ex. 12.35 and 12.36). The rest is introduction and coda. "Pirium."

No. 18, Peasant Dance

According to Lindeman, this tune is from Vang, in Valders, and was originally played after dinner at wedding receptions. Like *Dance from Jølster*, it is a

Ex. 12.34

Exx. 12.35 and 12.36

virtuoso number. It has an insistent rhythm that proceeds in a mad dash from the first open fifth in the left hand to the last chord. The piece is replete with *staccatos* of various kinds: wrist *staccato* (see Ex. 12.37a), lower-arm *staccato* (see Ex. 12.37b), and arm *staccato* (see Ex. 12.37c). The wrist *staccatos* in measures 5–8 are easier to produce if you rest heavily on the lower voice. The feeling is a little like standing on one leg and dangling the other.

Exx. 12.37a, b, and c

The trills in measures 11, 13, 17, 19, 36, 38, 42, and 44 can be tricky. Five-note trills are okay, but seven-noters are better. Practice them slowly (see Ex. 12.38).

In measures 25–28, the left hand must release quickly after playing each chord. You cannot play them as complete eighth notes without sacrificing some clarity (see Ex. 12.39).

Ex. 12.38

Ex. 12.39

The coda of this virtuoso piece requires great strength, with support in all the joints, including the wrists, yet relaxed (see Ex. 12.40).

Ex. 12.40

When *Peasant Dance* is well played, it can bring down the house (see Ex. 12.41).

Ex. 12.41

No. 19, Hølje Dale

The text of this song from Seljord is, "Day is dawning bright and clear, the witch's power begins to vanish. The song of birds singing again can be heard in the sky above, and the sun shines on the highest mountain peaks. It is Sunday morning. People are on their way to church, they know it is time for church." The story is about Hølje Dale, a man who became bewitched and was trapped by the witch in a mountain prison. His sad predicament can be underscored by the way you handle the vague motives that perhaps wafted up to him—the triplets in the left hand in measures 11–13. Play them *legato* and *pianissimo* (see Ex. 12.42).

Ex. 12.42

From his mountain prison, Hølje Dale heard the people on their way to church. Reflect this idea by giving an organlike character to the octaves and chords at the end of the piece (see Ex. 12.43).

Ex. 12.43

No. 20, Halling

This piece stands or falls on whether you can maintain an unfailingly even rhythm. Never give in and never allow it to become 4/4 (see Ex. 12.44).

Ex. 12.44

Measures 21–30, marked *pianissimo*, can perhaps be played *secco*, i.e., without pedal (see Ex. 12.45).

Ex. 12.45

No. 21, The Woman from Sætesdal

Judging from the accents in this piece, we can see that the woman is a real shrew. Play stubbornly and in strict rhythm—as if the woman is stamping her foot and shouting, "No! No! No!" Observe all the accents in measures 1–10 (see Ex. 12.46).

Ex. 12.46

No. 22, Cow Call

This little piece from Valdres is an authentic *lokk*, a tune originally used to call farm animals—in this case, cows. The text is, "Then we're calling over the marsh, to the peaceful hillside. Come all you wonderful animals: come cow, come calf, come cattle; come Raute, come Skaute, come favorite of Kari, come Kappelan's Mari, come Ronkebu's Kjersti, come Kålum's Berte, come Hullabrand."

Grieg is trying to convey the indescribable and undefinable Norwegian ethos—warm, lovely sounds without a trace of pretension. Bring out the *lokk* theme followed by an echo (see Ex. 12.47).

Be aware of the beautiful descending line in the bass shown in Ex. 12.48.

Create a shimmering but soft pedal effect in the last five measures. Grieg is an impressionist, so observe the *pedale sempre* and play softly (see Ex. 12.49). Do not underestimate this little jewel!

No. 23, Peasant Song

The English title of this humorous piece is *Peasant Song*, but a literal translation of the Norwegian title is "Have you seen anything of my old woman?" Grieg must have liked the tune, for he used it again in his *Symphonic Dances*, Op. 64. It is evident from the text that this woman is no beauty: "High up on the hillside, with a short skirt and a black hat, short, old, and limping."

Make the rolled chords as terse as possible. Play briskly, almost *alla breve*. Play measures 11–15, marked *piano*, in a tight *legato*, in sharp contrast to the lightning-fast chords in the *fortissimo* that follows. The final chord sounds almost as if it were muted. Did the woman finally stop yakking? (See Ex. 12.50.)

Ex. 12.50

No. 24, Wedding Tune

This tune from Vang in Valdres is said to have been played when the bride entered the church and when she left it. A young bride could be expected to walk lightly and delicately, so use a gently rocking, swaying rhythm. Play with controlled dynamics and a friendly, eighth-note rhythm. Don't spoil the wedding by letting the music get too heavy! (see Ex. 12.51.)

Ex. 12.51

No. 25, The Ravens' Wedding

The beautiful concluding piece in this long series of folk melodies comes from Sogn, in western Norway. The text reads, "Way out east in Ravenwood there is so lovely a town. All the animals are gathering there, out in the open air. The bridegroom is the grandest fellow in the forest." The scenery in western Norway is on a grand scale, with mountains and fjords and waterfalls surrounded by vast green forests. Some of that magnificent landscape is reflected in this heroic tune

The small notes in measures 3–9 and 14–15 should be released quickly, leaving the open octave. Perhaps they reminded Grieg of a raven's claws (see Ex. 12.52).

If the section marked *piano* (measures 11ff.) is played as a tight *legato*, distant, it will create an even greater contrast to the ending (see Ex. 12.53).

Ex. 12.52

Ex. 12.53

The last two measures are a physical challenge. Increase the volume from *piano* during the tremolo and connect it, without a break, to the final chord. To get a good, solid top note I recommend the fingering shown in Ex. 12.54. What a wedding!

Ex. 12.54

CHAPTER 13

Nineteen Norwegian Folk Songs, Op. 66

In Op. 17 it was Edvard Grieg the enthusiastic nationalist who arranged Norwegian folk tunes as no one before him had done. In Op. 66 it is the mature and world-renowned artist who is at work. The product of his labor demands the utmost of the interpreter. In this opus, more than in any other of Grieg's piano compositions, every note has expressive significance. To add or delete a single note or to change a single harmonization in this masterwork would mar it. Sublime musical poetry is brought to life with comparatively few notes.

Many of the harmonies in Grieg's works later came to be characteristic of impressionism. Op. 66, however, could be called an early example of expressionism. The colors are intensified, darker and bolder than those of Op. 17. The melodies are underscored, illuminated with varying harmonies, and placed in relief. They have been dramatized and at the same time made more intimate. Op. 17 is national romanticism pure and simple. It is to Norwegian music what the paintings of Adolph Tidemand, Hans Gude, and J. C. Dahl are to Norwegian art. It consists of clear, pure, ethereal sounds. Op. 66 is totally different; it stems from another time, and another kind of art speaks to us: that of Edvard Munch. The music no longer conjures up tableaus, scenes, or ideal pictures. Instead we find expressionistic sketches of people in special circumstances—human beings identified by some dominant psychological trait, surrounded by a menacing natural world.

Grieg conceived of Op. 66 as a unified whole—he even wrote *attacca* at the end of several of the pieces. All the melodies are authentic Norwegian folk tunes—*stevs*, lullabies, cattle calls, folk ballads. Some are secular, others religious. Grieg paints pictures of every facet of the Norwegian soul. The rich harmonies reflect the subtleties of nature and the various aspects of human life. For a good performance of Op. 66, you must create a vivid mental picture of each situation and draw inspiration from it.

To get closer to the expressionistic dimension, study the score to discover the techniques Grieg used to express himself in so powerful and personal a way. He was very partial to the descending chromatic scale, both in the bass line and in the middle voices, a characteristic that appears in such other works as *Ballade*, Op. 24. This compositional technique is especially prominent in the harmony of late Romanticism, and in an earlier age it was the typical way of depicting suffering. The music of the sixteenth-century Italian composer Don Carlo Gesualdo provides many examples. Grieg retained the technique of building harmonies around a descending chromatic scale from his early studies at the Leipzig Conservatory. In his old age, he returned to this insight from his youth and used it as a powerful principle of unity. This technique resulted in some late-Romantic chord progressions with interpolated secondary dominants. In a successful realization of the music, these elements should be audible in the tonal picture. They are prominent in Op. 66, especially in Nos. 1, 3, 4, 6, 8, 9, 10, 12, 13, and 17.

Grieg also makes use of pedal points, which must be emphasized if they are to be heard. The sound of the piano—unlike that of many other instruments—decays rapidly. The pedal points conjure up what could be called a *bourdon* feeling—a feeling of being on folk soil—even if they are a bit bizarre. But do not feel anxious about this element when you play Op. 66, for it will strengthen the expressiveness of the piece.

The melodies are often in the Lydian mode. Grieg harmonized them in a late-Romantic manner. A steady stream of dominant chords, the late-Romantic harmony, and the almost Medieval-sounding Lydian melodies create a highly picturesque conflict.

These characteristics recur again and again in Op. 66 and should be reflected in the interpretation of this opus. There is room for individuality in Op. 66, but not with respect to these aspects. They are so important to the central concept of this cycle that they must be emphasized.

Do not take too fast a tempo. Rather, delineate what is happening harmonically and with respect to voice leading. Bear in mind that the performer knows the material well, after endless hours of practice, but the listener may be hearing the piece for the first time. For the sake of the latter, keep the tempo on the slow side.

In addition to studying the melodies in the original (as well as the associated texts) and learning the material by heart, undertake your own analysis of the scores. Locate the pedal points, the ostinato figures, and the descending chromatic scales in Op. 66. You owe that much to Grieg if you are going to play these compositions.

No. 1, Cow Call

All the characteristics we have been discussing are present in this first piece in the set. Measures 3–7, for example, have a pedal point in the bass and an ostinato in the inner voices (see Ex. 13.1).

Ex. 13.1

In measures 7–13, the descending scale in the bass line covers almost two octaves (see Ex. 13.2).

Ex. 13.2

Note that in measures 13–17 the line progresses from F♯ to E to D. The inserted rolled chord in measure 14, a B-major triad, is followed by a seventh chord on E, and then, in measure 16, by a D^{6-5}_{4-3} progression, which resolves to a ninth chord on D in measure 17. The last four measures have pedal points in the bass. The pedal points and scales should not be emphasized unduly, but be aware of them as an important part of the total picture.

The opening measures of *Cow Call* are exceptionally beautiful. Observe the difference in dynamics, with measure 2 standing in the shadow of measure 1, like an echo fading away in the distance. It is also important to relate the bass chord and the figure in the right hand. They should be played in almost a single movement of the hand (see Ex. 13.3).

Ex. 13.3

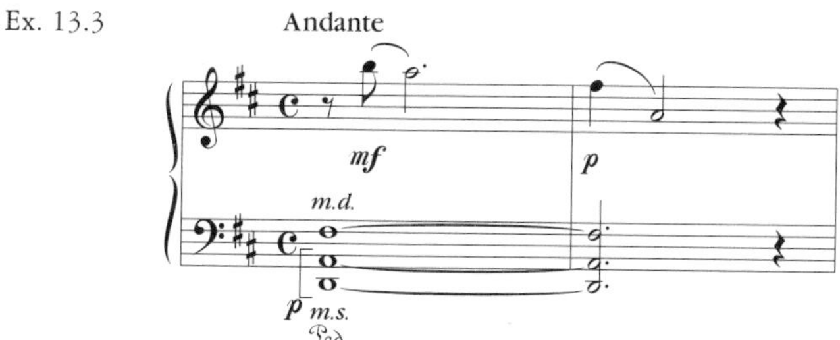

In the body of the piece, marked *Allegretto*, use a supple, slightly swinging *gangar* ("walking dance") rhythm. Keep the music "walking and walking" all the way to the rolled chord; sound the lowest and highest notes of the chord at the same time (see Ex. 13.4).

Ex. 13.4

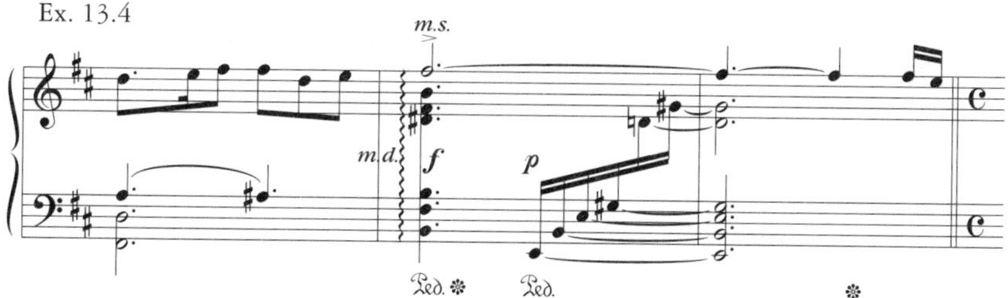

The embellishment in measure 3 should be relatively fast so that it does not sound just like the sixteenth-note triplet in the following measure (see Ex. 13.1). Do not lift your finger, but make the mordent an integral part of the melody. The same advice applies to the mordent in measure 12 (see Ex. 13.5).

Ex. 13.5

The pedal work in the transition between measures 14 and 15 can be tricky. To keep the bass notes alive as part of the B-major chord, play the high F♯ with the right hand as you begin playing the rolled chord with the left. That way you also avoid leaving a hole between E and F♯ in the melody line (see Ex. 13.4).

The *Andante tranquillo* should be a little calmer than the opening *Andante*.

Linger a bit over the notes marked with tenuto strokes in measure 16 by moving the wrist slightly as you play each note. Above all, be aware that *Cow Call* begins and ends with pedal points.

No. 2, It Is the Greatest Foolishness

The text of the song on which this piece is based comes from Valdres: "It is the greatest foolishness the world has ever seen, to waste one's love on someone that you cannot hope to win. What did you think those many times you took me in your arms? You thought to make a fool of me and blind me with your charms."

Give the beautiful melody a swinging rhythm to keep it from plodding. Think upward rather than downward as you shape the phrases. You can achieve some flexibility in the first phrase with the syncopations in the tenor and alto parts. They make the rhythm flow. The second phrase is a stroke of genius. Stress the melody in the middle range, but also give some attention to the counterpoint in the right hand (see Ex. 13.6).

Ex. 13.6

The melody in the tenor voice can be difficult to bring out. Sometimes you can do it by leaning on the outer edge of your hand, or by using an almost rigid second finger or the side of your thumb. One must do whatever is necessary to bring out the tenor part in a singing manner.

The part marked *pianissimo* (starting with the upbeat to measure 9) should be played with a bright soprano voice, but don't forget the pedal point on B♭. This phrase is somewhat indirect and distant. Use a bit of pedal to underscore the fact that harmonically you are at the balance point between two keys, each of which claims dominance. The augmented fourth lends a modal character and contrasts nicely with the typical late-Romantic chromaticism of the rest of the piece (see Ex. 13.7).

The inner voices in the concluding measures are especially lovely. Bring them out (see Ex. 13.8).

No. 3, A King Ruled in the East

The text of this song from Sogn is as follows: "A king ruled in the east, his name was Håkon the Brave. He had innumerable warriors the very sight of

Ex. 13.7

Ex. 13.8

whom was frightening. But he also had a daughter, whom everyone called Ragnhild the Fair."

Here again scalar lines are integral components of the composition, lending a feeling of austere strength and majestic dignity. There is no need to emphasize these lines dynamically, however, for then they would become too prominent. It is a matter of harmonic techniques almost in the same category as the use of the twelve-tone scale or strict counterpoint. But for the overall result, the performer must be fully aware of these lines.

Grieg begins with a descending scale from D to D in the bass (see Ex. 13.9). The bass line in the second section is a modified descending chromatic scale (see Ex. 13.10).

Ex. 13.9

Ex. 13.10

It is difficult to characterize this piece: it is not religious, nor does it seem to express tender human emotion. Perhaps one could say that it conveys a feeling of "inscrutable royalty." To preserve this feeling, observe the note values exactly as written. For example, the dotted rhythm in measures 1 and 2 should not be exaggerated (see Ex. 13.9); do not double-dot the eighths, as illustrated in Ex. 13.11a; nor should the sixteenth notes be played too soon, as if they were triplets, as in Ex. 13.11b.

Exx. 13.11a and b

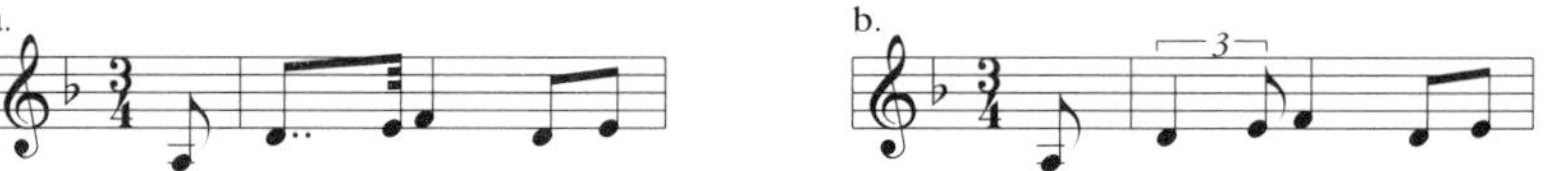

In measure 4, be careful to treat the C as a harmonic tone in contrast to the A, which is part of the melody. Thus the C must be relatively soft and the A relatively loud.

The first eight measures should be joined together in one great wave that sweeps the listener along to the chord in A major (see Ex. 13.12). Playing the anacrusis in the bass can be difficult. I recommend using the right hand for all four notes of the chord.

Grieg gives no instructions regarding the tempo of the second section, starting on measure 9, relative to the first. I recommend that the eighth notes be equal. However, he gave more than enough interpretation instructions in the second part of the piece: *pp molto legato*, then *più crescendo* leading up to the D^7 chord *fffz*, followed by *ritardando* and *diminuendo* to *piano* (see Ex. 13.13).

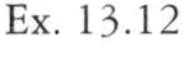

Ex. 13.12

Ex. 13.13

As is often the case in Grieg's music—in the second part of the *Piano Concerto*, for example, and in No. 18 of the present opus—it is best to make the anacruses short. That lends grandeur to the music (see Ex. 13.14).

Ex. 13.14

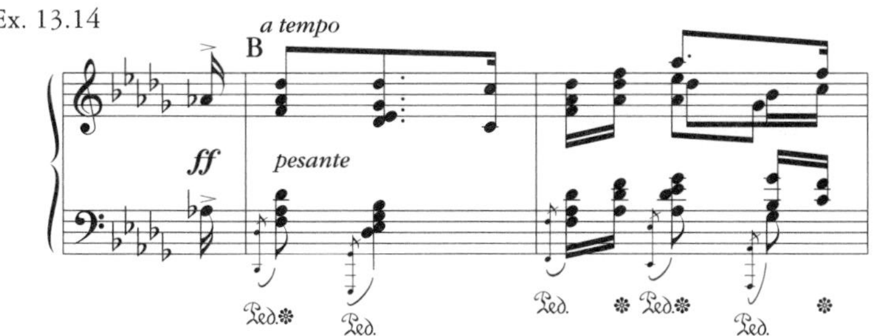

The piece concludes with pedal points in both soprano and bass. Be careful to give both D's (the root of the chord) enough volume to carry through to the last measure (see Ex. 13.14).

No. 4, The Siri Dale Song

In Op. 66, pay attention to the relative tempos in the various pieces. The main sections of the first three pieces have been *Allegretto*, *Andante espressivo*, and *Andante*. No. 4 is *Allegretto con moto*. If you play Op. 66 as a cycle, No. 4 should not be too slow. It should be a little faster than the *Allegretto* in No. 1; and No. 2 should be a little broader than the *Andante* in No. 3.

The Siri Dale Song is incredibly charming when it is played with a light touch and not too somber a tone in the main melody. As an aid to the phrasing, think of two kinds of slurs: short ones connecting the eighth notes to the following quarter notes, and a long one encompassing the entire phrase. This is not indicated in the score but is recommended to avoid choppiness (see Ex. 13.15).

Ex. 13.15

The many pedal points are important (see Exx. 13.16a and b).

Exx. 13.16a and b

From measure 15 onward there is an unbroken chromatic progression—first ascending and then descending—in the two inner voices (see Ex. 13.17). The phrase "ends" on G no fewer than four times. Make each G a little softer than the preceding one, the first one *forte*, then *diminuendo* through *mezzo forte* and *mezzo piano* to *piano* at the end.

Ex. 13.17

Nineteen Norwegian Folk Songs, Op. 66

No. 5, It Was in My Youth

This ballad tells a longer story than the preceding pieces in the set. You need to be personally engaged with it, using your imagination and loving the sounds you are producing.

The opening quarter-note arpeggio should perhaps begin *legato* but can become more assertive toward the end (see Ex. 13.18).

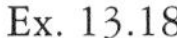
Ex. 13.18

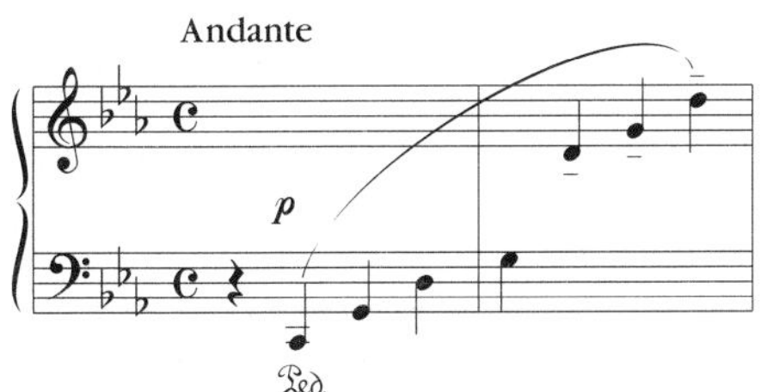

The piece reaches its high point in the *fortissimo* phrase that begins in measure 31 (see Ex. 13.19). Be sure to create a big, dramatic difference between this phrase and the soft, shimmering passage in the descant register with which the piece concludes. Because of the high register, you can use a good deal of pedal on the latter.

Ex. 13.19

It is worth studying the entire piece in detail to become aware of the many chromatic passages and pedal points. Be aware of them as you play.

Grieg's score is completely logical. The rest in measure 26 is effective (see Ex. 13.20).

Ex. 13.20

In measure 34, let the octave C in the right hand remain through the rest as the other notes die away. It is a nice detail when suddenly the octave stands there all by itself.

The piece ends with pedal points or inner voices in both hands. They must be loud enough to be heard to the end of the piece, yet extremely soft—so soft that you barely touch the keys. Everything is resplendent, everything is temperamental, everything is significant. Play accordingly (see Exx. 13.21a and b).

Exx. 13.21a and b

No. 6, Cow Call and Lullaby

As previously mentioned, the relationship of the tempos of the first four pieces should be planned. No. 6, however, is a challenge with respect to tempo all by itself. Grieg's intricate indications are: *Andante*, *Allegro*, *Più lento*, and *Andante molto*. I recommend first establishing a suitable tempo for the *Allegro* section. Next go to the *Più lento* section, which is still *allegro* but a little slower. Then find the *Andante* for the opening, which should not be as slow as the *Andante molto* of the last part. If this sequence does not work for you, try doing it in the opposite order: first practice the *Andante molto* at the desired tempo, then go a little faster in the *Andante*, faster still in the *Più lento*, and fastest of all in the *Allegro*.

These are the kinds of things every conductor has to deal with, and as a pianist, you are your own conductor onstage. By planning the tempos beforehand you can achieve more varied expression than if you thoughtlessly played through the piece. Think of all the trouble Grieg went to in developing these instructions!

For a good opening and a good conclusion—i.e., to make the *Andante* and the *Andante Molto* as supple as possible—think in terms of sixteenth notes while you are learning the piece. In time it will all seem quite natural and you will mentally place a long slur over the entire phrase. Put a little stress on the sixteenth notes at the end of measure 3. The figure A–B–C occurs three times in succession; vary the expression a little (see Ex. 13.22). Also stress the *ritardando* passage slightly in Ex. 13.23.

Ex. 13.22

Ex. 13.23

The *Allegro* section is undeniably Norwegian; note the accent on the second beat in measures 7 and 11 (see Ex. 13.24).

Ex. 13.24

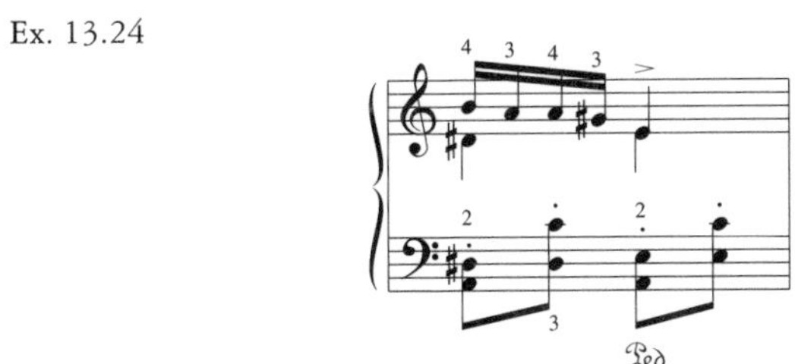

Other characteristics that are distinctively Norwegian are the bouncy second half of the phrase with a *staccato* on C in measures 8 and 12 and the light downbeat followed by a rest and a heavy second beat in measures 9 and 13. In measures 9 and 13, use an upward movement on beat 1 and a downward movement on beat 2 (see Ex. 13.25).

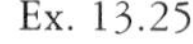
Ex. 13.25

The *Più lento* flits back and forth between C and C♯, and this combined with a pedal point on D produces a quite singular result.

It is said that a truly good pianist plays differently in the various registers of the piano. Most of the lowest octave (ascending from the C two octaves below middle C) are viewed as the gonglike bass register. The rest of this octave and all of the next one are the cello register, which requires a lot of *legato*. The most important level for melodies is the first and second octaves above middle C; here the natural openness and warmth of the notes can be emphasized with a singing tone. In the highest register the sound is more like that of a glockenspiel, and *legato* playing is no longer so important.

Not all of these generalizations apply to No. 6, but the opening certainly calls for a melodious *legato* (see Ex. 13.22). In the *Più lento* section, perhaps the bass should be emphasized (see Ex. 13.26). The second half of the *Più lento* lies an octave higher, so the right hand can be played in a more articulated and lucid manner (see Ex. 13.27).

Ex. 13.26

Ex. 13.27

The above generalizations also apply to the *Andante molto* section. In view of the difference in register, measures 29–33 should not be played in the same manner as measures 24–28 (see Exx. 13.28a and b). Some players can bring out the melody more clearly if they transfer the F♯ in measure 24 and the D♯ in measure 25 to the left hand.

Exx. 13.28a and b

The three rolled chords at the end of the piece can be of special interest by making each one a little slower than the previous one. The first two can convey intentionality, the last one a feeling of peace, of having arrived at your destination (see Ex. 13.29).

Ex. 13.29

No. 7, Lullaby

The tempo is *Allegretto con moto* in cut time, but despite the fast tempo, try to achieve a mood of tranquility, as though this lullaby is being sung not to put a child to sleep but to caress a child who is already sleeping. Give some color to the octaves. Some performers like to emphasize the lower note, others the upper, and still others like to give them equal weight (see Ex. 13.30). Note the repetitions of the notes on A, later on E, and so on. Play compactly so the piece does not become disjointed. In general, play compactly when repeating a note or making jumps, more openly when the music is diatonic.

The *sforzando* in measure 17 should be seen in relation to the last preceding dynamic indication, i.e., the *piano* in measure 10 (see Ex. 13.31).

Although this piece is relatively unassuming both harmonically and melodically, Grieg did include some diatonic—almost chromatic—lines in the

Ex. 13.30

Ex. 13.31

inner voices in measures 10ff. (see Ex. 13.32) and a descending line in measures 17–18 (see Ex. 13.31).

Ex. 13.32

No. 8, Cow Call

Grieg is a strange fellow. In measure 14 of this piece he has written *molto* before the rolled chord (see Ex. 13.33). I think it means that we should put our whole soul into this broken chord, not simply dash it off without thinking. Linger over it, caress it, make it say something.

Ex. 13.33

The piece has many other elegant features. The opening consists of two virtually identical statements of the same motive. Phrase them differently. The first two measures should grow dynamically toward the D, then *diminuendo* in measures 3–4 (see Ex. 13.34).

Ex. 13.34

Another challenge for the performer is to begin *piano* and then play *pianissimo* in the *Poco mosso* (measures 5ff.). The pedal point on F in measures 1–4 should also be emphasized.

In the *Poco mosso* section, note the stepwise descent in thirds in measures 8–13. It is a nice duet (see Ex. 13.35).

Ex. 13.35

At the beginning of the *Poco mosso*, emphasize the alternation between C and B in the bass line (measures 5–8), as if Grieg were trying out the descending line—C–B, C–B, C–B—before finally succeeding on the third try.

The main theme is sounded many times, and it is a real challenge to keep it from lapsing into banality. The last statement is clearly the most important, as is evident from both the harmonic change and the dynamic marking *mf*.

The rests in measures 9, 11, 13, and 18 can be very effective.

The conclusion of the piece is quite remarkable: the melody disappears in the foreground, but in the distance, more softly, we hear the chordal progression continuing.

Note that the *staccato* on E that begins in measure 8 continues to the very end of the piece. In measure 19 it is played first, then a fraction of a second later comes the underlying arpeggiated D-minor chord, and then the final D of the melody.

No. 9, Small Was the Lad

In this piece there is a lot to sketch in a short time without allowing one's interpretive efforts to become distracting. The playing should be like a Chinese drawing: delicate but detailed, subtle yet explicit. There must not be too much of anything, still every tiny detail must be in place. Practice everything in an exaggerated way so that you can retain the subtleties in the condensed form Grieg has given to this piece. Small was the lad, and small was the piece.

Andantino, *Andante tranquillo*, *Adagio* are the tempos indicated at three specific points. The metronome equivalents are a matter of personal taste, and they can vary from day to day and from one period of one's life to another. Therefore, one cannot give metronome settings that are valid for all performers at all times. What is *not* variable, however, is the relationship between and among the various tempos. Arrange them so as to generate excitement. No. 9 must not begin too slowly, for the *Andante tranquillo* is slower, but not too slow, for if it is the concluding *Adagio* will fail to achieve its intended effect. Note the *stringendo* in measure 11 and the *ritardandi* in measures 6 and 14. Measure 6, however, calls for little more than an organic rounding off of the phrase (see Ex. 13.36).

Ex. 13.36

The *Andante tranquillo* section has a steady *stringendo*, as the melodic figure in measure 10 is repeated verbatim in measures 11 and 12 (see Ex. 13.37).

Ex. 13.37

Answer the *stringendo* with an equally steady *ritardando* in the three measures preceding the *Adagio* (see Ex. 13.38). To achieve a perfectly even *stringendo* and *ritardando*, think in terms of the smallest units—sixteenth notes, in this case. Think of them even when they are not there.

Ex. 13.38

No. 10, *Tomorrow You Shall Marry Her*

With Op. 66, No. 10, we finally reach a virtuosic piece, one that can be played pianistically. It is difficult, so practice for clarity from measure 28 on, but with sonorous chords and a lively tempo, for these young folks about to get married are bursting with vitality! (See Ex. 13.39.)

Ex. 13.39

Grieg is very explicit about which notes to accent: beat 1 in the first part, beat 2 in the second (see Ex. 13.40). The situation becomes more complex when you also make an effort to retain a feeling for the measure. Even when you accent beat 2, beat 1 must get a little emphasis as well (see Ex. 13.41).

The excitement is further heightened by bringing out the descending bass line in measures 3–10 and 28–35 (see Ex. 13.39). The hemiola feeling is also very effective (see Ex. 13.42).

Ex. 13.40

Ex. 13.41

Ex. 13.42

Try to make the *pianissimo* passage in measures 11–18 sound like a distant echo (see Ex. 13.40). Note the accents alternating between the hands in measures 35–39.

Plan the dynamics of the piece so that you have something left for the *fortissimo* conclusion (see Ex. 13.43).

Ex. 13.43

No. 11, There Stood Two Girls

The first eight measures are four-voiced throughout. Play them as you would a chorale, i.e., *legato* and with absolutely even rhythm. Emphasize the soprano line, and provide solid support in the bass.

Measures 7–8 are reminiscent of *Veslemøy*, No. 2 in Grieg's song cycle *The Mountain Maid* (see Ex. 13.44). This similarity may subtly influence one's

Ex. 13.44

sense of the basic mood of the piece. Similarly, the piano introduction in the second movement of Grieg's *Cello Sonata* concludes with a quotation from his song *From Monte Pincio*. Now one cannot play the passage in the *Cello Sonata* like the corresponding phrase in *From Monte Pincio*, nor can one play *There Stood Two Girls* in the same manner as *Veslemøy*. But it is interesting to draw comparisons, perhaps to be inspired by the words of the songs or to ponder why Grieg inadvertently—or intentionally—quoted himself. Perhaps he was in the same frame of mind on these pairs of occasions.

The second half of No. 11 is many-voiced. It is really a piano arrangement of a four-voiced piece, with various notes doubled in the manner one uses in playing chorales on the piano. Work at getting a good sound in the chords, i.e., precise attacks and a good balance between the upper and lower voices. Note that in measure 15, beat 3 does not have the dotted rhythm of measure 7 (see Ex. 13.45). It appears that the second half of the piece is intended to be broader and more significant than the first. Emphasize this quality.

Ex. 13.45

It is important to distinguish between harmonic and melodic sound. In measure 2, for example, the G is melodic, while the F and E are harmonic and should be softer (see Ex. 13.46a). The same sort of thing occurs in measure 10 (see Ex. 13.46b).

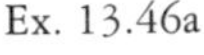
Ex. 13.46a

Ex. 13.46b

The rich harmonies of this short piece warm one's heart. At the same time, the even marching rhythm gives it a majestic character. It is a picture painted with bold colors—like Edvard Munch's *Girls on a Jetty*.

No. 12, Ranveig

Everything in Op. 66 is not equally sad. Grieg had reached a point where he saw a need for a little salt in the soup. He is said to have remarked, "Now and then I need a really stiff drink!" This painfully short piece is a welcome variation in the cycle. It is a shadowy little strain from a spiteful young woman who is taunting us.

The pedal point on A that underlies the first five measures needs the tiniest bit of emphasis: Ranveig is stubborn! The rest of the piece contrasts harmonically with the first part, with a long descending, mostly chromatic, line in the bass (see Ex. 13.47).

Ex. 13.47

In the last measure, once again be aware of what is melody and what is harmony: the A is melodic, the C♯ the harmonic resolution.

No. 13, A Little Gray Man

Starting with No. 13, all the remaining pieces in Op. 66 are longer than the previous ones. It is a relief for the interpreter to have a few more notes to work with, to spread your wings after the long series of miniatures.

The text of No. 13 comes from a lullaby. It tells about a little man who "walked and walked" (*Allegretto*) until at last he got home again (*Andante*). Let the piece sound like one long walk until the little man "comes home" in the brief concluding *Andante*.

No. 13 is an interesting study in *staccato*, especially in the difference between a *staccato* eighth note and a *staccato* quarter note. It is a little crude to play them equally short (see Ex. 13.48).

Ex. 13.48

The accompaniment should be played a little softer than the melody. In measures 9–13 and 17–24 emphasize the nice descending line in the bass (see Exx. 13.49a and b).

Exx. 13.49a and b

This piece is an example of the Norwegian *gangar* ("walking dance"), but the walker seems a little weary. Play the descending bass line in measures 23–25 very *legato* (see Ex. 13.50).

Ex. 13.50

No. 14, In Ola Valley, in Ola Lake

Grieg's friend Frants Beyer recorded the story that lies behind this song, as told to him by Gudrun Skattebo of Østre Slidre:

> Way up in Østre Slidre, in a little valley with steep mountains on either side—in the vicinity of the Jotunheimen mountains—there is a lake that is called "Ola Lake," and next to this lake is a *seter* [a summer dairy farm] called "Ola Seter." One summer a woman named Siri lived there with her son. One day the boy drowned in Ola Lake, but no one knew what had happened to him. They looked everywhere for him, but to no avail. At last they concluded that he must have been kidnapped by the trolls—bewitched. So they had the church bells from the village brought up to Ola Seter, and they began to ring and ring, ring and ring, ring and ring. In the end the bells sang this song: "In Ola Valley, in Ola Lake, there Siri lost her beloved boy; they searched in the valley, they rang o'er the lake, but Siri never found her boy again."

This poignant background presents some interesting details for the performer. Work the rolled chords into the texture so that there are no irregularities or breaks in the flow of the melody. At first, practice them rhythmically, as integral parts of the rhythmic context. When the upbeat is in the right hand (as in measure 3) it can be played like a sixteenth note and two thirty-seconds so you can reach the melody note on the first beat of the next measure.

Use this technique each time the pattern occurs. Later, when the same pattern appears in the left hand, it is better to think in terms of triplets (see Exx. 13.51a and b). When there are four notes, treat them as thirty-seconds (see Ex. 13.52a and b).

Exx. 13.51a and b

Exx. 13.52a and b

Think of the *fortissimo* rolled chord in measure 24 as belonging to what lies ahead, not to what has passed. Play it relatively fast and with a forward impulse (see Ex. 13.53).

Ex. 13.53

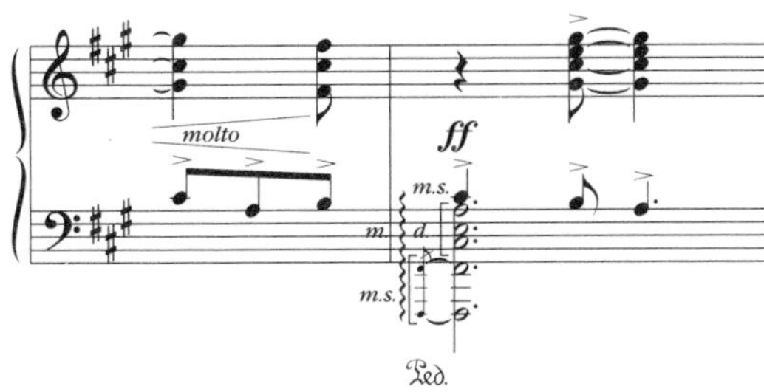

In the transition from measure 25 to measure 26, think of a sixteenth note plus a thirty-second note triplet and play the E with the right hand (see Ex. 13.54).

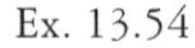
Ex. 13.54

In the recapitulation (*Tempo I*), think of the rolled chords as quintuplets flowing from the right hand to the left and back to the right hand again (see Ex. 13.55).

Ex. 13.55

This detailed advice on playing the rolled chords may frighten some readers, but it is useful. Regard it as a preparatory exercise. Once you have mastered it, forget the details. Its purpose is to achieve a smooth integration of the rolled chords and prevent No. 14 from becoming choppy as a result of lingering too long at too many places.

Play the open fifths as light upbeats, not heavy downbeats. Feel the beat at the rest, and play the chord with an upward movement (see Ex. 13.56).

Ex. 13.56

Throughout the piece, make a clear distinction between *piano* and *pianissimo* (see Ex. 13.57).

The middle section, marked *poco più mosso* (starting at measure 15), should flow. *Tempo I*, starting in measure 34, is marked *molto tranquillo*, indicating Grieg's intention that the *molto tranquillo* be quieter than the opening *Andante tranquillo*, which, in turn, is more tranquil than the *poco più mosso*.

The last two rolled chords have a lot of notes, and they have to be played on the upbeat and very fast. In order to get the D in the bass of measure 42,

Ex. 13.57

I play A–D–F♮–A–D–F♮–A on the upbeat and the low D along with the C♯ in the treble on the downbeat (see Ex. 13.58). You can do the same thing with the A-major chord in measure 44: strike the low A in the left hand at the same time as you play E and A in the right hand.

Ex. 13.58

Practice the tremolo figure in the right hand in measures 44–47 loud at first, then soften it down to *pianissimo*. Practice the second finger separately because of the repetitions. The result—a kind of vibration—adds a nice touch. Meanwhile, the rhythm in the left-hand accompaniment must be entirely independent and in tempo (see Ex. 13.59).

Once you have mastered the technical details you can open your soul to the poignancy of the story in a setting of unsurpassed natural beauty (see Ex. 13.60).

Exx. 13.59 and 13.60

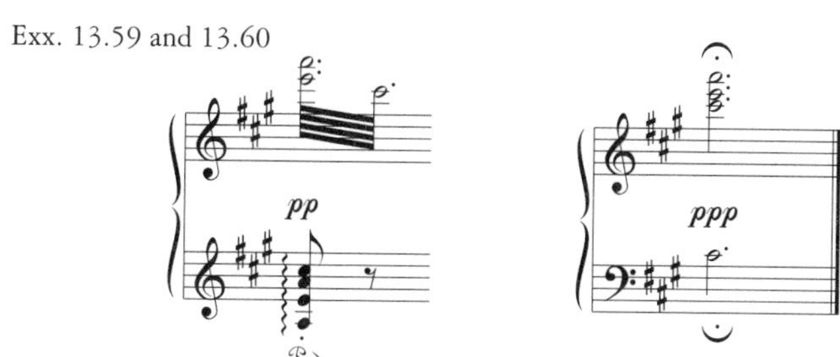

No. 15, Lullaby

Give a feeling of calm and intimacy to the opening *Andante molto tranquillo* and the recapitulation (*Tempo I*, measure 34). The accompaniment is characterized by ostinato figures and numerous repetitions of the same note, i.e., pedal points (see Ex. 13.61).

Ex. 13.61

The lovely melody first appears in the middle register (see Ex. 13.62). Then we hear it in a lower range (see Ex. 13.63). Finally, to brighten things up, it comes in octaves in the descant register (see Ex. 13.64). These differences should be underscored by playing differently in the various registers (see above under No. 6).

Ex. 13.62

Ex. 13.63

Ex. 13.64

The middle section, *Allegro*, is rhythmically complex. Measures 16 and 17 have an accent and a *staccato* on the first beat, but in measure 19 the accent is on the second beat. These two patterns are effectively alternated.

The length of the fermatas is an interesting question—perhaps two beats, even three. They can be handled in a variety of ways, but decide in advance how long to make each one (see Exx. 13.65a and b).

Exx. 13.65a and b

The conclusion is very subtle, especially the last measure, where the D is the resolution of the melodic line in the tenor voice (see Ex. 13.66). The final G, standing in the shadow of what preceded it, yields a shimmering effect.

Ex. 13.66

No. 16, Little Astrid

This piece is known in some areas as "Little Kari." Regardless of what you call it, it contains many awkward and uncomfortable passages. In playing the repeated notes, it is best to keep a loose wrist (see Exx. 13.67a and b).

In the accompaniment in measures 15–19, swing toward the notes occurring on the beat—as if the sixteenth notes were anacruses to the dotted eighths that follow (see Ex. 13.68).

In the right hand of measures 28–30, be sure to hold the chords in the middle voices through the rests in the upper voice (see Ex. 13.69).

Exx. 13.67a and b

Ex. 13.68

Ex. 13.69

A difficult challenge is to play clearly the *pianissimo* passages with sixteenth notes and thirty-second notes in tricky rhythmic combinations (see Exx. 13.70a and b). To make matters worse, Grieg has indicated syncopated accenting on the thirty-second notes. It is no slip of the pen, for he specifies an accent on the second thirty-second note no fewer than four times.

Exx. 13.70a and b

In the opening *Allegro giocoso* introduce a *diminuendo* so that the fifths sound like echoes growing softer and softer (see Ex. 13.71). Articulate the right hand clearly while the left maintains *alla breve* phrasing, and bring out the descending scale in the accompaniment in measures 7–10 (see Ex. 13.72).

The piece has the same tempo throughout, but a few measures have three

Ex. 13.71

Ex. 13.72

beats instead of two. It adds interest to emphasize this a bit when it occurs (see Ex. 13.73).

Ex. 13.73

In measures 20 and 21 the accents in the left and right hands are fighting each other. Bring this out by keeping the two hands independent (see Ex. 13.74).

Ex. 13.74

In measures 41–45, marked *crescendo molto e stretto*, play right into the rest. Let the rest be the goal, such that the fermata feels like part of the melodic line. It's effective!

The three chords with which the piece concludes demand great power and precision. Play with infectious enthusiasm. The only problem is the uncomfortable position of the fourth finger on D♯. You may find it easier to play the D♯ almost simultaneously with the rest of the notes, lifting the fourth finger quickly just as you attack the chord (see Ex. 13.75).

Ex. 13.75

No. 17, Lullaby

In Op. 66, No. 17 moves downward and inward toward the weightiest and most important piece in the entire set, No. 18. There is a wistfulness in the downward movement that the piece represents in the total collection. In the *Andante tranquillo* it is tempting to think *con tristessa, ma semplice.*

The principal characteristics are the same ones that have recurred throughout Op. 66: pedal points and descending chromatic lines (see Exx. 13.76a and b).

Exx. 13.76a and b

One unique feature of this piece is the impressionistic pedal effect in measures 15–17 and 53–55 (see Ex. 13.77). Play way out on your fingertips here in order to get a subdued tone, but give a little emphasis to the first bass passage to provide a foundation for what is to follow. Do not play too loud, but cover the whole with a shimmering magic veil. Grieg has not indicated where the pedal is to be released, but presumably it is at the rest in measure 18.

Ex. 13.77

In the middle section, *Allegro con brio*, the melody line has an unusual, intricate rhythm in measures 21–22. Its peculiar pattern of dotted and undotted rhythms lends a special effect. As usual, Grieg's notations are very detailed: *poco ritardando* at the end of the first phrase, *poco ritardando* with a fermata at the end of the second. The first phrase is *mezzo forte*, the second an echo. This pattern appears again in measures 28–38, so emphasize the contrast between *forte* and *piano*.

In the recapitulation (measures 39ff.), experiment with some variations in the sonority. You might, for example, emphasize the bass line a little differently. Perhaps the *fortissimo* could be a little louder or differ in some other way from the first iteration.

The conclusion of the first *Andantino tranquillo* (measures 18–19) ends on a dominant seventh, whereas the end of the recapitulation (measures 56–58) resolves to the tonic. Thus there is something unresolved, something expectant about the earlier conclusion. At the end of the piece, make a point of the fact that the seventh chord is not left hanging but resolves to the tonic. The tonic is not just the conclusion of No. 17 but also the subdominant of the next piece. This minor subdominant is so important in relation to No. 18 that it seems as if Grieg wanted to hold it back at measure 19, as if he did not dare to reveal it yet, but wanted to save until the last moment the secret that the final chord will lead to D major. For now we are about to behold the crown jewel of Op. 66.

No. 18, I Wander Deep in Thought

The text, which appears in A. P. Berggreen's collection of Danish folk songs, is as follows: "I wander deep in thought, I love one whom I cannot win. While he goes merrily on his way, I have only sorrow. It is a great sorrow that I did not get you, whom I love so dearly. So many deceitful people are the cause of my failure." The tempo is *Adagio religioso*. Think of the piece as an elaborate arrangement of a chorale tune.

Give some thought to the position of the piece in the collection as a whole. No matter how beautiful, how important, how strong the preceding pieces may have been in their own right, when we come to No. 18 everything that went before it seems preparatory. When you perform the entire set, therefore, try to build an enormous slur from the beginning of No. 1 and leading up to No. 18. To put it another way: even in No. 1, the relatively innocent *Cow Call*, there must be something hidden, a concealed element that is part of the big picture—part of the national tableau that is Op. 66. In this great musical epic poem, No. 18 is the focal point toward which Grieg aims from the very beginning. It is the deepest lake and the highest mountain.

The interpretation will vary—one person might play quite introspectively, another in a more outgoing manner—and the intensity will be different on different occasions. But many performance details have been prescribed by Grieg himself. In rapid succession he has written *p*, *pp*, *f*, *ff*, *fff*, and *fz*—not to mention *diminuendo*, *crescendo molto*, *stretto*, *ritardando*, and *la melodia ben tenuto*. This multiplicity of instructions surely indicates that Grieg intended No. 18 to be intense and vari-colored. Indeed, the colors are very bold—*pianissimo* and *ff* appear in close proximity—and it is a big leap from the compact *legato* of the four-part texture at the beginning to the majestic anacrusis octaves starting in measure 39 (see Exx. 13.78a and b).

Exx. 13.78a and b

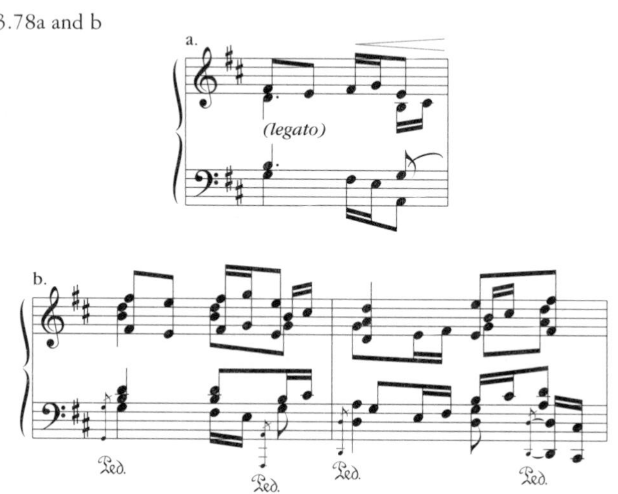

Musicians, including pianists, can learn from great performers in the theater. Note how a dramatic actress develops a role, the way she brings out the subtleties of her character without losing a sense of the whole. Her command of the whole dynamic spectrum, her ability to highlight the details of the individual phrases and motives are worthy of emulation. It is better to find one's model in another art form than among other concert pianists. Comparisons with the latter might be misunderstood or regarded as too direct. A great actress demonstrates by her example that a performing artist must immerse herself in her art in order to realize her potential. It takes a generous portion of natural talent and a lot of hard work to succeed as an artist.

Your approach should be to practice flexibly and at the same time in a disciplined manner, so that in the end you can free yourself from the tyranny of the printed score and perform the music with a heartfelt personal engagement. When you have mastered the technical aspects, the expressive and spiritual elements can come to the fore and give life to a three-dimensional interpretation uniting the score, the moment, and your personal temperament. But you must still observe Grieg's explicit instructions in the score.

While you are learning No. 18, think in terms of the smallest note values for awhile. Following the principle of "give and take back," these units can be varied in a controlled *rubato*, one that conveys the feeling of an uninterrupted stream despite the freedom you are exercising.

Work hard on the *legato* passages. You must have a good feeling of solidity in the keys, regardless of the dynamic level. It may be necessary almost to "pinch" the melody line to give it sufficient intensity. But remember, intensity is not loudness. Playing *legato* means connecting each note to the succeeding one, but the moment of attack is also a part of it. There must not be a trace of an accent; everything should be as smooth as possible. Press the key as slowly as you can, with a sweeping motion and with your arm extended over and toward the keys. A continuous movement of the arm helps to achieve what could be called an attached *legato*. Ferruccio Busoni used to say that he tried to play as if he had no fingers, just a dangling wrist. Your weighted wrist and relaxed fingers should glide along the keys, and the cushions of your fingers should feel like heavy globules of liquid as you let them sink gently down. After you have mastered the *legato* attack, think about the connection of each note to the next. Follow the preceding key upward without losing contact with the surface. This matter of being concerned with the upward as well as downward movement of the key is impractical and almost unattainable while one is playing. For the performer, however, it is an aid to detaching oneself from the technical aspects of the performance in order to concentrate on the spiritual and the musical dimensions. *I Wander Deep in Thought* is a sublime piece of music with many challenges to be overcome and many details worthy of attention, but the most important thing is the attitude of the performer.

Try to "feel yourself into" the friction between the various harmonies. This is different from understanding a harmonic analysis, and it is of the utmost importance for achieving a sensitive interpretation.

Make the tenor voice in measures 18–36 very *legato*; hold each note as long as possible before moving on to the next one (see Ex. 13.79).

Ex. 13.79

Give the ascending figure in F♯ in Ex. 13.80 a nice shimmering color in *pianissimo*. It should be so soft that the A♯ of the melody continues to be heard.

Ex. 13.80

Do not play the anacruses too slowly, i.e., too soon, before the big, majestic chords in measures 39ff. Properly executed they create an entirely different effect than if they are thrown in haphazardly (see Ex. 13.81).

Ex. 13.81

There is enormous tension between the melody when it occurs in the lower octave and when it is in the tenor register. In the third variation it appears in octaves in the soprano. Color it accordingly (see Ex. 13.82).

Ex. 13.82

Toward the end of the piece, dark and light sounds are juxtaposed. Note the *fff* in measure 58 and the *pianissimo* on the concluding chord (see Exx. 13.83a and b). Primarily, dark colors mean bass clef and below (see Ex. 13.84), but the last three measures should be light and clear.

No. 18 is the culmination of Op. 66. What follows is an afterthought.

Exx. 13.83a and b

Ex. 13.84

No. 19, Gjendine's Lullaby

Gjendine Slaalien was a milkmaid whom Grieg met on a trip to the mountains in 1891. According to Julius Röntgen, Grieg transcribed the melody after hearing Gjendine sing it to her sister's child, but the harmony is his.

The text reads, "My mother takes me in her lap, dances with me back and forth. Dance, then, with the little one, dance, then, then the child will dance. The child is laid in the cradle, sometimes it cries and sometimes it laughs. Sleep, now, sleep now in Jesus' name. Jesus, watch over the child."

No. 19 is a bit like an appended "moral" after the story is over. At the end of No. 18 one might ask, "What is life?" No. 19 answers, "A puff of wind in the rushes." That is how *Gjendine's Lullaby* appears, coming right after No. 18, which has plumbed the depths of human experience.

It is most important to make a subtle distinction between *pianissimo* and *piano*. The *pianissimo* tends to get a little slow, but keep to the tempo indication of *Allegretto semplice*, which is fairly fast.

A pedal point on G underlies the entire first phrase. It might enhance the freedom of the melodic line to play the chords entirely with the left hand (see Ex. 13.85).

Ex. 13.85

How should the embellishments be played—before the beat, or on it? Perhaps they should be played differently each time—for example, before the beat in measure 2, on the beat in measure 6. Playing them on the beat in measure 6 adds a little depth, and it works well in *piano*. Emphasize the low notes in measures 5–8 (see Ex. 13.86).

Ex. 13.86

Measures 9–13 also have some nice little subtleties. Played *pianissimo*, the sound is almost like humming. In measures 14–18 you can sing out a little more. When playing *pianissimo* you must try to strike the keys with an upward movement. Now, in *piano*, perhaps you can use a downward movement or play a little more toward the fingertips (see Exx. 13.87a and b).

Note the different harmonies on beat 2 in measures 11 and 16—the first time with A in the bass, the second time with A♭. The latter implies heightened tension (see Exx. 13.88a and b).

Gjendine's Lullaby is not ponderous harmonically, but it has a few chromatics—for example, in measures 9 and 10 (see Ex. 13.87a).

In the concluding three measures the middle voices move in parallel chro-

Exx. 13.87a and b

Exx. 13.88a and b

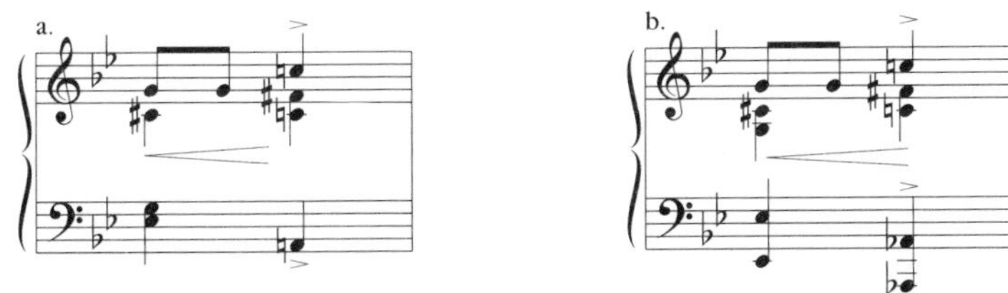

matic lines. Stress them just enough so that an attentive listener will be vaguely aware of them (see Ex. 13.89).

Ex. 13.89

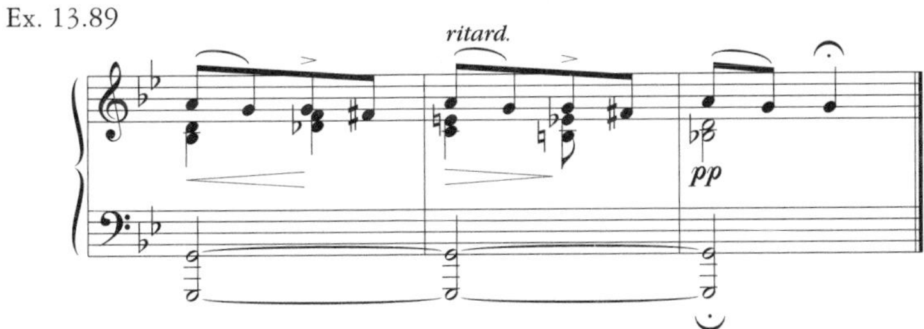

It is useful to locate the various contact points on the key, depending on whether your hand is moving upward or downward. In an upward move the arm moves slightly away from the key without too much bending of the wrist. In a downward move, let the arm be relaxed and free, but again do not bend the wrist very much. The wrists should fall naturally into place so that you feel a continuous line from your shoulder to the end of your finger. This imaginary line need not go away even if the movement is relaxed. If it does, the movement is too pronounced, and you cannot control the quality or the dynamic level of the note. If you achieve a good transmission of the impulse from arm to key in both an upward and a downward movement of the arm, you will possess a valuable resource for subtly varying tone color. This brings us to the heart and at the same time the principal danger in *Gjendine's Lullaby*: Differentiate between *pianissimo* and *piano*, and emphasize the pedal points and the gently accented chromaticism without allowing the dynamic spectrum to become too large.

Nothing in Grieg's entire production surpasses Op. 66 in genuine and subtle nuances. To master this opus, no effort is too great. Contrary to popular belief, the age of the skaldic poets did not end with the writing of the so-called *Younger Eddas*, for in Op. 66 they are reborn in glorious, immortal sound.

CHAPTER

14

Six Norwegian Mountain Melodies, EG 108

Grieg composed many pieces based on tunes in L. M. Lindeman's extensive collection of Norwegian mountain melodies (*Norske fjeldmelodier*), among them the six pieces discussed in this chapter. The arrangements are simple, and at first hearing one might think that Grieg dashed them off in haste. Upon closer analysis, however, one is struck by the sensitivity with which he handled these tunes, as though he wished to preserve their inner essence, to render them playable on the piano without marring them in any way. *Six Norwegian Mountain Melodies* are like wildflowers that are carefully illuminated so as not to alter them in the process.

No. 1, Springar

This piece is reminiscent of Op. 17, which was composed five years earlier. It has some unpretentious embellishments in the left hand and some fragmentary bass passages (see Ex. 14.1).

Measures 9–10 are much like Op. 17, No. 1, except that the movement is upward instead of downward (see Ex. 14.2).

In measures 23–26, use some pedal, especially in measures 25–26. Imagine fog hovering over a mountain lake.

Ex. 14.1

Allegro

p

Ex. 14.2

In measures 29–36, marked *pianissimo*, hold back a bit so as to provide a lot of contrast with the *fortissimo* section that follows.

Maintain a pleasant tone at all times, in both the soft and the louder passages. Nothing must be too direct or harsh. Each individual note must be clear as crystal and light in timbre. The two hands must be perfectly coordinated. Think vertically, and be sure that notes intended to sound simultaneously really do so. You must, however, retain the horizontal dimension as well.

No. 2, Lullaby

This charming tune from Valdres is very well known in Norway, where it is still often sung as a real lullaby. Grieg's arrangement is so simple that it might have come from a children's song book. If you look more closely, however, you can see the hand of the master in the delicate harmonies and the careful voice leading.

Ex. 14.3 shows a little duet in thirds, which can be brought out by giving a bit of emphasis to the tenor voice.

Ex. 14.3

The pedal point on C in measures 13–15 and the inverted pedal point on F immediately following should also be brought out. Emphasize them gently and circumspectly, so that they provide a firm harmonic foundation, but try to preserve the illusion that we are hearing a folk instrument, not a piano. Grieg may have been thinking here of the *langeleik*, a zitherlike stringed instrument commonly played (in Grieg's time as well as today) in the Valdres region of Norway (see Exx. 14.4a and b).

Exx. 14.4a and b

The *legato* should be as smooth as possible. There should be some emphasis on the soprano voice, but it should never be overpowering. Most important in playing this piece is to produce a sweet, tender sound by pressing down on the keys with a plastic and gentle movement of the wrist and arm.

The saying "*crescendo* is talent, *diminuendo* is art" certainly applies here. To create a real *diminuendo* at the end of the piece is not easy. Gently does it. Remember that you are trying to put a child to sleep.

No. 3, Springar

Modal harmonies—minor dominants alternating with Lydian chords—give this fascinating little piece a mixed major/minor feeling. The esoteric harmony is charming but never distracting. Think of a pen-and-ink drawing, a quick little sketch, that is so artistic and genuine that it could hang in an art gallery. Grieg was very familiar with this dance form—he knew what people did with their feet—but he did not exaggerate these characteristics in the music.

Internalize the harmonic progression in the left hand—each individual chord—as something carefully chosen by Grieg and, therefore, important. He worked hard to avoid a thick sound, weeding out inessential notes. What remains is only that which is absolutely necessary to characterize and color the melody. A *crescendo* leads to the *fortissimo* in measure 13; thereafter the music recedes in a *sempre diminuendo* to *pianissimo* at the end (see Exx. 14.5a, b, and c).

Exx. 14.5a, b, and c

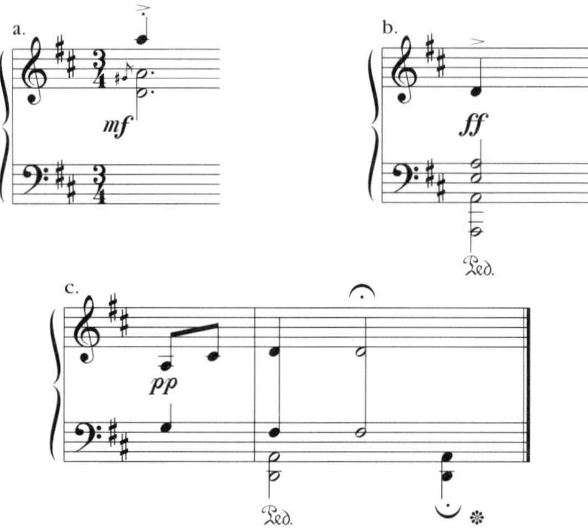

No. 4, Sjugurd and the Troll Bride

This lofty and beautiful folk ballad from Hallingdal was, among other things, the inspiration for Grieg's *Old Norwegian Melody with Variations* (for two pianos) Op. 51. Again we are impressed by the simplicity, the way Grieg makes use of so few of the resources available to him! Every note in the harmony, every harmonic twist—indeed, each tiny detail is significant. In that respect it is like *Gjendine's Lullaby*, the last piece in Op. 66. Everything is important, but this very fact can become a burden when you perform these pieces, for you must resist playing loudly, ponderously, or slowly. If you are aware of what is going on harmonically, you will come to feel that you are reading between the lines, hearing between the sounds, feeling something between the notes. More important than the notes are the ethereal harmonies that we sense, above and beyond those that are written and played.

This beautiful folk tune comes from the very heart of Norway. It begins solemnly, earnestly, on a $^6_4$ subdominant chord (see Ex. 14.6). Despite the

Ex. 14.6

predominantly solemn tone, the last two measures, in 6/8 time, are in a lighter mood (see Ex. 14.7).

Ex. 14.7

No. 5, Halling

Grieg's arrangement of this delightful tune from Østerdalen is a stroke of genius. It seems to be chiseled out of stone. The potentially monotonous melody is spiced up with clever variations in the accompaniment: pedal points, appoggiaturas, lush and long-held chords. The harmony is definitive, and the voice leading is equally convincing. Do not play inordinately loud, but loud enough to leave no doubt that you are completely in control. You must be very alert, with a clear grasp of both sound and phrasing. Both of these elements are prominent in measures 25–28, where G♯, the Lydian subdominant, clashes with the prevailing A-major harmony (see Ex. 14.8).

Ex. 14.8

This sharp dissonance reminds one of the *Norwegian Peasant Dances*, Op. 72, No. 13 (see Ex. 14.9).

Ex. 14.9

No. 6, The Boy and the Girl in the Hayloft

This is the same tune that Grieg arranged in *Improvisata on Two Norwegian Folk Songs*, Op. 29, No. 1. The text is given on p. 132.

The first part, in which the boy is singing, resembles a *gangar* ("walking dance") and should be played with a forward-rocking motion of the arm and rhythm. The boy is affectionate but a little reserved. The girl is a little spitfire—full of mischief, ready for anything. When it is her turn to sing, the rhythm changes to that of a much livelier *springar*.

In measures 1–3, pay careful attention to the pedal point in the bass and the inverted pedal point in the alto. The melody should be played with a nice, flowing *legato* (see Ex. 14.10).

Ex. 14.10

Portraying the girl requires a cleverly developed accompaniment. Think of a downward movement on the half note and a quick upward movement on the quarter note (see Ex. 14.11).

Ex. 14.11

In the dotted rhythms of the *Vivace* section, think of the sixteenth notes as belonging to the note that follows—almost as if they were anacruses (see Ex. 14.12). The quarter-note chords in measures 17 and 19 should be played fairly *staccato*. And do not slow the tempo toward the end.

Ex. 14.12

No. 6 is not a long piece, but it offers a lot of color in the space of a few measures. Play it, then, with simple but subtle sound effects. Develop the rhythm, and listen to the countermelodies that Grieg has added here and there. His pen-and-ink drawings are very clear, not at all impressionistic. Strive for clarity rather than frequent use of the pedal, articulation in preference to thickness of any kind. This little bouquet of six pieces constitutes a modest collection, but with respect to clarity and quality it is on a par with many of Grieg's larger works.

CHAPTER 15

The Lyric Pieces

SOME GENERAL OBSERVATIONS

For a Norwegian pianist it is as important to play Grieg's *Lyric Pieces* as it is to master Bach's Preludes and Fugues, Beethoven's Sonatas, and Chopin's Etudes. The performer's musicality and ability to create moods are put to the test. The most important clue to the special nature of these pieces is the very title that Grieg chose. He did not write Romantic works, as Dvořák and Schumann did. The use of the adjective *lyric* rather than *romantic* clearly was deliberate. What does "lyric" mean? Something heartfelt, but also something light, something Nordic, in contrast to the heavier character of Continental Romanticism. It has a parallel in the climate of Norway. To be sure, winter is dark and long, but from spring to early autumn everything is light and green and beautiful—in short, lyrical. Summer in Norway is warm but fresh. The high humidity and summer storms common on the Continent are almost unheard-of in Norway. And it is so light, for in the southern part of the country the sun barely dips below the horizon, and northern Norway is the land of the midnight sun.

The difference in climate between Norway and central Europe may have something to do with the differences between Norwegian and Continental music. Perhaps the predominately humid and stormy weather in such countries as Germany, Austria, and Czechoslovakia during the summer months is partly responsible for the heavier, Romantic music characteristic of those countries. Musical emotions, like the weather, are sometimes violent. Now Nordic music is not lacking in emotion, but the colors are pastels rather than bold pigments.

Let this lightness shine through when you play Grieg's *Lyric Pieces*. These pieces also reflect Norway's wild and rugged landscape, with more sharply hewn rhythms and accents than in Schumann, for example. Schumann is more Romantic, more ponderous, and friendly, whereas Grieg tends to be lyrical and majestic. Playing his music also requires seriousness, but one should hold to a relatively sparse sonority even in the *forte* passages. As a rule there is something frisky and folkish lurking nearby, and this lightens the coloring.

It is impossible to overdo the subtleties and shadings when playing the *Lyric Pieces*. You need as varied a palette as you can muster.

Unfortunately we have only a few recordings of Grieg's own playing, and they hardly do him justice. They were made when he was old, quite feeble, and ill. His wife, Nina, confided that Grieg himself was not pleased with the recordings. The recording company wanted him to do another take, but it is reported that Grieg merely coughed and said, "No, I am too sick. I can't manage any more. It can't be used." But after his death, commercial interests dictated otherwise. There was money to be made from his recordings, whether he approved of them or not. For that reason, we must not judge Grieg as a performer on the basis of these recordings. Critics who attended his concerts by and large painted a picture of a great artist. In both Paris and London they wrote about the subtle elegance of his playing. He was not described as a virtuoso, but that is not surprising, for he was not trained as a concert pianist. Beyond all doubt is the richness of his palette and the fine shading of the sound.

Most of the *Lyric Pieces* have descriptive titles. Let your imagination run free. Conjure up pictures and stories. Imagine something looming before you, listen to your fantasies, and recreate something of what you see and hear in your playing. Then your listeners will perceive them as effective character pieces. Some of the pieces are waltzes; play several of them in succession for a while. Then go on to the *hallings*, and master them one by one. Those that have the character of a *springar* and those that are marked *alle marcia* might also be practiced in their respective groups. There are a few virtuoso pieces, the most virtuosic being *Brooklet*. It requires a great deal of practice, but it is worth it. Op. 65 is the longest collection of *Lyric Pieces*, Op. 12 the shortest.

The first and biggest problem in learning the *Lyric Pieces* is to develop a feel for Grieg's short phrases. They rarely exceed four measures, and often they comprise only two. The music becomes choppy if you use *rubato* at the end of each phrase. Instead, craft lines encompassing more than one period, lines that unite several smaller elements.

Secondly, let the *rubato* follow the chord progression, the harmonic turns, the modulations. Get intimately acquainted with the relations between and among the various positions on the circle of fifths. Movement to the right on the circle lends a warming effect; movement to the left tends to cool things down. The aesthetics of an earlier age called the dominant (or keys notated with sharps) the sun, the subdominant (or those notated with flats) the moon, and the tonic (or the root key) the earth. You may find some helpful insight in this old idea. In any case, you will not go wrong if you listen for a rich, round tone when you move to the right and a thinner, more Medieval, sound when the harmonies move leftward, i.e., toward the flat keys or those with fewer sharps. The main point is that the feeling must follow the harmonic progression and not be introduced haphazardly.

The *Lyric Pieces* are miniatures; like Asian ink drawings they use just a few strokes to create explicit characterizations. Every stroke in the drawing makes a contribution to the whole; and when we play the *Lyric Pieces* we must focus on the mood and make a precise presentation in a short time. In the shorter pieces this can be difficult, so it is wise to approach the small forms slowly. Start out by exaggerating your interpretation, then gradually moderate it. Then it will be easier to present your ideas in a nutshell.

Many of the *Lyric Pieces* are easy to play and have been ruined by poor performances. When they became popular, piano playing and singing were common in almost every home, and most of the players were amateurs. It is a challenge to interpret these pieces artistically and consciously keep them at a high artistic level. Draw inspiration from whatever you think the piece is representing, and listen carefully. Combine short phrases into longer units, longer lines, i.e., place them in a larger context. If possible, play an entire opus rather than just one or two pieces from it. That way you can paint larger pictures. The miniatures remain, of course, but as part of a larger whole. Grieg was probably thinking cyclically when he wrote the *Lyric Pieces*. In any event the juxtaposition within each opus is tasteful and well considered: the sequence of keys always makes sense, and the various moods complement one another. Seldom does he place two virtuoso pieces, or two static pieces, side by side. A lyrically tuned and sensitive spirit is the first requisite. Imagination, articulation, and *rubato* are extremely important, but one also needs a solid, underlying rhythm.

The *Lyric Pieces*, despite their apparent simplicity, demand piano playing of the highest order. Bring out the beautiful colors of these tone pictures: yellows and blues vie for dominance with reds and an occasional black stroke—but little or no brown. Approach them with alert senses and a listening mind. Peer beyond the obvious; experience that which cannot be seen. Look for a third dimension between the lines and give your imagination free rein.

THE LYRIC PIECES CLASSIFIED BY CHARACTERISTIC

(Numbers in parentheses indicate the position of each piece in the entire collection of the 66 *Lyric Pieces*.)

Musical Types

Character Pieces

- Arietta, Op. 12, No. 1 (No. 1)
- Watchman's Song, Op. 12, No. 3 (No. 3)
- National Song, Op. 12, No. 8 (No. 8)
- Canon, Op. 38, No. 8 (No. 16)
- Butterfly, Op. 43, No. 1 (No. 17)
- Solitary Traveller, Op. 43, No. 2 (No. 18)
- In My Native Country, Op. 43, No. 3 (No. 19)
- Little Bird, Op. 43, No. 4 (No. 20)
- Erotikon, Op. 43, No. 5 (No. 21)
- To Spring, Op. 43, No. 6 (No. 22)
- Melancholy, Op. 47, No. 5 (No. 27)
- Shepherd's Boy, Op. 54, No. 1 (No. 30)
- Notturno, Op. 54, No. 4 (No. 33)
- Scherzo, Op. 54, No. 5 (No. 34)
- Vanished Days, Op. 57, No. 1 (No. 36)
- Gade, Op. 57, No. 2 (No. 37)
- Illusion, Op. 57, No. 3 (No. 38)
- Secret, Op. 57, No. 4 (No. 39)
- She Dances, Op. 57, No. 5 (No. 40)
- Homesickness, Op. 57, No. 6 (No. 41)
- Sylph, Op. 62, No. 1 (No. 42)
- Gratitude, Op. 62, No. 2 (No. 43)
- French Serenade, Op. 62, No. 3 (No. 44)
- Brooklet, Op. 62, No. 4 (No. 45)
- Phantom, Op. 62, No. 5 (No. 46)

Homeward, Op. 62, No. 6 (No. 47)
From Early Years, Op. 65, No. 1 (No. 48)
Peasant's Song, Op. 65, No. 2 (No. 49)
Melancholy, Op. 65, No. 3 (No. 50)
Salon, Op. 65, No. 4 (No. 51)
Ballad, Op. 65, No. 5 (No. 52)
Wedding Day at Troldhaugen, Op. 65, No. 6 (No. 53)
Sailors' Song, Op. 68, No. 1 (No. 54)
Grandmother's Minuet, Op. 68, No. 2 (No. 55)
At Your Feet, Op. 68, No. 3 (No. 56)
Evening in the Mountains, Op. 68, No. 4 (No. 57)
Once Upon a Time, Op. 71, No. 1 (No. 60)
Summer's Eve, Op. 71, No. 2 (No. 61)
Peace of the Woods, Op. 71, No. 4 (No. 63)
Gone, Op. 71, No. 6 (No. 65)

WALTZES

Waltz, Op. 12, No. 2 (No. 2)
Waltz, Op. 38, No. 7 (No. 15)
Waltz-Impromptu, Op. 47, No. 1 (No. 23)
She Dances, Op. 57, No. 5 (No. 40)
Sylph, Op. 62, No. 1 (No. 42)
Salon, Op. 65, No. 4 (No. 51)
Grandmother's Minuet, Op. 68, No. 2 (No. 55)
Valse mélancolique, Op. 68, No. 6 (No. 59)
Remembrances, Op. 71, No. 7 (No. 66)

SPRINGARS (NORWEGIAN "WALKING" DANCES)

Norwegian, Op. 12, No. 6 (No. 6)
Folk Song, Op. 38, No. 2 (No. 10)
Springar, Op. 38, No. 5 (No. 13)
Springar, Op. 47, No. 6 (No. 28)
Homesickness (middle section), Op. 57, No. 6 (No. 41)
From Early Years (middle section), Op. 65, No. 1 (No. 48)
Once Upon a Time, Op. 71, No. 1 (No. 60)

HALLINGS

Halling, Op. 38, No. 4 (No. 12)
Halling, Op. 47, No. 4 (No. 26)
Halling, Op. 71, No. 5 (No. 64)

Folk Songs

Folk Song, Op. 12, No. 5 (No. 5)
Folk Song, Op. 38, No. 2 (No. 10)
Once Upon a Time (first part), Op. 71, No. 1 (No. 60)

"Troll" Pieces

March of the Dwarfs, Op. 54, No. 3 (No. 32)
Wedding Day at Troldhaugen, Op. 65, No. 6 (No. 53)
Puck, Op. 71, No. 3 (No. 62)

Lullabies

Cradle Song, Op. 38, No. 1 (No. 9)
At the Cradle, Op. 68, No. 5 (No. 58)

Melodies

Melody, Op. 38, No. 3 (No. 11)
Melody, Op. 47, No. 3 (No. 25)

Elegies

Elegy, Op. 38, No. 6 (No. 14)
Elegy, Op. 47, No. 7 (No. 29)

Album Leaves

Album Leaf, Op. 12, No. 7 (No. 7)
Album Leaf, Op. 47, No. 2 (No. 24)

Marches

Homeward, Op. 62, No. 6 (No. 47)
Sailors' Song, Op. 68, No. 1 (No. 54)

Gangars

Gangar, Op. 54, No. 2 (No. 31)

Pieces for Advanced Pianists

Virtuoso Pieces

Fairy Dance, Op. 12, No. 4 (No. 4)
Butterfly, Op. 43, No. 1 (No. 17)
Scherzo, Op. 54, No. 5 (No. 34)
Brooklet, Op. 62, No. 4 (No. 45)

Homeward, Op. 62, No. 6 (No. 47)
Wedding Day at Troldhaugen, Op. 65, No. 6 (No. 53)

EXCEPTIONALLY LONG PIECES
Vanished Days, Op. 57, No. 1 (No. 36)
Wedding Day at Troldhaugen, Op. 65, No. 6 (No. 53)

Pieces with Particular Musical Characteristics

PRONOUNCED OPEN FIFTHS IN THE BASS (BOURDON EFFECT)
Waltz (conclusion), Op. 12, No. 2 (No. 2)
Fairy Dance, Op. 12, No. 4 (No. 4)
Folk Song, Op. 12, No. 5 (No. 5)
Norwegian, Op. 12, No. 6 (No. 6)
Cradle Song (middle section), Op. 38, No. 1 (No. 9)
Folk Song, Op. 38, No. 2 (No. 10)
Halling, Op. 38, No. 4 (No. 12)
Springar, Op. 38, No. 5 (No. 13)
Solitary Traveller, Op. 43, No. 2 (No. 18)
In My Native Country, Op. 43, No. 3 (No. 19)
Little Bird, Op. 43, No. 4 (No. 20)
Waltz-Impromptu, Op. 47, No. 1 (No. 23)
Album Leaf, Op. 47, No. 2 (No. 24)
Melody, Op. 47, No. 3 (No. 25)
Halling, Op. 47, No. 4 (No. 26)
Melancholy, Op. 47, No. 5 (No. 27)
Springar, Op. 47, No. 6 (No. 28)
Shepherd's Boy, Op. 54, No. 1 (No. 30)
Gangar, Op. 54, No. 2 (No. 31)
March of the Dwarfs, Op. 54, No. 3 (No. 32)
Scherzo, Op. 54, No. 5 (No. 34)
Bell Ringing, Op. 54, No. 6 (No. 35)
Vanished Days, Op. 57, No. 1 (No. 36)
Gade, Op. 57, No. 2 (No. 37)
Homesickness, Op. 57, No. 6 (No. 41)
Brooklet, Op. 62, No. 4 (No. 45)
Phantom, Op. 62, No. 5 (No. 46)
Homeward, Op. 62, No. 6 (No. 47)
From Early Years, Op. 65, No. 1 (No. 48)
Salon (middle section), Op. 65, No. 4 (No. 51)

Wedding Day at Troldhaugen, Op. 65, No. 6 (No. 53)
Evening in the Mountains, Op. 68, No. 4 (No. 57)
At the Cradle, Op. 68, No. 5 (No. 58)
Valse mélancolique (middle section and conclusion), Op. 68, No. 6 (No. 59)
Once upon a time (middle section), Op. 71, No. 1 (No. 60)
Summer's Eve, Op. 71, No. 2 (No. 61)
Puck, Op. 71, No. 3 (No. 62)
Peace of the Woods, Op. 71, No. 4 (No. 63)
Halling, Op. 71, No. 5 (No. 64)
Remembrances, Op. 71, No. 7 (No. 66)

Inverted Pedal Points

Folk Song, Op. 38, No. 3 (No. 11)
Halling, Op. 38, No. 4 (No. 12)
Springar, Op. 38, No. 5 (No. 13)
Elegy, Op. 38, No. 6 (No. 14)
Canon, Op. 38, No. 8 (No. 16)
Solitary Traveller, Op. 43, No. 2 (No. 18)
Little Bird, Op. 43, No. 4 (No. 20)
Album Leaf, Op. 47, No. 2 (No. 24)
Melody, Op. 47, No. 3 (No. 25)
Halling, Op. 47, No. 4 (No. 26)
Melancholy, Op. 47, No. 5 (No. 27)
Elegy, Op. 47, No. 7 (No. 29)
Shepherd's Boy, Op. 54, No. 1 (No. 30)
March of the Dwarfs, Op. 54, No. 3 (No. 32)
Notturno, Op. 54, No. 4 (No. 33)
Scherzo, Op. 54, No. 5 (No. 34)
Vanished Days, Op. 57, No. 1 (No. 36)
Gade, Op. 57, No. 2 (No. 37)
Illusion, Op. 57, No. 3 (No. 38)
Secret, Op. 57, No. 4 (No. 39)
She Dances, Op. 57, No. 5 (No. 40)
Homesickness, Op. 57, No. 6 (No. 41)
Sylph, Op. 62, No. 1 (No. 42)
French Serenade, Op. 62, No. 3 (No. 44)
Phantom, Op. 62, No. 5 (No. 46)
Homeward, Op. 62, No. 6 (No. 47)
From Early Years, Op. 65, No. 1 (No. 48)
Salon, Op. 65, No. 4 (No. 51)

Wedding Day at Troldhaugen, Op. 65, No. 6 (No. 53)
Evening in the Mountains, Op. 68, No. 4 (No. 57)
Valse mélancolique, Op. 68, No. 6 (No. 59)
Once Upon a Time, Op. 71, No. 1 (No. 60)
Summer's Eve, Op. 71, No. 2 (No. 61)
Puck, Op. 71, No. 3 (No. 62)
Peace of the Woods, Op. 71, No. 4 (No. 63)
Halling, Op. 71, No. 5 (No. 64)
Remembrances, Op. 71, No. 7 (No. 66)

Prominent Pedal Points
Arietta, Op. 12, No. 1 (No. 1)
Waltz, Op. 12, No. 2 (No. 2)
Folk Song, Op. 12, No. 5 (No. 5)
Norwegian, Op. 12, No. 6 (No. 6)
Album Leaf, Op. 12, No. 7 (No. 7)
Cradle Song, Op. 38, No. 1 (No. 9)
Elegy, Op. 38, No. 6 (No. 14)
Erotikon, Op. 43, No. 5 (No. 21)
Halling, Op. 47, No. 4 (No. 26)
Melancholy, Op. 47, No. 5 (No. 27)
Shepherd's Boy (conclusion), Op. 54, No. 1 (No. 30)
Gangar, Op. 54, No. 2 (No. 31)
March of the Dwarfs, Op. 54, No. 3 (No. 32)
Scherzo, Op. 54, No. 5 (No. 34)
Gade, Op. 57, No. 2 (No. 37)
Gratitude, Op. 62, No. 2 (No. 43)
Brooklet, Op. 62, No. 4 (No. 45)
Homeward, Op. 62, No. 6 (No. 47)
From Early Years, Op. 65, No. 1 (No. 48)
Peasant's Song, Op. 65, No. 2 (No. 49)
Melancholy, Op. 65, No. 3 (No. 50)
At Your Feet, Op. 68, No. 3 (No. 56)
Evening in the Mountains, Op. 68, No. 4 (No. 57)
At the Cradle, Op. 68, No. 5 (No. 58)
Peace of the Woods, Op. 71, No. 4 (No. 63)
Halling, Op. 71, No. 5 (No. 64)

Prominent Chromatic Passages
Melody, Op. 38, No. 3 (No. 11)
Butterfly, Op. 43, No. 1 (No. 17)

Erotikon, Op. 43, No. 5 (No. 21)
Elegy, Op. 47, No. 7 (No. 29)
Shepherd's Boy, Op. 54, No. 1 (No. 30)
Notturno, Op. 54, No. 4 (No. 33)
Gade, Op. 57, No. 2 (No. 37)
Illusion, Op. 57, No. 3 (No. 38)
Secret, Op. 57, No. 4 (No. 39)
She Dances, Op. 57, No. 5 (No. 40)
Gratitude, Op. 62, No. 2 (No. 43)
Brooklet, Op. 62, No. 4 (No. 45)
Peasant's Song, Op. 65, No. 2 (No. 49)
Melancholy, Op. 65, No. 3 (No. 50)
Wedding Day at Troldhaugen, Op. 65, No. 6 (No. 53)
At Your Feet, Op. 68, No. 3 (No. 56)
Evening in the Mountains, Op. 68, No. 4 (No. 57)
Valse mélancolique, Op. 68, No. 6 (No. 59)
Summer's Eve, Op. 71, No. 2 (No. 61)
Puck, Op. 71, No. 3 (No. 62)
Peace of the Woods, Op. 71, No. 4 (No. 63)
Halling, Op. 71, No. 5 (No. 64)
Gone, Op. 71, No. 6 (No. 65)
Remembrances, Op. 71, No. 7 (No. 66)

Abrupt Key Changes and Harmonic Transitions
Watchman's Song, Op. 12, No. 3 (No. 3)
Butterfly, Op. 43, No. 1 (No. 17)
Erotikon, Op. 43, No. 5 (No. 21)
Melancholy, Op. 47, No. 5 (No. 27)
Gangar, Op. 54, No. 2 (No. 31)
March of the Dwarfs, Op. 54, No. 3 (No. 32)
Notturno, Op. 54, No. 4 (No. 33)
Scherzo, Op. 54, No. 5 (No. 34)
Vanished Days, Op. 57, No. 1 (No. 36)
Phantom, Op. 62, No. 5 (No. 46)
Homeward, Op. 62, No. 6 (No. 47)
From Early Years, Op. 65, No. 1 (No. 48)
Salon, Op. 65, No. 4 (No. 51)
Wedding Day at Troldhaugen, Op. 65, No. 6 (No. 53)
At Your Feet, Op. 68, No. 3 (No. 56)
At the Cradle, Op. 68, No. 5 (No. 58)
Valse mélancolique, Op. 68, No. 6 (No. 59)

Once Upon a Time, Op. 71, No. 1 (No. 60)
Summer's Eve, Op. 71, No. 2 (No. 61)
Puck, Op. 71, No. 3 (No. 62)
Peace of the Woods, Op. 71, No. 4 (No. 63)
Gone, Op. 71, No. 6 (No. 65)
Remembrances, Op. 71, No. 7 (No. 66)

Impressionistic Passages
Album Leaf, Op. 47, No. 2 (No. 24)
Melancholy, Op. 47, No. 5 (No. 27)
March of the Dwarfs, Op. 54, No. 3 (No. 32)
Notturno, Op. 54, No. 4 (No. 33)
Bell Ringing, Op. 54, No. 6 (No. 35)
Secret, Op. 57, No. 4 (No. 39)
She Dances, Op. 57, No. 5 (No. 40)
Sylph, Op. 62, No. 1 (No. 42)
Gratitude, Op. 62, No. 2 (No. 43)
Phantom, Op. 62, No. 5 (No. 46)
From Early Years, Op. 65, No. 1 (No. 48)
Salon, Op. 65, No. 4 (No. 51)
Wedding Day at Troldhaugen (middle section and conclusion), Op. 65, No. 6 (No. 53)
At the Cradle, Op. 68, No. 5 (No. 58)
Summer's Eve, Op. 71, No. 2 (No. 61)
Peace of the Woods, Op. 71, No. 4 (No. 63)

Unaccompanied Melodies or Recitativic Parts
Waltz, Op. 38, No. 7 (No. 15)
Waltz-Impromptu (transitions), Op. 47, No. 1 (No. 23)
Elegy, Op. 47, No. 7 (No. 29)
Shepherd's Boy, Op. 54, No. 1 (No. 30)
Gade, Op. 57, No. 2 (No. 37)
She Dances (beginning), Op. 57, No. 5 (No. 40)
Homesickness, Op. 57, No. 6 (No. 41)
From Early Years, Op. 65, No. 1 (No. 48)
Melancholy, Op. 65, No. 3 (No. 50)
Grandmother's Minuet, Op. 68, No. 2 (No. 55)
Evening in the Mountains, Op. 68, No. 4 (No. 57)
Valse mélancolique, Op. 68, No. 6 (No. 59)
Peace of the Woods, Op. 71, No. 4 (No. 63)
Remembrances, Op. 71, No. 7 (No. 66)

TRANSITIONS BETWEEN PARALLEL MAJOR/MINOR KEYS
Waltz, Op. 12, No. 2 (No. 2)
Watchman's Song, Op. 12, No. 3 (No. 3)
Norwegian, Op. 12, No. 6 (No. 6)
Cradle Song, Op. 38, No. 1 (No. 9)
Canon, Op. 38, No. 8 (No. 16)

MODAL (LYDIAN OR DORIAN) TINGE
Homesickness (Lydian, middle section), Op. 57, No. 6 (No. 41)
Brooklet (Lydian, ending), Op. 62, No. 4 (No. 45)
Ballad (Dorian), Op. 65, No. 5 (No. 52)
Puck (Lydian), Op. 71, No. 3 (No. 62)
Halling (Lydian), Op. 71, No. 5 (No. 64)

AUGMENTED MIDDLE SECTIONS
March of the Dwarfs, Op. 54, No. 3 (No. 32)
Scherzo, Op. 54, No. 5 (No. 34)
Homeward, Op. 62, No. 6 (No. 47)
Wedding Day at Troldhaugen, Op. 65, No. 6 (No. 53)

IMITATION AND CANON
Canon, Op. 38, No. 8 (No. 16)
Gone, Op. 71, No. 6 (No. 65)

HEMIOLA EFFECTS
Salon, Op. 65, No. 4 (No. 51)
Once Upon a Time, Op. 71, No. 1 (No. 60)

CHAPTER

16

Lyric Pieces I, Op. 12

Grieg's *Lyric Pieces* are a large collection of small pieces. There are 66 in all, grouped into ten opus numbers. Op. 12 is the shortest of the lot, a miniature collection of miniatures. It is as if Grieg deleted things as he was composing, eliminating everything that was not essential. Each piece in its own way is incredibly successful. Op. 12 brought Grieg his first great success. The publishing houses got excited, and the public became aware that there was a new master on the scene. Op. 12 stands at the beginning of a uniquely successful and productive creative project. Do not view it as Grieg's first pieces for piano students. The emphasis is on evoking certain moods or scenes, but the playing should never be exaggerated. Let the interpretation be understated rather than overstated. If you hold back a bit, your hearers will get the impression that you could have emphasized many details a bit more, but that you had the wisdom to set limits. The miniature pictures of the Orient would never be in oil. They are not Rembrandts. Something comparable goes on here. Op. 12 should be small and select, but genuine. The pieces are sweet and beautiful, but wonderfully light and coolly refreshing.

No. 1, Arietta

The lovely theme of this piece reappears in modified form in the very last lyric piece, *Remembrance*, Op. 71, No. 7, thereby drawing an enormous cyclic slur over all ten opuses.

Arietta has three independent voices, and an important secret to success is to make this three-voicedness a reality. Give your attention first to the melancholy, gently murmuring soprano voice, but practice the arpeggio figure in the middle voice and the bass line individually as well. You can also practice the two outer voices together, then the soprano and middle voices, and lastly the bass and the middle voices. Everything will then come together in a unified trio in which each voice nonetheless retains its individual identity.

Pay close attention to the dynamics of the bass line, and use the pedal to make sure that it is present without being too loud. The harplike figure in the middle voice should be even and soft, and the soprano voice should sing out gently on the top.

Pay careful attention to the phrasing. Note that the first part consists of two-measure phrases in which the first measure is like an upbeat in preparation for the second. After the first four measures, the flow becomes more differentiated. Note the articulation in the counterrhythm, and try to execute it independent of the other voices. This is one of subtleties of the piece (see Ex. 16.1).

Ex. 16.1

The first and last measures contain exactly the same notes. Practice them side by side, and make them different in the ways Grieg has indicated. The first measure should emerge out of silence, and the concluding one should disappear into silence once again.

Measures 9 and 11 are identical except for pitch. Each should be given its own distinctive coloring. Measure 11 might be played almost as an echo of measure 9.

In measure 14 you can partially release the pedal to clean up the sound without allowing the deep E♭ from measure 13 to disappear altogether.

From measure 17 forward give a little added emphasis to the bass line, which is a nice warm counter-melody. All in all, let *Arietta* be a beautiful dream (see Ex. 16.2).

No. 2, Waltz

This is the first of many waltzes in the *Lyric Pieces*. Although it is often played by children, it is also suitable for the concert hall. For a concert performance,

Ex. 16.2

think about porcelain and light ballet. Technically, this implies articulating meticulously and gently from the fingertips.

The phrasing in the right hand is at all times independent of the left hand's typical 3/4 waltz character.

Do not play the *forte* passages too loud. Remember that this is a miniature. Miniaturize the dynamics as well.

The *piano subito* on the fermata in measure 18 gives a nice effect (see Ex. 16.3).

Ex. 16.3

Note that the principal theme is stated twice *piano*, but the third time it is *pianissimo*. This subtlety is important for the form of the piece. The same dynamic contrast reappears in the coda—*piano dolce* in measure 71, *pianissimo* in measure 77.

Measures 63ff. sound as if the waltz is about to turn into a Norwegian *springar* (see Ex. 16.4).

Ex. 16.4

It seems appropriate to play the *staccato* quarter notes with a bit of a swinging rhythm (see Ex. 16.5).

Although Grieg has not so indicated, one might consider making the coda a shade slower than the rest of the piece. Try to achieve a kind of pastoral character. The middle section in A major might be played the same way. These differences should, however, be minute (see Ex. 16.6).

Ex. 16.5

Ex. 16.6

No. 3, Watchman's Song

Watchman's Song was very popular during Grieg's lifetime and still is. Though simple, it is a true masterwork. Pay attention to the *alla breve* notation: let us hear a definite 2/2 beat, not 4/4. That will also make it easier to bring out the simplicity that Grieg asks for. Maintain a good *legato* in the opening section, which is sometimes in unison, sometimes three-voiced, and sometimes four-voiced. Play in an unassuming way, as if you were unaware that a fateful event is about to occur (see Ex. 16.7).

Ex. 16.7

The *Intermezzo* is famous. Imagine owls hooting as a murder is committed in the darkness of the night. Grieg composed it after watching a performance of Shakespeare's *Macbeth*, so try to incorporate some of the *angst* and terror of that mighty drama in your performance. Think of an evil deed observed, or just glimpsed, by the night watchman as he makes his rounds. Did he hear the whole thing, or did something occur stealthily inside as he walked by? Perhaps the latter supposition is preferable.

The septuplets in thirty-second notes must be very soft, but clear. A little arm movement is needed here, but keep the hand stationary as much as possible. The ascending triplets must not be suddenly loud. Start out *piano* and increase the volume gradually.

No. 4, Fairy Dance

This charming little virtuoso piece is reminiscent of Mendelssohn. Everything has to be done with the fingertips in order to achieve a light, fast *staccato*. You will need a little help from your arm, but keep your hands close to the keys at all times. Sideways movements help when playing the eighth notes, but minimize them in fast tempo so that you do not upset your coordination. Such movements easily lead to a muddy sound and imprecise rhythm. *Fairy Dance* should be soft, light, and rhythmically precise.

Do not overdo the *forte* passages. You don't want to scare away the fairies until the very end. But you should practice this passage loud at first, then tone it down to just a shade louder than *pp* (see Ex. 16.8). In the scene that Grieg is trying to evoke the little fairies swarm around, hide, reappear, and finally disappear for good.

Ex. 16.8

Only in measures 29–30 and 70–72 does Grieg call for pedal. It gives the piece an extra dimension—an impressionistic veil, or perhaps a wispy bit of fog into which the fairies disappear (see Exx. 16.9 and 16.10).

Ex. 16.9

Ex. 16.10

No. 5, Folk Song

Grieg had an uncanny ability to invent melodies with an authentic Norwegian sound. Although *Folk Song* was undoubtedly inspired by the rich store of folk music of his native land, it is in fact his own invention.

Do not play it too slowly: note that Grieg has indicated *Con moto.* One characteristic of Norwegian temperament is melancholy, and to bring this out the piece should be played with simple sincerity. Unite the two four-measure phrases at the beginning into an eight-measure period, so that the second phrase sounds like an answer to the first. You might increase the volume gradually during the first four measures, then allow it to recede in measures 5–8, so that the entire eight-measure passage will sound like a single period.

In measures 3 and 4 it is natural to let the tone be a little brighter. In measure 7 it grows darker. Try to imitate a kind of chest tone (see Ex. 16.11).

Ex. 16.11

Folk Song is dreamlike from beginning to end. Norway's great national poet, Henrik Wergeland, once described his native land as a beautiful, majestic lyre filled with the hope of becoming something warm and musical. This hope hovers over the notes of Grieg's *Folk Song*.

No. 6, Norwegian

This piece is a powerful *springar*, the most distinctively Norwegian of the national dance forms. It abounds with pedal points and ostinatos, which give it a decidedly folklike quality. You can almost hear the undertones and the *bourdon* bass of the Hardanger fiddle, the Norwegian folk instrument *par excellence*. Practice it first in strict rhythm, and later introduce a bit of rhythmic variation. Note that there is sometimes a *sforzando* on the first beat (measures 1, 3, 5, 7, 14, etc.), sometimes on the second (measures 11, 15, 43, 47), and sometimes on the third (measures 16, 26, 27, 28, 30, etc.). The result is a varying and bouncy effect. The strength of the accent should be adjusted to fit the circumstances. Thus, for example, the accents in the middle section, marked *pp*, should be weaker than those elsewhere, but they should be there—on the third beat (see Ex. 16.12).

Ex. 16.12

The *staccato* quarter notes in the middle section should be soft, compact, and precise, as a contrast to the pedal points elsewhere in the piece. Some of the tied notes in the left hand act as pedal points, those in the right hand as inverted pedal points, and together they create a texture with its own harmonic tension. Play with accented rhythm but no *rubato* until the *sempre ritardando* near the end—and here it will help to achieve a uniform *ritardando* if you think in terms of eighth notes (see Ex. 16.13).

Ex. 16.13

No. 7, Album Leaf

What kind of an album leaf might this be? A secret little love letter from Grieg's youth, perhaps? There is something of the fickleness of teenage mentality about the piece. Whether he is writing to her or she to him is unknown, but it seems clear that both are involved. A dialogue proceeds for the most part in eight-measure periods. To be sure, "he" (melody in the tenor voice) has the floor for sixteen continuous measures, but then "she" (melody in soprano) has both the first and the last word.

The anacruses should not be too long, or the piece will sound archaic. To make them short, think to the right, i.e., think of them as belonging more to the following note than to the previous one. Practice playing them almost simultaneously, then separate them by degrees.

In the dialogue between the two hands, never play a given motive the same way twice. Use your imagination! You can make this piece into an enchanting little conversation, recorded in all secrecy on a page of someone's private album (see Exx. 16.14a and b).

Exx. 16.14a and b

No. 8, National Song

It was Christmas Eve, and Bjørnstjerne Bjørnson is reputed to have rushed up the stairs to Grieg's apartment in Oslo shouting, "I have found the text to Norway's national anthem!" Grieg had already composed No. 8 and had played it for Bjørnson, who liked it so much that he resolved to write words for it—32 verses, no less! It did not in fact become Norway's national anthem, but it should be played like one. It must be rhythmic in every detail in order to live up to the title and the indication *maestoso*. Attack the half notes in a swinging manner and with enough pedal to produce a bell-like sound, and hold them for their full value (see Ex. 16.15). Play the contrasting *piano*

Ex. 16.15

passage as *legato* as possible—like a brass ensemble playing softly and smoothly (see Ex. 16.16).

Ex. 16.16

Say it all with a small number of notes—and be thankful that Grieg did not make a through-composed setting of all 32 verses!

CHAPTER

17

Lyric Pieces II, Op. 38

Op. 38 was received with considerable anticipation after the great success of Op. 12. Grieg felt sure of himself. He had matured as an artist, and in the new pieces the form and the dimension were somewhat enlarged. For that reason Op. 38 may be easier to perform than Op. 12.

No. 1, Cradle Song

The title of the piece implies that the predominant rhythm is like the rocking of a cradle. Nothing should disturb the tranquility, but measure 3 can pose a problem. It is only a matter of three notes against two, but the relations among the notes are a bit intricate. If you find it difficult to play as written, try taking some of the alto notes with the left hand (see Ex. 17.1).

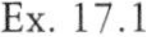
Ex. 17.1

In measure 7 it is difficult but important to connect the D and the E in the soprano voice, i.e., with the fifth finger followed by the fourth, but it helps to think primarily about the top voice. Release the lower voice if necessary.

Nearly always in Grieg's music, anacruses and small notes should be relatively short, never casual or sluggish. That is the case here in measure 9 and elsewhere, in imitation of the delicate figurations used on folk instruments.

In measures 13–16, play each rolled chord more slowly than the preceding one. This fits in nicely with the *ritardando* and brings the first section to a proper conclusion (see Ex. 17.2).

Ex. 17.2

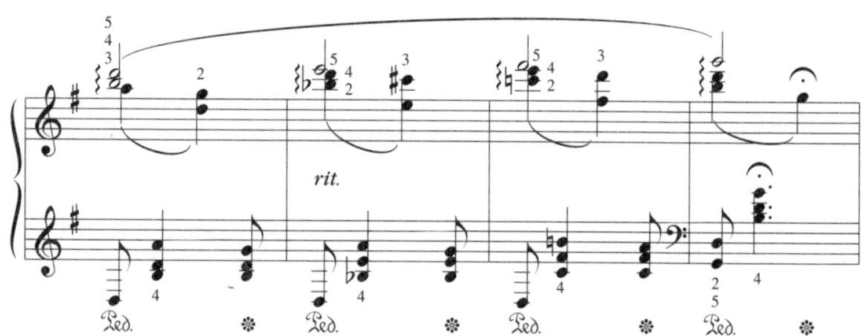

The accompaniment in the left hand should be quiet and peaceful, but don't be afraid to bring out the pedal point on G. Later the root of the chord is D, and this, too, should be allowed to support the harmony. Be careful not to make the last chord in the accompaniment too short.

In measures 15–16, bring out the fine passage in the tenor voice. Measures 17–32 repeat measures 1–16, but this time *ppp*, as a soft and gentle echo.

In the *Con moto* section, beginning in measure 33, Grieg gives us a restrained little *halling*—the first example in the *Lyric Pieces* of a piece in this distinctively Norwegian dance form. One is tempted to say that it is more like a little story about the *halling* and its character rather than an example of one. Gentle accents and contrasting emphases—in measures 33–34, for example, accent on beat 1 in the right hand, *tenuto* on beat 2 in the left—give the right feel. But remember, everything in moderation. Don't get too wild! (see Ex. 17.3.)

Ex. 17.3

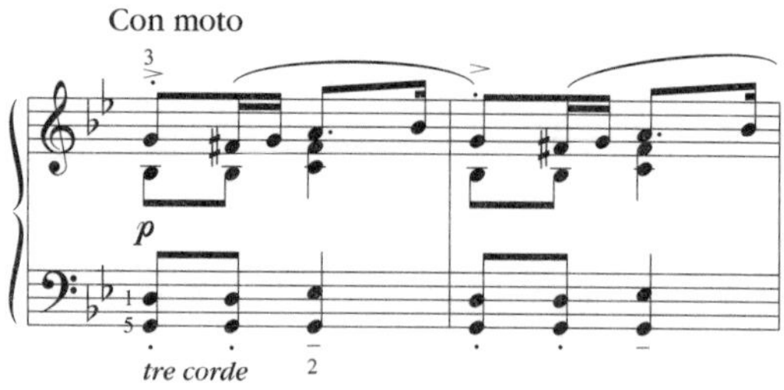

The breathless phrasing in measures 33–36 stands in contrast to measures 37–38. The focus of this two-measure phrase is on the second measure, so measure 37 feels almost like an upbeat, notwithstanding the *ritardando*. Measures 39–40 are a mere rounding off of the phrase, but a little rocking motion is needed in the right hand in measure 39. The mood is a little more animated when the *halling* is transposed up a third in measures 41ff. Schubert, Bruckner, Grieg, and pop composers do that sort of thing!

There is a musical and melodic connection between measures 47–48 and 49–50, especially between the F and the E in the soprano voice. Thus you must be careful that the C♯-minor arpeggio, which is written out in small notes, does not become too ponderous or interrupt the established rhythm. Listen to the one-beat rest (see Ex. 17.4).

Ex. 17.4

Often in Grieg's music, pedal points and inverted pedal points serve an integrating function even as they give the music a national flavor. For example, there is a pedal point on G from measure 51 all the way to measure 67. Be aware of the beautiful descending chromatic line in the bass (measures 67–70), just before the reversion to G major.

No. 2, Folk Song

The rhythm here is that of a *springar*. The left hand controls the rhythm throughout the whole piece, unifying the form and providing the energy (see Ex. 17.5).

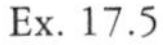
Ex. 17.5

There should be a slight emphasis on the first beat of the accompaniment throughout the entire piece. The right hand often teases us with a counterrhythm: a gentle stress on the second beat that creates an effective bounce (see Ex. 17.6).

Ex. 17.6

You can toy with the second beat in the right hand, in contrast to the first-beat accent in the left (see Ex. 17.7). The duet in the right hand in a dotted

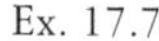
Ex. 17.7

rhythm can best be executed by leading slightly from the elbow. Move it out and in a bit. To master the fingering, practice the upper and lower parts by themselves, then try to combine them with as much precision as possible (see Ex. 17.8).

Ex. 17.8

The middle section (measures 15–29) is light and open. If you find it difficult to play measures 15 and 17 as written, play the alto G with your left hand. To keep the piece from becoming too breathless, try inserting a long slur over measures 15–18 (see Ex. 17.9).

Be very careful about the *ritardando* passages. Use more *ritardando* the second time than the first. Stay within the framework of a folk song.

Ex. 17.9

No. 3, Melody

This piece is decidedly Schumannesque. It is important that it not be played too fast; 4/4 is not *alla breve*! Don't be too tempestuous: this is a calm sea with gently rolling waves.

The anacrusis in measure 3 must not be too long or casual. It belongs to the note that it precedes, not the one that it follows.

In measures 2 and 4 Grieg has clearly indicated four voices. Play the music exactly as it is written, with a good *rubato* and no unnecessary pause before the resolution (see Ex. 17.10).

Ex. 17.10

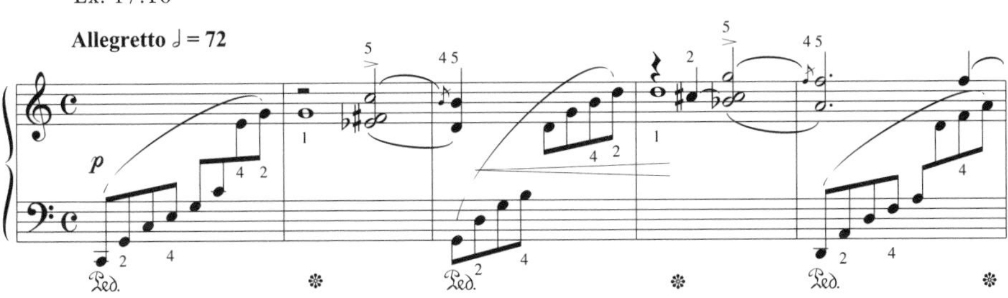

Melody has a fragmentary, improvised character. There is a constant shifting between melodic arpeggios and dissonances with suspensions, some of which broaden out into long melodic lines (see Ex. 17.11).

Ex. 17.11

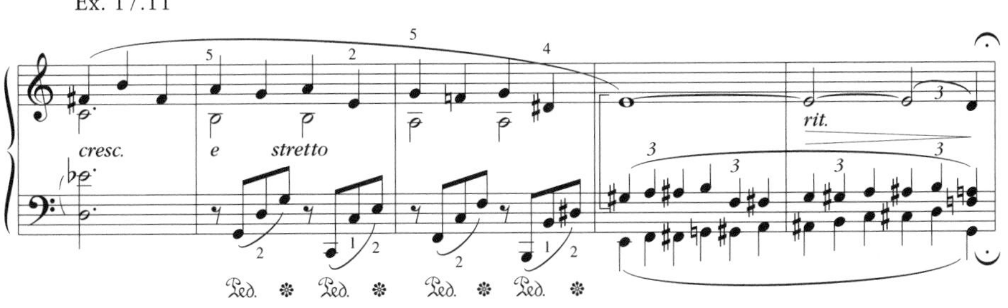

This piece often requires you to play four notes against three. Carefully work out the relations between and among half notes, quarter notes, eighth notes, and quarter-note triplets, practicing everything in strict rhythm. Only when you have learned this firmly should you begin to introduce a bit of your own *rubato*. Even then, think carefully about what you are doing. Start with the *ritardandi*, the fermatas, the *poco stretto*, etc., indicated in the score. You may find that you do not need much *rubato* in this piece beyond what Grieg has indicated. "Through strictness to freedom" is a well-worn motto that is applicable here. The idea is to convey the impression of a freely improvised piece, but it must be kept in check so that it does not fall apart (see Ex. 17.11).

Make *Melody* into a gesture of linear and vertical improvisation with elasticity in the chords and the moving passages. Vary the expression in the parts that are repeated, and distinguish between melodic and harmonic sound. At the end, for example, don't let the last two C's drown out the lingering sound of the final C in the melody (see Ex. 17.12).

Ex. 17.12

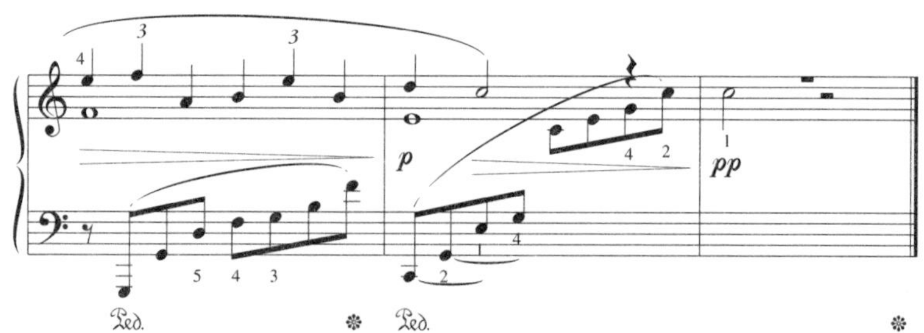

No. 4, Halling

Grieg gave us a foretaste of what was to come in the middle section of No. 1, but No. 4 is the first real *halling* dance among the 66 *Lyric Pieces*. It is jerky and a full-blown country yokel! It should be light throughout, extremely articulated, and played with rapid finger movement. First practice with absolutely even rhythm, then add the many syncopated accents. Measures 1–2 and 5–6 have accents on beats 1 and 2, whereas measures 3–4 and 7–8 call for accents alternating between the hands. In measure 4, be careful that the slur over the first two sixteenth notes does not include the third sixteenth, but separate the last three notes. It adds to the merry-making (see Ex. 17.13).

The middle section, in B♭ major, has syncopated emphases on the upbeats in measures 9–10 and 13–14 (see Ex. 17.14). The *pianissimo* passages in this section have no accents at all—a nice effect.

Plan how you will handle the relationship between the B♭-major and the

Ex. 17.13

Ex. 17.14

D-major *pianissimo* passages, measures 11–12 and measures 15–16. The latter should be a little softer, with a gentle *ritardando* (see Exx. 17.15a and b).

Exx. 17.15a and b

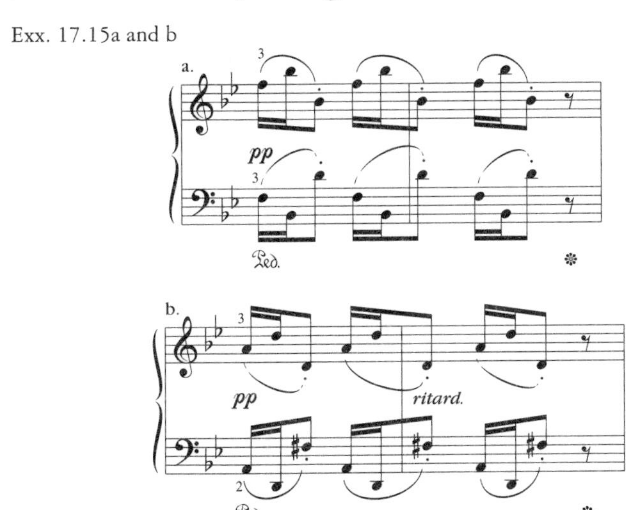

After you have practiced the piece thoroughly and everything is precise and under control, introduce a springy lilt in the rhythm. To dance the *halling*, it is not enough just to get the steps and the leaps right. It needs to be supple and elegant with no exaggeration of the movements.

No. 5, Springar

This is the third *springar* in the Lyric Pieces, and it is a little demon, a fiend from the realm of the trolls. As in No. 2, the left hand controls the rhythm.

Its pattern of half and quarter notes in 3/4 time provides the foundation on which the little demon can perform his dance (see Ex. 17.16).

Ex. 17.16

In measure 6, the third beat serves as an upbeat to the new section (see Ex. 17.17).

Ex. 17.17

Beginning in measure 11 we get a series of syncopated accents on the third beat. The syncopation is effective and charming, but it is also necessary to identify beat 1, at least on the chords marked *fp* in measures 11 and 15. Play the mordents *on* the beat to keep the rhythm under control (see Ex. 17.18). In measures 20, 22, 24, and 26 you will be able to play the mordents more clearly if you take one of the notes in the treble clef with the left hand.

Ex. 17.18

A dynamic sweep encompasses the whole piece: it begins softly, builds steadily to *fortissimo*, then recedes to *pianissimo* at the end. However, the polyrhythmics are its most distinctive stylistic characteristic. Accents, *marcatos*, and *sforzandos* occur throughout the *springar*, sometimes on the first beat, sometimes on the second, sometimes on the third; and, near the end of the piece, there are even accents on the upbeat. The accents are difficult to bring out. Practice the fundamentals first: clap the rhythm, keep time with your foot—preferably more than one rhythm at a time to get the accents "in your bones." For example, beat a steady three beats with one foot while following the left-hand pattern of half and quarter notes with the other. Then clap the accents with your hands. If you can do all of this and sing the melody at the same time, you will have mastered the art of polyrhythmics sufficiently to present the inner tension and drive of this piece.

Although the open fifths in measures 1 and 2 are marked *piano leggiero*, they should have a definite, firm rhythm and a sense of drive.

The last two notes of the piece are an afterthought and should sound like a ram's horn, or perhaps a *lur* (see Ex. 17.19).

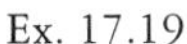
Ex. 17.19

No. 6, Elegy

The title suggests a mood of sadness. *Elegy* has some features that will help you get at its inner nature. The first one is the long E with which the piece begins and which returns five times. Keep it tranquil; listen to it, and notice how long it continues to sound. The rests in measures 9–10 and 28–29 are a second important element. Try to create an especially tension-filled, listening effect, as if you are waiting for something to happen.

This piece has great rhythmic variation. It contains all the note values shown in Ex. 17.20. Grieg varies these patterns and sets them against one

Ex. 17.20

another; sometimes they even occur simultaneously. Concentrate on getting the relations between these various patterns as precise as possible. A lot of musical expression can be wrung out of rhythmic relationships, especially when the patterns are as varied as they are here. Start out with strict adherence to the score with no *rubato*. Once you have mastered the notes you will unconsciously introduce a bit of freedom.

Bring out the dialogue between the right hand and the cellolike tenor voice in measures 2–3 and parallel passages (see Exx. 17.21a and b). Express your own sadness in *Elegy*.

Exx. 17.21a and b

No. 7, Waltz

This second waltz in the collection of *Lyric Pieces* is larger and more flexible than the one in Op. 12. The central section of the first one was almost elegiac, whereas the virtuoso intermezzo in this one, marked *Presto*, is elegant and Chopinesque. The waltz is not very fast, and its melody should soar beautifully. It ends with a long ritardando in measures 11–15; when the *ritardando* returns in measures 48–51, it should be even longer (see Ex. 17.22).

Ex. 17.22

Play the *Presto* section *leggiero*—clear as crystal and light as gossamer.

Tempo I, starting in measure 33, is a quasi *ritardando*, a transition, a little recitative that takes us to the recapitulation. Many pianists think of *Tempo I* as starting five measures later. Try it.

No. 8, Canon

This important piece is like an inner dialogue between two voices. It is worthy of comparison with the world's finest piano music. The music wells forth, wave upon wave, building up to an *agitato* in measure 19. The *rubato* should be gradual and even, both when the tempo is accelerating and when it is slowing down—like a rubber band that is stretched and then relaxed. Play the accompaniment figures softly so as not to destroy the canon effect. That will create a three-dimensional sound picture, with two independent voices and an accompaniment in between (see Ex. 17.23).

Ex. 17.23

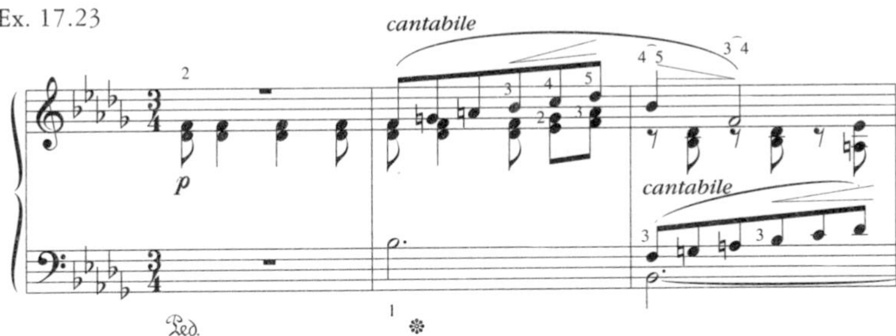

It is common practice to omit measure 32 the first time through, using it as a second ending after playing the *Da Capo*.

The middle section, *Più mosso, ma tranquillo*, gives the piece the stamp of greatness; indeed, it elevates the entire opus. Choralelike and hymnlike, it must be played *legato*, but with a bell-like tone in the chords. Bring this out with a loose wrist, hanging hands, and a round tone. With respect to phrasing, think of two types of slurs: one from the quarter note to the half note in the next measure, and one encompassing the whole period (see Ex. 17.24).

Ex. 17.24

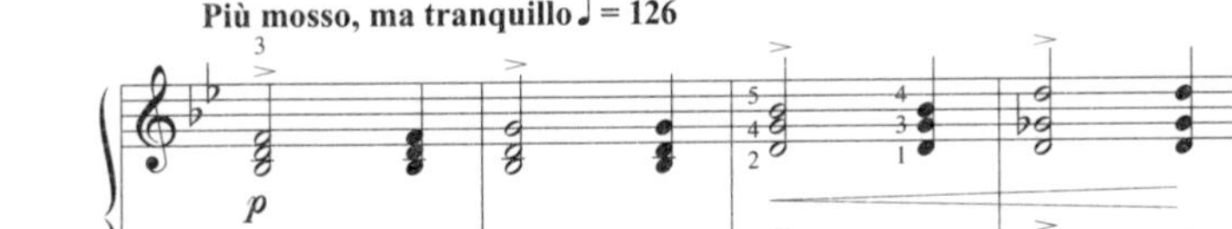

You may surprise your listeners with the sustained depth of the canon.

CHAPTER

18

Lyric Pieces III, Op. 43

However successful Opp. 12 and 38 may have been, Grieg's lyrical miniatures first came into full bloom in Op. 43. Each of the six pieces is a little gem—tuneful and flawlessly crafted. Collectively, they are a priceless treasure in the repertoire of any pianist and well worth the practice needed to master them.

No. 1, Butterfly

This is one of Grieg's best-known piano pieces, bursting with charm and elegance. Start by practicing *Butterfly* as an etude in order to lay a solid technical foundation. The first requirement is to make the sixteenth notes absolutely even, both rhythmically and dynamically, with perfect coordination between the hands (see Ex. 18.1).

Ex. 18.1

At first practice everything *forte*, then gradually decrease the volume to *piano*. As you move toward a more *leggiero* style of playing, to maintain that style, you may often have to go back and practice the piece firmly.

Measure 7 can be fingered in such a way that the accented notes are played by the left hand. The fingering suggested here is that used by several generations of pianists in Norway (see Ex. 18.2).

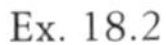

Ex. 18.2

Pay close attention to the phrasings, i.e., the slurs notated by Grieg. They encompass one measure, sometimes two, sometimes half a measure, sometimes just a quarter of a measure. The time between many of these slurs is not long, but it should be audible. The result is a charming and beautiful plasticity (see Ex. 18.3).

Ex. 18.3

Some of the sixteenth notes are accompaniment and should be subordinated to the melody (see Exx. 18.4a and b).

Ex. 18.4a

Chopin once said that all of his runs are melodic. The same can be said about *Butterfly*, although there is no *crescendo* or *diminuendo* in the first measure or in similar places elsewhere in the piece. Even so, never play it without expression. Play the chromatic passages as *legato* as possible, with the first, second, and third fingers held very close together. After you have achieved

Ex. 18.4b

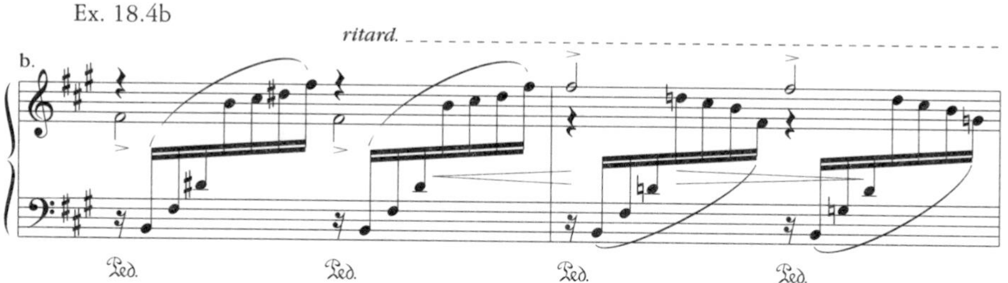

evenness, try to free up the expression in the direction of a roguish unevenness; it will be quite different from the unevenness of a beginner. As a butterfly moves from flower to flower, and bush to bush, it flutters and is thrown this way and that by the summer breeze. This charming picture is conveyed here.

No. 2, Solitary Traveller

Solitary Traveller is one of Grieg's best-known character pieces. It is often played too slowly. It makes the strongest impression if the tender melody is played at the tempo Grieg specifies, *Allegretto semplice.*

The first requisite is a flowing *legato* in the melody. Emphasizing the pedal points brings out the national coloring (see Ex. 18.5).

Ex. 18.5

In measure 14, marked *stretto*, there is a hint of a Norwegian folk dance. Be careful that the slurs are not extended into the resolution. Put a little space between each pair of slurs.

The first part of the melody is characterized by heavy upbeats, but we should not totally alter the rhythmic pattern: there should also be some emphasis on the first beat. In the middle part, there is no such stress on the upbeats; on the contrary, the accents are on the first and fourth beats.

The very first phrase, measures 1–4, presents problems with respect to accent/no accent. There are accents on the upbeats to measures 1 and 2, then two measures with no accents on the upbeats; then the pattern repeats (see Ex. 18.6). Unless otherwise indicated, the accent is of course on the first beat. Think of moving your hand downward at each accent.

Ex. 18.6

It is difficult to make the sixteenth-note figure in measure 3 and elsewhere perfectly smooth. I prefer the fingering indicated in Ex. 18.7.

Ex. 18.7

In measures 16–17 the pedal can present a problem. If the passage is played exactly as written, with the notes assigned to the hands as indicated, the pedal can be released at the second F♯, i.e., on beat 4 of measure 17. If your hands are big, you can play both moving parts with the right hand and use the left to hold down the tied notes. Then there is no problem with the pedal, and you can clean up the sound as you see fit (see Ex. 18.8).

Ex. 18.8

In measure 17, play G–B with the left hand to free the right hand to play the mordent. I feel that the principal melody should be colored by the left hand at the octave from time to time. In the middle section, however, a lighter color is preferable, with emphasis on the right hand.

Measures 13–15 and 24–26 should be phrased like a reverberation until the last F♯-major chord in measures 15 and 26 respectively. Then, like a musical Janus, the passage serves both as a conclusion of what preceded it and the beginning of what is to follow.

Solitary Traveller also contains repetitions of motives; similar figures appear and reappear. Do not play them identically each time, but make a story out of the whole. Then this familiar and beloved piece will be gripping.

No. 3, In My Native Country

This beautiful hymn to the composer's homeland should be played with a flowing, pliable *legato.* At the same time, a deliberate firmness in the lower part of the fingers is needed to produce a bright, brilliant tone. The music is mostly in four voices, and to bring out the character of a string quartet keep the wrist relatively low. To avoid monotony think carefully about the difference between *piano* and *pianissimo.*

The opening section has a long, unbroken line (see Ex. 18.9), but the phrasing in the middle section should be more angular, with undulating dynamics swelling toward the second beat (see Ex. 18.10).

Ex. 18.9

Ex. 18.10

When the theme returns *pianissimo* for the last time the mood is one of reflective calm.

Use the changing registers in the last four measures to vary the color: dark, bright, middle register (see Ex. 18.11).

No. 4, Little Bird

This intricate little rascal is effective only if the execution is flawless and crystal clear. Here, as elsewhere, it is wise to practice first with solid attacks

Ex. 18.11

and open fingers, then gradually decrease movements and volume. If you practice it only *piano*, it easily gets too airy and you start losing notes.

I think it works best to play the trills as written, using the first and third fingers as much as possible. The four thirty-second notes should be absolutely even, absolutely clear, and the right hand must be in perfect sync with the left. First practice the left hand alone, then both hands together with the left louder than the right. Then practice with the left hand playing softly—but continue to *think* left hand, for it must lead.

The first part is dancelike with a game between a slightly delayed first beat and a frisky third. The accent in the first section is on the first beat (see Ex. 18.12).

Ex. 18.12

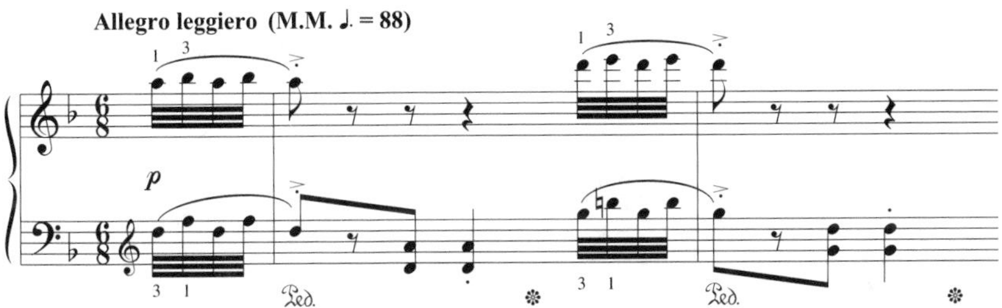

In the middle section there is also a little accent on beat 2, and later on beats 3 and 6. They are not easy to execute, but they give the piece its twittering charm. Exaggerate the accents when you practice, then dampen them bit by bit so that they become nothing more than a hint (see Exx. 18.13a and b).

Ex. 18.13a

It seems best to use the pedal exactly as Grieg specified. As you create the

Ex. 18.13b

illusion of a little bird, remember that birds generally have a bit of little echo around them when they are chirping. They do not sing in a carpeted living room filled with upholstered furniture. They sing outdoors, in the birch tree on the hillside. So use a little pedal!

No. 5, Erotikon

It is said that Grieg was thinking of a poem as he wrote this piece: "All things ripen in their own way. The scent of the rose, now as in youth's springtime, is reflected in song, in a glance, in erotic love." It certainly is not a crass "let's get right down to business" sort of thing. Rather, it suggests the passionate glow that two people might feel when exchanging loving words, or perhaps merely an affectionate glance. It expresses longing rather than an overt act. Keep this in mind while playing.

Use a smooth *legato* that glides stealthily over the keys. Never interrupt the flow of the sound. Note that the opening theme is first stated *piano* then *pianissimo* and sounds good that way (see Ex. 18.14a and b).

Exx. 18.14a and b

The lovely rolled chords, spanning both clefs, must be planned very carefully and executed so that neither the rhythm nor the flow of the melody is interrupted. In this respect they are similar to the rolled chords in Op. 66, No. 14.

In general, *Erotikon* should have a warm tone, and the harmony should find support in the bass voice.

In the middle section, *più mosso e sempre stretto*, the inner voices are *agitato*, but they are accompaniment and should be subordinate to the other voices (see Ex. 18.15).

Ex. 18.15

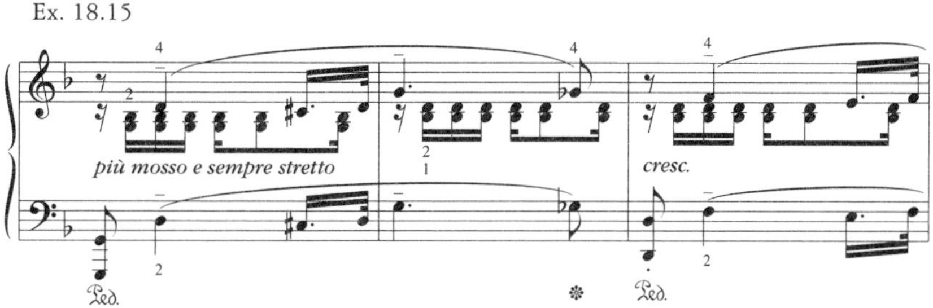

The *subito piano* effect in *Tempo I* is very effective (see Ex. 18.16).

Ex. 18.16

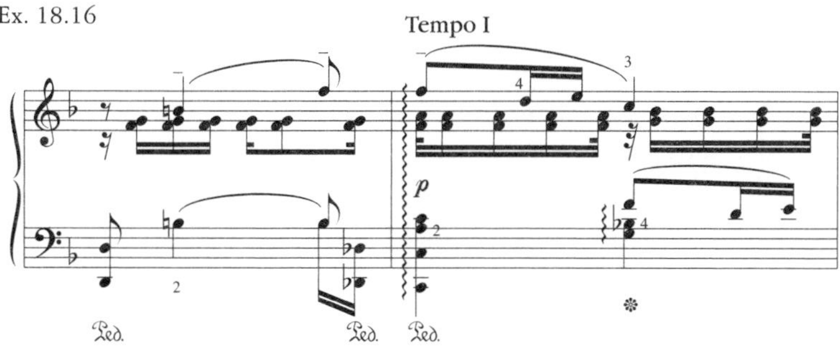

No. 6, To Spring

Now we arrive at one of Grieg's best-known and most frequently played pieces. The world has taken it to its heart, but it is still a distinctively Norwegian piece. It might well have been called "To a Norwegian spring" or "To spring after a long winter."

It must not be played too directly. There is no rumbling or crashing in this piece. It is a picture of ice crackling and sparkling beneath the warm spring sun, but happening so subtly that we can scarcely believe it is real. We feel a deep, inner joy as we behold the melting ice and snow. Let the joy be real, but play *dolce*.

The piece begins and ends in a whisper. Note Grieg's performance indications at the beginning: *Allegro appassionata*, but *pianissimo*. The piece should be performed in a relaxed manner, but when you are just learning it you should maintain a steady tempo—six quarter notes to a measure. Work out the rhythmic relationship between duplets and triplets (see Ex. 18.17).

Ex. 18.17

Structurally, *To Spring* can be described as a heterophonic right-hand voice that reproduces and embellishes the melody in the left. The *rubato* must be incorporated as part of a coherent, continuous flow.

Be careful to make the eighth-note accompaniment in the *Tempo I* recapitulation clear and even. Create a picture of spring brooklets just beginning to form. Never play hard, but always beautifully and with a round tone, even in the middle section, *forte agitato* (measure 37).

Grieg himself indicated a number of *ritardandi* in the piece: *ritardando molto*, *poco ritardando*, *ritardando stretto*, *animato poco ritardando a tempo*, *ritardando a tempo sostenuto*, and so on. Try to observe most of them. You may wish to take a few liberties of your own, but probably not many. It takes a bit of thought to master all these details, but it is worth it (see Ex. 18.18).

Ex. 18.18

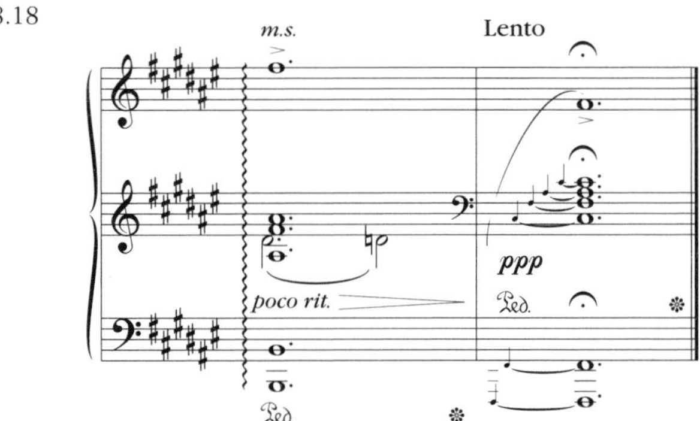

CHAPTER 19

Lyric Pieces IV, Op. 47

The fourth collection of *Lyric Pieces* is painted in pastel colors. Narrative, longing, and billowing expressions predominate. Some people might describe these pieces as salon music. I would say instead that they are illusive, but with wonderful gestures and asymmetric lines. They are harder to get hold of, especially *Waltz-Impromptu*, *Album Leaf*, *Melody*, *Melancholy*, and *Elegy*. *Halling* and *Springar*, however, are made of sturdier stuff. They are concrete, animated, and full of life. Approach Op. 47 obliquely—hinting at rather than declaring, using side lighting rather than an overhead lamp.

No. 1, Waltz-Impromptu

The composer immediately establishes a somewhat nervous and indirect mood with a long, quivering line in the right hand. The mordents should be played with clear finger movement, but do not allow them to break the flow of the melody. Since embellishments occur frequently in this piece, remember that their purpose is to provide ornamentation, not to interrupt the melodic line (see Ex. 19.1).

The *stretto* section, starting in measure 27, is virtuosic in a Chopinesque kind of improvisation.

As so often in Grieg's music, there is a dialogue between the bright descant register and the cellolike left hand (see Exx. 19.2a and b).

Ex. 19.1

Exx. 19.2a and b

Tempo I

a.

pp

b.

f

Make the long trill (measures 69–72) as even as possible, including the *ritardando*, but never too loud.

The accompaniment in the left hand is very simple throughout. Play lightly, distinctly, and with precision. The left hand controls the tempo, but it must be soft. Pay attention to the harmonic changes.

A number of repeats are not identified as such, i.e., passages that are restated a number of times. As always, these repeats are a challenge to the performer. Play them differently each time; tell a story.

Waltz-Impromptu is nervous, trembling, indirect. It is as fleeting as the mythical genie in the bottle: remove the cork and it is gone.

No. 2, Album Leaf

What is an album leaf? Perhaps a special page in a personal diary? I have the feeling that the diary belongs to a restless, somewhat immature person—perhaps someone like Hilda in Ibsen's *The Master Builder*. She is filled with an inner turmoil and is giddily awaiting the future.

Pianistically, the piece requires a highly developed technique. It contains many tricky passages that depend heavily on the third, fourth, and fifth fingers. There is a special danger that a note will become unclear when the fourth finger is responsible for a repeated note (see Ex. 19.3).

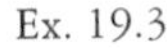
Ex. 19.3

In measures 9 and 10, focus on F♯ and F respectively, subordinating the other notes (see Ex. 19.4).

Ex. 19.4

Measures 13, 14, and 15 are just a kind of footnote to what has preceded. Note the accents on the first beat in measure 16 and the second beat in measures 17 and 18 (counting two beats to a measure).

The second section (starting in measure 21) is somewhat broader but is still a feather-light trifle with little substance. To play it well, you must be totally comfortable with every passage. Your finger and wrist movements must be convincing to produce the *leggiero* effect called for here (see Ex. 19.5).

Ex. 19.5

The figure in the right hand is very tricky. Too much hand movement will reduce its clarity. The hand need not move very much if you play the figure *legato* (see Ex. 19.6a). When the reach becomes wider, use a tremolo wrist movement (see Ex. 19.6b).

Exx. 19.6a and b

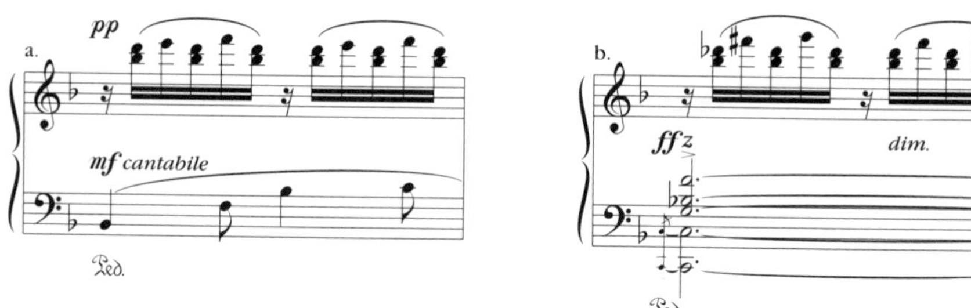

Draw a long slur, or a long descending line, over measures 90–102. Think of stardust sifting down.

This *Album Leaf* is a sequel to Op. 12, No. 7. If the earlier one was a glimpse into the secret thoughts of a teenager, this one depicts the breathless excitement of a young person on the edge of adulthood, and the story is told more fully.

No. 3, Melody

This melancholy little piece has a trembling restlessness created by the relentless throbbing of the accompaniment. Op. 38, No. 3, was also called *Melody*, but its melody was fragmentary, with melodic episodes interspersed with arpeggios. It hinted at the melody rather than singing it out. Here, the melody goes on and on without end. The soprano voice is the most important, as the texture is uniformly homophonic, in contrast to the more complex texture in Op. 38. Work carefully on the melody line, paying attention to the tone, the phrasing, the attack. The frequent syncopated accents on the second beat (counting two beats to a measure) give flexibility to the subdivision of the melody and its gestures (see Ex. 19.7).

Ex. 19.7

Later editions of this piece often omit the repeat sign preceding *Tempo I* (see Ex. 19.8). Grieg's original score specified that the first forty measures be repeated, resulting in a great deal of similar-sounding music. Take it as a challenge to create long melodic lines to structure a tune full of fantasy.

The accompaniment supports the form, discreetly, but carrying the music forward rhythmically as if on a wave, or like the beating of a heart. Grieg's instructions include *più mosso*, *poco ritardando*, and *stretto*. Be flexible. Make these variations in tempo and dynamics organic parts of your interpretation. Think of the melody as coming from a distant place. It comes closer, intensifies, then recedes and finally disappears into an eternal silence. The rest is the goal, the *telos* toward which it has been moving all along (see Ex. 19.9).

No. 4, Halling

This piece is another little gem from Grieg's hand. You may have trouble keeping the time absolutely correct in the syncopated bass line because it constantly clashes with irregularities in the right hand. The whole piece is a rhythmic duel. Once again, work out the rhythmic details before you start playing; for example: tap out the two-beat rhythm with one foot and the syncopated bass line with the other. Then try to sing the melody line and clap the accents. It is an interesting study in polyrhythmics. The rhythmic planes are of varying lengths and are constantly shifting.

Next, concentrate on getting a briskly articulated sound from your instrument. The accents must not be too crass and direct. They should be generated by the finger, even if you use your arm to some extent. Never use a straightforward arm accent in *forte* and *fortissimo* without simultaneous finger articulation (see Ex. 19.10).

Ex. 19.10

It is the most agile young man in the valley who is dancing the *halling*, as if he were about to fly. Practice until you are able to convey such a picture.

No. 5, Melancholy

You do not need particular association to understand this piece: the title says it all. With respect to form, it has a four-measure introduction and a three-measure coda (see Exx. 19.11a and b). Otherwise, the piece consists of a simple

Exx. 19.11a and b

series of unresolved iterations, like gentle sighs. Phrase accordingly (see Ex. 19.12).

The first section is written over a pedal point on G. Bring it out enough to make your listeners aware of it. The second section has an inverted pedal point on D, and later E♭ in the soprano voice (see Exx. 19.13a and b).

Ex. 19.12

Exx. 19.13a and b

If you emphasize the pedal points—first the one in the bass, then those in the soprano—the whole piece will be nicely framed by them. Practice the introduction and the coda together, skipping over everything in between, to help develop a sense of unity in the overall form. In the middle section hold down the volume at first, then turn it up a notch for the *forte* and *fortissimo* in measures 33–34. Most important, however, is to give musical expression to a truly melancholy passion.

No. 6, Springar

The *springar* gets its name from a solo dance form with leaps and jumps in a three-beat irregular rhythm. It should be played as a display of elegant sport. This *springar* is the fourth in the *Lyric Pieces* thus far. It is more full-bodied than the earlier ones and is more difficult to play. The left hand, as usual, is primarily responsible for carrying the rhythm, but its part is more complex than in the earlier examples. Indeed, there are places where the left hand has the melody (see Ex. 19.14).

The second section, starting in measure 11, is highly virtuosic, with huge

Ex. 19.14

leaps in the left hand. Here, too, everything should be controlled by the bass, which requires real pianistic skill.

Pay careful attention to the vertical coordination of the hands. Except as otherwise indicated, play the open fifths in the left hand lightly and precisely. The *staccato* on the third beat, i.e., on the second open fifth in the left hand, gives the piece its gymnastic character.

The middle section is lyrical and more linear. It is followed by a section of irregular syncopations.

The introduction is to be played *piano*, but it must be stubbornly active, even agitated—in contrast to the concluding four measures, which are more restful. Practice the introduction and the ending side by side so that you are aware of the differences.

Practice the parallel sixths one part at a time (see Exx. 19.15a and b). They should also be practiced as tied exercises (see Ex. 19.16).

Exx. 19.15a and b

Ex. 19.16

No. 7, Elegy

The somber mood suggested by the title is brought out by observing a brief *tenuto* on the first beat of each measure (see Ex. 19.17).

You can give the middle section, starting with the *poco mosso* in measure

Ex. 19.17

17, a little more movement. Make it like a recitative, tell a story, express your passion.

Viewed in relation to the middle section, the accents in the introduction and later in *Tempo I* are easier to understand. Treat the identical parts as repeats, i.e., vary the expression each time (see Ex. 19.18).

Ex. 19.18

The nature of the tragedy in *Elegy* is not clear. Indirect thoughts and feelings may be sensed in this opus. Perhaps the person depicted is disturbed at a subconscious level, not with physical pain, but rather with a troubled mind.

As in No. 3, a repeat sign just before the first *Tempo I*, which was in the original score, is often omitted in modern editions. The repeat makes the piece quite long, but it can also give it an unsuspected dimension if there is sufficient variation. You can create the illusion of a troubled mind murmuring its complaint within the confines of a closed circle, from which there is no exit. This form of expression may correspond to the piece, a suppressed elegy that never quite comes to the surface. Its complaint is powerful and gripping, albeit indirect.

CHAPTER 20

Lyric Pieces V, Op. 54

Grieg is in top form in Op. 54, one of his most popular collections of piano pieces. These crowd pleasers belong in every pianist's repertoire. They can be used almost any time, are always well received, and are worth whatever effort it takes to master them. Everything must be worked out down to the tiniest detail.

Grieg has acquired greater depth in his musical language since Op. 43. Its light colors have been intensified and darkened in Op. 54, resulting in a mature, personal, and distinctively Norwegian set of pictures. Grieg has elevated his nationalistically inspired themes to a high harmonic plane. He has developed the pieces polyphonically, and has introduced a more advanced late-Romantic harmony than in any of the earlier *Lyric Pieces*. Many passages call for pianistic brilliance.

No. 1, Shepherd's Boy

Although the theme—an unusually beautiful melody—sounds like something that might have been played on a willow flute, this piece is dramatic in concept. To Norwegian ears it is reminiscent of Grieg's song *The Princess*, a setting of a poem by Bjørnstjerne Bjørnson:

The princess looked down from her lofty height,
A lad stood there playing in evening's soft light.
"O why must you blow on your horn, silly boy,
I want just to dream, and my thoughts you annoy,
As the sun goes down."

The princess looked down from her lofty height,
The lad had ceased playing in evening's soft light.
"Why stand you in silence? Play on, silly boy!
The sound suits my dreaming, your tunes I enjoy,
As the sun goes down."

The princess looked down from her lofty height,
The horn again sounded in evening's soft light.
Then weeping and trembling she bitterly cried,
"O why am I filled with such sadness—God, why?"
And the sun went down.

The harmonic advances, chromaticism, and imitations should be emphasized. Make the *rubato* as gradual as possible. Several passages lend themselves to echo effects (see Ex. 20.1).

Ex. 20.1

The theme is first sounded *piano cantabile*, as if it were being played out of doors for the benefit of the birds and wild animals. The repeat is *pianissimo*, as if it were to be heard only by oneself (see Exx. 20.2a and b).

Ex. 20.2a

The introductory section (measures 1–16) is a little breathless, with short periods, but the middle section can be formed as a coherent whole with a steady

Ex. 20.2b

crescendo leading to the *fortissimo* in measure 28. Note the dialogue between the hands in Ex. 20.3.

Ex. 20.3

The *fortissimo* in measure 28 is followed by a long, gentle *diminuendo* all the way to *ppp* in measure 35. This *diminuendo* is a wonderful vignette of nature, as the chords recede steadily into the distance and at last disappear over the horizon.

At the end you get one last chance to display the contrast between the low open fifth and the high G (see Ex. 20.4).

Ex. 20.4

No. 2, Gangar

The main idea of *Gangar* ("walking dance") is that it must "go and go" without interruption. Although one must maintain absolutely steady rhythm from beginning to end, there is a rocking feeling, as if the walker's knees were giving out. The last twelve measures, marked *diminuendo e più tranquillo*, are a bit calmer.

The pulsating beat, i.e., the pattern of dotted quarter notes, is sometimes in the left hand, sometimes in the right, but the tempo should be unvaried in either case. The sixteenth-note figuration must be fast and clear (see Ex. 20.5).

Ex. 20.5

The middle section (starting with the upbeat to measure 18) is a dialogue. Think of it as mutual flirtation, a concept that you will find useful onstage, in which *fortissimo* is the boy and *piano* is the girl (see Ex. 20.6a and b).

Exx. 20.6a and b

The sixteenth-note figures in measures 18, 20, 22, etc., are difficult to play with precision. It helps to give good lower-arm support to the fingers (see Ex. 20.7).

Ex. 20.7

Starting with the upbeat to measure 108, marked *ppp*, think in terms of a steady *crescendo* to the *fortissimo* in measure 139. At that point use the whole body for support, for the whole instrument must participate in the *gangar*. Still, the tone should be rich, not harsh; you are not trying to express anger.

The coda (the last twelve measures) transforms the whole piece into a tableau, a picture that is like a reflection (see Ex. 20.8).

Ex. 20.8

No. 3, March of the Dwarfs

March of the Dwarfs is one of the high points in the entire collection of *Lyric Pieces*. This piece alone would have made Grieg world-famous, just as *Rustle of Spring* made Sinding a household name in his day. Great virtuoso pianists have used *March of the Dwarfs* as a sparkling encore. Performed with bravura, it is a sure winner.

The form of *March of the Dwarfs* is ABA, with an incisive rhythm and brilliance in the A part and lyric freedom in the B part. As in *Gangar*, plan for a long *crescendo* and a long *diminuendo*. The *staccato* chords, whether *pianissimo* or *fortissimo*, must be precise with emphasis on the upper voice (see Ex. 20.9).

Ex. 20.9

The thirty-second notes must be as clear and metallic as those of a steel guitar. Move downward on the first note and upward on the last to prevent the rhythm from getting reversed (see Ex. 20.10).

The octaves in measures 30ff. should be strong, firm, and precise, but they should also be disconnected, almost *staccato*. Measures 40–41 are fiendishly difficult because of the huge leaps. Practice these left-hand octaves until you

Ex. 20.10

can play them in tempo with your eyes shut to ensure that you won't mess them up when performing.

Play the B section, starting in measure 71, with sincerity, freedom, and a lyrical tone. The arpeggio figure is rhapsodic and harplike. No doubt it is the troll maiden with her harp who is depicted here—mischievous and in good humor. Part of this section is in D major, part in G major, with the latter the brighter of the two.

March of the Dwarfs, well performed, never fails to please an audience. It is worth the effort to practice it, for the result is virtuosity in the grand style.

No. 4, Notturno

Grieg gave this piece its Italian name. It is one of his most important and successful character pieces. Your listeners should scarcely be aware of upbeats or downbeats, but it is important for you always to feel an inner pulse based on the eighth-note figures in the accompaniment. They should be soft but still control the flow. Some *rubato* is permissible, even desirable, but always as an organic part of the whole—i.e., the time value of the smallest units in the measure should be gradually altered. Feel this both mentally and aurally.

The contour of the melody is three-dimensional. One level is the C below middle C, a second is A above the treble staff, and the melody is spun out in the register between these two extremes. It is the aesthetic equivalent of nature's abhorrence of a vacuum: no space is left unfilled, everything works together in perfect balance (see Exx. 20.11a and b).

Exx. 20.11a and b

An effective performance requires the correct relationship between the duplets and triplets. They must be executed very smoothly, lest the effect be amateurish (see Ex. 20.12).

Ex. 20.12

In measures 1–4 and elsewhere there is an uninterrupted chromatic descent in the bass. This is the first of the *Lyric Pieces* in which Grieg employed this harmonic device, which appears often in his works—for example, in *Ballade*, Op. 24, and in *Nineteen Norwegian Folk Songs*, Op. 66. This descending chromatic line, which is thoroughly integrated into the harmonic texture, gives the piece an added dimension. Make these bass notes the foundation of the sound, but do not overemphasize them.

The middle section is an imitation of the chirping of birds, and is not particularly virtuosic. Note Grieg's placement of the slurs and phrase accordingly: this is the secret to the charm of this section (see Ex. 20.13).

Ex. 20.13

The *Più mosso* in measures 21–33 starts out *pianissimo*, recedes to *ppp*, builds steadily to *fortissimo*, then recedes once more until it ends in a 3/8 measure of rest in which we are waiting for the next note to be played.

In playing the duet in the right hand, keep a loose wrist. Practice it with finger articulation, with *legato* in the upper voice and almost *staccato* in the lower, but with a loose arm. One's ear should be attuned primarily to the upper voice.

In the recapitulation, the theme announced at the beginning is broadened. The A in measure 46 is louder than the E in measure 12 (*fortissimo* vs. *forte*), and shortly thereafter the piece winds down with an astounding chromatic descent in all voices. When the chirping birds return on A and A♭ in measures 57 and 60, they should sound a little dejected in contrast to their first appearance, when they sang out more cheerily and brightly on D and F, in measures 16 and 19. The *Adagio* at the end should be warm and restful (see Ex. 20.14).

Ex. 20.14

To develop an inner feeling for the accompaniment, practice it by itself, making it as *legato* as possible. Try to hear the other voices with your inner ear as you play the accompaniment. Use a little Italian freedom and warmth. *Notturno* is the wonderful kind of piece that can produce complete silence in an audience.

No. 5, Scherzo

This festive piece is a Mendelssohnian virtuoso number. Like *Fairy Dance* in Op. 12, it is marked *leggiero*, but it is more undulating, more varied, and broader harmonically and melodically. However, it must be practiced in strict tempo and with great precision.

The middle section (measures 17–70), marked *feroce*, is utterly enchanting: wild in the *fortissimo*, mischievous and expectant in the rests (see Ex. 20.15).

Ex. 20.15

The ensuing *diminuendo* reminds me of a beautiful troll maiden, as the music, *dolce*, dies out to *ppp* and then to silence (see Ex. 20.16).

The quarter note retains the same value when the time signature changes to 2/4. Do not play as if 3/4 = 2/4 (see Ex. 20.17).

The melody in the *Più tranquillo* section, starting in measure 71, is an augmented version of the one at the beginning. Grieg liked this technique and used it often—for example, in the *Norwegian Peasant Dances*, Op. 72. It gives the composition a unity that would otherwise be lacking. The lowest voice in the bass descends diatonically. The middle section of the *Più*

Ex. 20.16

tranquillo rests on a pedal point and flits around from one key to another. The descending bass line and the pedal point give this piece an added dimension and should be emphasized. It is a scherzo—but a significant one!

No. 6, Bell Ringing

Grieg concluded Op. 54 with a unique piece, a composition that is a true stroke of genius. With the simplest of means—a long series of fifths—he achieves an impressionistic effect that invites comparison with such composers as Debussy.

The tempo indication is *Andante* 2/4, but to keep it from getting too marchlike try to feel a quasi *alla breve* tempo.

Hold back the *crescendo* as long as possible. Grieg calls for nothing louder than *pianissimo* until measure 37. Keep it soft until then (*pp* and *ppp* as indicated) so that there is room to grow during the *crescendo poco a poco* leading up to *fff* in measure 49. To *crescendo* evenly, aim for *p* in measure 37, *mf* in measure 41, *f* in measure 44, and *ff* in measure 47. Let the left hand lead in executing the *crescendo*.

The half-note chords starting in measure 77 resemble a chorale played by a brass choir, with the volume increasing from *pianissimo* to a thundering *fortissimo* in just five measures. It is also important to take short breaths in the *piano* and *pianissimo* near the end.

Pay close attention to the kind of attack you use in this piece. You must create a bell-like sound that is not too sharp. Start the attack with your finger on the key, then move upward and inward toward the lid of the piano. Think of the way you would strike a bell or a gong: you would start the stroke close up, and then move away. If you move your arm upward at the same time you can execute a fast attack without losing contact with the key because of a big arm movement. Use your ears, and don't give up until you have achieved a gonglike effect.

The anacruses should be relatively short so as to create maximum tension throughout the piece.

Bell Ringing has a broad perspective. Play it with a broad outlook and show your grand ideas onstage.

CHAPTER

21

Lyric Pieces VI, Op. 57

Dark colors are in evidence in Op. 57. A shadow hangs over the music, albeit not in a negative sense, as if Grieg has developed a new affinity for Brahms and his style of composing. The picture is colored by low bass notes and dense chords. The pencil strokes are broader than before, and the pianist has to interpret in wide expanses, in broadly conceived color contrasts.

No. 1, Vanished Days

This piece could have been given the subtitle "Ballade." Think of a story of wide scope, a narrative in ABA form in which the B part is the event itself and the A parts are commentaries on it. The A sections invite one to use a lot of *rubato*, but first one should sort out the relationships between the note values: dotted halves, quarter and eighth notes, triplets, sixteenth notes, sixteenth-note triplets, and triplets consisting of a quarter note and an eighth. This diversity can be used to bring out the narrative and balladic character of the piece. The narrative is concealed in an even, unbroken inner line in the first part, resulting in substantial tension leading up to the high point in measures 39–42. Thereafter you should execute a finely tuned *poco diminuendo e molto ritardando* to an *Adagio* conclusion in measures 45–47.

Plan the tempos carefully: *Allegro vivace*, *Più lento* (not very slow, but slower than *Allegro vivace*), and *Molto vivo* in the middle section (starting in measure 73). First establish *Molto vivo* by determining how fast you can play this part. Then make the *Allegro vivace* a shade slower, and make the *Più lento* another step slower. Lastly, establish the *Andantino* and *Allegro* of the A part.

The principal technical challenge is to achieve perfect precision in playing the thirds with which the piece abounds. Practice them with good arm support and unwavering firmness in the lowest joint of each finger (see Exx. 21.1a and b). As always when playing a double line, practice each voice by itself (see Ex. 21.2).

Exx. 21.1a and b

Ex. 21.2

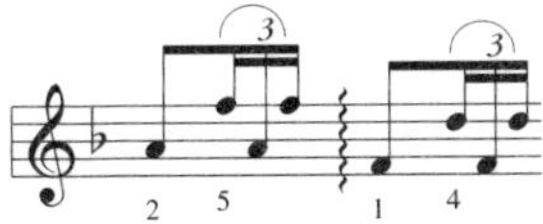

In the ascending arpeggio figure in measures 54 and 62, tilt the right hand slightly toward the right. As a general rule, help the thumb when playing a descending passage and the fifth finger when playing an ascending one, as in Ex. 21.3.

Ex. 21.3

The accompaniment figures in measures 9–12, marked *pianissimo*, should be played as evenly and as *legato* as possible. Keep your finger on the key even after you release it. Use the same technique for the chords shown in Exx. 21.4a, b, and c).

Exx. 21.4a, b, and c

Everything gets easier during the *crescendo* starting in measure 37. Add weight bit by bit.

There are also some fine bass lines to take care of in *Vanished Days:* E–D–C–B♭–A (see Ex. 21.5).

The sixteenth notes in the left hand in measures 25–31 should be integrated into the whole as smoothly as possible. Think of the notes in the right hand on the first beats of measures 25 and 26 as the beginning of the figure that follows in the left hand. Note the fine articulation in the right hand in measures 26–27 and the imitation in the left hand immediately following (see Ex. 21.6).

There is a hidden chromatic modulation in the harmony, *pianissimo*, in measures 32–34. A shift to the left on the circle of fifths often has a cooling effect, and in this case it sounds almost like a sudden falsetto (see Ex. 21.7).

A big climax builds in measures 35–39, but hold back a little so you can create an even bigger climax in the recapitulation.

I recommend using the first finger on the high E♭ in measure 70—just preceding the *Più lento* (see Ex. 21.8).

In many editions, the fingering suggested for the first three notes of the ascending figure in measure 98 is 2–3–4. I prefer the fingering indicated in Ex. 21.9.

No. 2, Gade

This piece is a tribute to Danish composer Niels W. Gade, who was not exactly Grieg's teacher but had an important influence on him. In the first edition it was titled "Danische Idylle." A Danish landscape with the gently rolling contours of Zealand, not the steep, jagged mountains of Norway, is depicted in the long, smooth lines. Grieg's dynamic indications should be interpreted in relation to this understanding of the piece. An *f* does not always mean a true *forte*, nor does *fortissimo* necessarily have its ordinary meaning. Here they can signify an inner intensity rather than an overt increase of volume. *Gade* can be a supple and beautiful piece if the dynamics are toned down a bit. The tempo is fluid and *alla breve*.

The focal point of the first partial phrase is F♯, of the second partial phrase, B. Thus there should be a slight accent on the second beat of measure 2 and on the first beat of measure 4. The same kind of asymmetry can be used later as well, for a similar pattern recurs again and again.

Note the duet between the soprano and the tenor (see Exx. 21.10a and b).

Starting at measure 17, the periods consist of just three measures, but they, too, should flow like an endless stream. With *rubato*, remember to "take and give back." In measures 17–19, for example, accelerate a little in measures 17–18 and give back the stolen time in measure 19 (see Ex. 21.11).

Think of a long slur extending all the way from measure 23 through

Exx. 21.10a and b

Ex. 21.11

measure 49. This entire section is an effective dialogue in sequences between the hands (see Ex. 21.12).

Ex. 21.12

The transition in measures 46–49 is like a recitative. Listen to the F♯ and shape the eighth-note figures in a gradual flow. The smaller rhythmic unit provides the pulse, but the rendition should not be metronomic (see Ex. 21.13).

Ex. 21.13

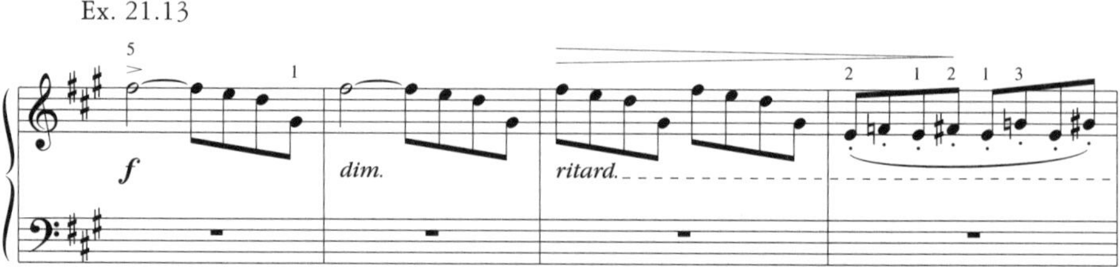

The recapitulation, which begins at measure 50, can be played with almost no pedal.

The coda is somewhat Schumannian, but note Grieg's irregular accents (see Exx. 21.14a and b).

Exx. 21.14a and b

Throughout the piece, maintain a round and friendly tone, which requires a relaxed wrist and elbow. Let your fingers caress the keys. Hold the wrist at an angle that will help the fingers achieve a smooth touch. Gade is a nice, tuneful intermezzo.

No. 3, Illusion

Grieg does not tell us what kind of illusion he has in mind; presumably it is a *lost* illusion, perhaps a love affair that did not work out. The piece is dominated by a pessimistic-sounding descending line, a series of suspensions that vanish into the abyss.

The beginning—a single note with a fermata—is typical of Grieg. It gives the piece a national feel, like the sound of a solitary *lur* (an indigenous instrument that resembles an alpenhorn) echoing across the valley. That single note can say a lot if you attack it appropriately and think of it as long and significant.

The tempo indication is not self-contradictory, but it shows two sides of the problem: *serioso*, but don't forget the *allegretto*! The piece can easily become excessively melancholy, get bogged down in sticky sentimentality.

Illusion is not technically difficult, but it requires a smooth *legato* in the parallel sixths (see Ex. 21.15). The attack and general sonority must never be direct. It should be practiced, therefore, with a loose arm and a light touch.

Ex. 21.15

Grieg often uses short motives. With one-measure motives it is important to keep things moving and save the *rubato* for the resolutions. Think of measures 2–9 as constituting one coherent unit and measures 10–17 another. Then comes a thirteen-measure unit—measures 18–30—that should hang together.

Observe the indicated *ritardandi*, especially at measure 27 (marked *più tranquillo*), and let the *sempre ritardando* in measures 29–30 be an indication of the tempo as a whole. In observing these indications think backwards: play *più tranquillo*, then make the main tempo faster. The *ritardando* in the recapitulation should be a little more pronounced than that in measures 29–30. The second repetition, which also acts as a coda, should be played in a somewhat restrained manner and extra softly.

No. 4, Secret

Although the harmony in this exciting character piece is very chromatic and late-Romantic, its mood is somewhat archaic, Medieval, indeed, Sphinx-like. The feeling is of a secret that is not told—"like a little box that is opened just for a moment, but is closed again," as a child might say. Think of it as a national secret rather than a merely personal one. Since the piece is episodic, to keep it from falling apart you must feel a strong artistic spirit throughout that keeps pace with you as you play. One motive takes over from the other, and the long notes have an inner life that is—appropriately—hidden from view.

There are many rests, but don't think of them as interruptions of the flow of the music but as listening pauses. Just as a river disappears from view when it flows under a bridge, even if we cannot see it, it is still flowing. Here, the forward progress continues during the rests, albeit inaudibly.

A velvety-soft *legato* yields the desired sonority. A supple *dolce* character with no rough edges is the greatest asset you can have. Note the kind of sound that Grieg invites us to produce in Ex. 21.16. Leaving the pedal down during the entire passage will produce a cluster effect. Measures 23–29 also provide a nice contrast to the following *Tempo I ma recitando*. It starts out as an unaccompanied solo voice that is especially interesting precisely because it is preceded by lush harmonies and a rich-sounding, veiled effect.

Ex. 21.16

Play the octaves and two-note chords as *legato* as possible. If you cannot connect both voices, play the upper one *legato* and do the best you can with the lower one (see Ex. 21.17).

Ex. 21.17

For a subtle nuance, play the *stretto* portion of the *Più mosso* a little faster the second time; similarly with the two *recitando* passages, practice them in various ways so you can play them differently the second time.

No. 5, She Dances

This piece has often been disparaged as an example of salon music. It is rather facile and must never be allowed to get too heavy, too lumpy. The "she" who is dancing is young, beautiful, and a flirt. We would also bet that she is slender and graceful and that she is wearing elegant shoes. Play accordingly.

At the piano it is always the same: to play very lightly and delicately in a technically demanding piece, practice the piece quite loud until you have mastered the notes. The sixteenth-note fifths should be practiced as written and also as tied exercises, i.e., holding down one open fifth while repeating the other (see Exx. 21.18a and b).

Exx. 21.18a and b

Some arm support and arm movement are useful when playing these fifths, but if the downward arm movement is too pronounced the playing gets too heavy. Norwegian pianist Agathe Backer-Grøndahl once said that she could not perform a piece until she had the feeling that every note was right in the tips of her fingers. One's arm must feel light without being stiff. A constantly moving arm is best in *She Dances*. Practice using the whole finger, i.e., with a straight line from the knuckle to the fingertip. Feel the fingers transmitting energy to the key. The music acquires a warmer character with the entry of a masculine cello voice in measure 42 (and again in measure 86), and a bright female voice replies. The dialogue is under way (see Ex. 21.19).

Measures 62ff. are not exactly a Viennese waltz, but give the passage a playful flirtation with a fairly pronounced accent on the first beat (see Ex. 21.20). The waltz rhythm in the left hand should be smart and elegant. Play

Ex. 21.19

Ex. 21.20

the two-note chords that alternate between the hands in measures 66–69 lightly and clearly.

Pay attention to the subtle nuances. Imagining that you are a spectator, watching the dance and the coquetry from the gallery, will enhance the lightness. The *forte* passages must be clear and distinct, but not too direct.

The conclusion is virtuosic, brilliantly clear and light. Our little Cinderella has danced her best, and she now blows her audience a final kiss and disappears into the wings (see Ex. 21.21).

No. 6, Homesickness

Grieg was spending the winter abroad when he wrote this piece, but it seems that his thoughts were turning toward the snow-capped mountains and sparkling streams of his native land. Surprisingly, the piece is rarely played in Norway. It was Walter Gieseking's favorite of all the *Lyric Pieces*, and he made a brilliant recording of it.

Ex. 21.21

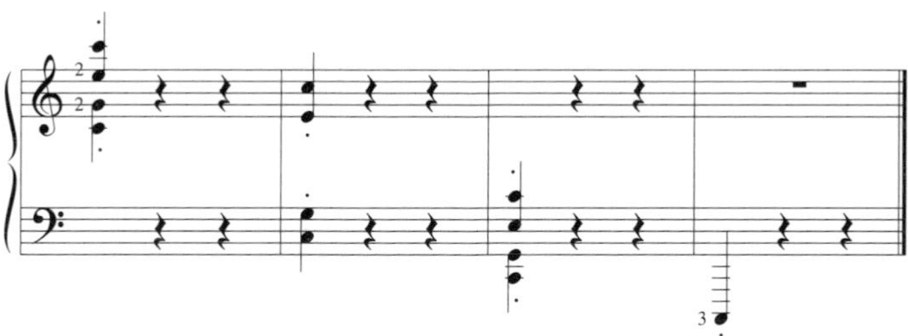

The form is ABA. There is an undertone of protest in the A melody, which reflects the folk music from which Grieg drew his inspiration. The B section is a little *springar* that is quite difficult and tricky to play. It is like a stubborn little goat, yet so soft and delicate that it seems to be a memory of a *springar* rather than the *springar* itself. Imagine a picture of a dance painted with impressionistic, muted colors. Grieg has also played it safe by indicating *piano* and *pianissimo* as the desired volumes.

Begin the piece with an overt complaint, but use a more restrained tone for the repeat of the theme in *Tempo I* (measure 68). Play the A section with a smooth *legato* and carefully attuned chords. Make the bass notes strong enough to provide a firm foundation. The broken chords should be even and clear. Grieg has indicated that the last part of the first phrase (measures 7, 25, etc.) is to be declaimed. That is best achieved by a little downward movement from the wrist.

To execute the imitation between the hands in measures 9–15, keep the wrists low. The recitative in measures 17–18 should be played lightly and freely, controlling the flow with a loose arm. The A section concludes with dark tones, which can be emphasized in the bass so as to maximize the contrast with the B section, which follows.

The *springar* is highly dependent in the first instance on a completely even and precise accompaniment (see Ex. 21.22). The upper voice should be like that in *She Dances*: soft, but clear. Practice it with active fingers.

In the middle part of the B section Grieg plays with varying rhythms and

Ex. 21.22

phrases of different lengths, imitating the hilarious irregularity of the authentic *springars* he has heard. Thus in three periods we get 2/4 and 4/4 rhythms one after the other (see Ex. 21.23). Following that, in a very sophisticated effect, there are quarter-beat groups that contradict the underlying rhythm (see Ex. 21.24).

Ex. 21.23

Ex. 21.24

The intricate little trill in the recapitulation must be precisely coordinated with the accompaniment figure in the left hand (see Ex. 21.25). You can play the alto E in measure 44 and the alto B in measure 46 with the left hand, freeing the right hand to concentrate on the trill. In this case the right-hand fingering in measure 44 will be 2–3–1–3–1–3–2, and in measure 46 it becomes 2–1–3–1–3–1–2 (see Ex. 21.26).

The B section must be as brilliant and clear as possible. It is playfully virtuosic.

Ex. 21.25

Ex. 21.26

The first A section has a *poco ritardando* near the end, the recapitulation has *poco a poco più lento al Fine*—a very gradual *ritardando* that continues to the very end. These two different ways of concluding the A section will keep the interpretation interesting. Grieg has also written in a number of fermatas, some with *poco*, some with *longa.* Varying them will help to produce a plastic and genuinely artistic interpretation. Think about this as you are practicing and feel it as you are performing onstage.

CHAPTER

22

Lyric Pieces VII, Op. 62

After the dark colors of Op. 57, in Op. 62 Grieg returns to more cheerful moods. The musical language is polished, cultivated, cosmopolitan. There are still some distinctively Norwegian features—in *Brooklet* and *Homeward*, for example—but the nature moods and national elements are adapted to the tastes of a sophisticated, big-city audience. The pieces are virtuosic, luxuriantly pianistic, and replete with impressive bravura passages. To play Op. 62 you must be in good form; your technique and fingers must function at their best to bring these pieces to life.

No. 1, Sylph

This is a playful but understated waltz, perhaps a characterization "in the manner" of a waltz. The waltz keeps disappearing as the music wanders off into cadences, gestures, and unwaltzlike time signatures. Perhaps it is a ballet, but it certainly is not a dance for amateurs.

Sylph should be played primarily with the fingers. Even the attack should be from the fingers, not the arm. As I have stated many times, if you practice the soft, shadowy pieces loud and firm at first, later you will be able to dance lightly over the keys. There must be no muddiness in the tone or the rhythm. Experiment with a bit of coquettish *rubato*. You can also enhance the mood by making something out of the rests, not only in the introduction but between the phrases as well. Listen, but keep your hand moving in a steady movement, even during the rests. Then the *rubato* will not become unnatural (see Ex. 22.1).

Ex. 22.1

The cadences on C$\sharp^7$ in measure 10 and on G$\sharp^7$ in measure 18 will be charming with a *poco ritardando*, as Grieg indicates. Try to sound flirtatious! In the ascending chromatic passage in measure 19, dance smoothly and springily over the keys with your hand tilted a bit toward the right. The cadences are transformed into long lines in measures 26–29 and 32–33 (see Ex. 22.2).

Ex. 22.2

Tempo I should be played very fluidly, preferably as a cascade in the pedal, as if the sylph were taking a bath. Then this picture fades away, and the original dance tune returns after two lush broken chords in the left hand in measures 40 and 42 (see Ex. 22.3).

Ex. 22.3

With precise finger activity and a whimsical attitude, *Sylph* has the potential to be an elegant, pastel-colored, fanciful little seascape.

No. 2, Gratitude

In this wonderfully pleasing and intimate piece, nobody knows what the gratitude is for, but it can hardly be for something merely ordinary. Perhaps it is a word of thanks that one hopes will not come too late, or a country's gratitude for a great philanthropist. Or find something in your own experience that fits the serious mood of this piece.

Start out with a smooth *legato*. Sing out the melody line, keeping the fingers close to the keys. Attack each note with a slow downward movement, generating the sound at the bottom of the key, and keep your finger on the key as it comes back up. Keeping your fingers on the surface of the keys even when they are not playing may help to induce an attitude of thankfulness.

The first section is intense, but the middle section—a remarkable impressionistic flight of fancy—starts inconspicuously and quietly, like a thought that one scarcely dares to express. It slowly becomes more concrete and eventually develops into something big. The principal theme returns three times and the contrasting section twice. Practice the several iterations of the main theme in succession, omitting the contrasting sections, and then the contrasting section without the main theme, so that each tells its own story. Vary the phrasing in accordance with your understanding of what each part is trying to say.

In the recapitulation, a modulation from G major to C major brightens the picture and raises the intensity (see Ex. 22.4).

Ex. 22.4

Try varying the phrasing. In measures 65–66, for example, the phrase can be thought of as leading to E, as written, but you could phrase to the half note on B in measure 66. It is also possible to accent the E on beat 4 of measure 65. There is no need to adopt a particular phrasing and stick to it. You can use different phrasings on different occasions. In so doing you create periods of unequal length in the various repetitions of the same passage. Another way to create variation is to let the lowest voice in the left hand lead, thereby giving the music a darker color. The melody in measures 73–74 can also be phrased in various ways depending on whether you put the emphasis on C or G in the first measure or on A in the second one (see Ex. 22.5).

Ex. 22.5

The coda is like a mirror image of the impressionistic section; there the movement had been upward while in the coda, it is downward (see Exx. 22.6a and b).

Exx. 22.6a and b

The chromaticism of the conclusion should be emphasized. Play the three concluding broken chords quite slowly, and vary the loudness as indicated. The last one should be the most tranquil.

No. 3, French Serenade

Take this piece as a challenge to execute salon music in an elegant manner. Don't make a fool of yourself in the hall of mirrors, but dress nicely—and use a proper technique! The pieces that have been deprecated the most are often the most enjoyable. *French Serenade* is said to describe a little episode in the life of Grieg's friend Gerhard Schjelderup. The aging Schjelderup fell in love with a young Parisian woman and became like a young man again. The piece expresses a good deal of coquetry. We hear it first in the graceful introduction, which is like an invitation to dance (see Ex. 22.7).

Ex. 22.7

Andantino grazioso

p

The coquetry appears again in the *scherzando* passages (measures 14, 26, 44, 62), which seem to portray flirtatious young eyes and the playing of a guitar. Draw an elegant and ingratiating sketch amidst these ornate surroundings.

First work out the accompaniment, which must be light and precise. The score abounds in ties and slurs (see Exx. 22.8a and b). Play precisely and softly,

Exx. 22.8a and b

as if you were plucking the strings instead of striking them. Then, against this background, add the sophisticated, fragmentary melody. Don't create too forthright a sound with a lot of arm weight, but use a light, pliable arm that gently shapes the melody.

Which part of the hand determines the quality of the sound? Only the lowest part of the fingers, the fingertips, can do that, because only they are in contact with the surface of the keys. Be aware of this fact. Flexibility in the knuckles, wrists, elbows, and shoulders can facilitate what in the last analysis can be done only by the fingertips, so try to achieve a delicate control of them.

When you practice the piano, you develop a muscle feeling in your hand that is similar in many ways to yoga. Just as the aim of yoga is that mind and thought shall control muscles subject to the autonomic nervous system, pianists have—in a way completely different from that of other people—direct contact with the farthest extremities of their hands. This is not just a vague thought but a conscious feeling. To bring this out, I often pinch the ends of my fingers, even to the point of making them hurt. This kind of feeling has to be an everyday experience for a pianist. If you have such an oversensitivity in your hand, you can connect it to a similarly oversensitive variability in your mind to conjure up pictures. If you can do that, you can make *French Serenade* into a surprisingly fine piece. The same notes fall flat if they are played imprecisely or muddily. First practice in a firm tempo to achieve elegance, for without elegance there is no *French Serenade.*

Measures 14–15 and 26–27 are replete with slurs and staccatos and are incredibly elegant. These passages call for a very smooth *legato* in the sixteenth-note runs and a coquettish, guitarlike conclusion in which the fingers play actively and lightly. The wrist should move upward as well (see Ex. 22.9).

Ex. 22.9

The piece winds down in a guitarlike passage in measures 63–64, with soft broken chords and gentle articulation.

No. 4, *Brooklet*

This piece is the most technically demanding of all the *Lyric Pieces*. As an etude it is on a par with the most difficult works of Chopin and Liszt. It occupies an inconspicuous place among Grieg's *Lyric Pieces*, but it should not be underrated.

The advice that is often given about learning virtuoso pieces by Romantic composers is to practice everything slowly and thoroughly, over and over again, for an indeterminate period of time. Such is the case with *Brooklet*. It is not a piece to get ready for a specific occasion on short notice.

To learn *Brooklet* place it on your daily practice schedule alongside your other pianistic studies. Practice firmly and loudly, one hand at a time, rhythmically, and place accents on different parts of the measure. (Compare Cortot's advice regarding Chopin's Etudes.) Thereafter, practice with a soft right hand and a loud left. Performances of this piece frequently lack clarity in the left hand, and some notes get lost. To get a lively tone, practice the finger *staccato* in a slow tempo. Little by little move to a phrasing movement in the arm: down on beat 1, up on beat 3 (see Ex. 22.10).

Ex. 22.10

For the tremolo effect starting in measure 25, use a little rotating movement in the wrist—not too much, or you will sacrifice clarity. The fingers must do the articulation, and they must be in top shape. *Brooklet* is lively: it jumps, ripples, almost stands still, then rushes off again. For a moment it is hidden in the marsh grass, then suddenly it emerges and tumbles over the cliff into a deep, fresh pool. But *Brooklet* is mischievous and can tear itself away, to escape those who try to learn it.

It takes a lot of patience to master its tricky runs. One way to sneak up on them is to play the intervals simultaneously (see Exx. 22.11a, b, c, and d).

Exx. 22.11a, b, c, and d

No. 5, Phantom

This piece was originally called "Dream Vision," and it hovers between *piano* and *pianissimo.* There are no technical challenges, and the music has a highly refined sound. Grieg himself once said that the motives are nothing—everything depends on how they are handled. In *Phantom*, a simple motive is clothed in late-Romantic and impressionistic harmonies. Grieg constantly employs tonal shifts, i.e., a motive is shifted without modulation from one chromatic step to another. Thus we start out in A major, but the prominent sixth creates a subdominant character. This harmonic ambiguity allows the composer to depart from A major in measure 6 without an overt break, but emphasize the shift in the harmony. He has written *pianissimo* at this point, and it sounds best if you make it *subito pianissimo*, as if you were shifting from singing to humming. The trill in measures 18–19 and 42–43 should have a dreamy sound. It should not be a virtuoso trill, but a gentle vibration.

The transition in measures 20–24 is one of the most important passages in the entire piece—more important than what precedes it—because it contains the first unadorned triads we have heard up to this point. It is the first time that anything feels like a tonic.

The next section is just like the first except that the melody appears in octaves (see Exx. 22.12a and b).

Exx. 22.12a and b

Because of the triads and the reiterated tonic, the coda (measure 44 to the end) is the most substantial part of the piece. Here at last the composition achieves a harmonic foothold. Each of those insistent E's in the coda should have its own unique sound. The importance of the coda is further enhanced by the steadily descending line in the bass, which provides the harmonic framework.

The dreamy character of *Phantom* makes this piece difficult to grasp, but it is surpassingly beautiful.

No. 6, Homeward

One is in good humor heading for home in *Allegro giocoso alla marcia*. Is it a fellow walking by himself, or is it a group? Maybe it is a whole gang of people in a carriage. Whatever you imagine it to be, the rhythm must be steady regardless of the motives or the technical difficulties. The enthusiasm in the *Molto Allegro* at the end should suggest that you can finally see the goal.

In the middle section, Grieg makes use of motivic augmentation (compare measures 3 and 53). In this respect *Homeward* is similar to *March of the Dwarfs*; however, in the latter the middle section is light and shimmering, while *Homeward* is darker and more melancholy. This section is like an open wound, like a longing for one's home and homeland. Toward the end of the middle section, Grieg uses a brighter register. Try to make it sound like a willow flute (see Ex. 22.13).

Ex. 22.13

The principal technical problems are in the main section. First, last, and always you must establish the rhythm with the left hand; it must never abdicate this role. It has the simpler part to play, but the simple voice must set the pace for the more difficult one to follow. If the left hand fails to do this, everything gets topsy-turvy.

That said, we can turn our attention to the right hand. Try some tied exercises. Ex. 22.14a may be practiced as indicated in Ex. 22.14b. Try to achieve perfect coordination between the hands (see Ex. 22.15). It is very important to have a free arm and a loose wrist, which dances along in the *staccato* passages (see Ex. 22.16).

Exx. 22.14a and b

Ex. 22.16

Arm movement can help you achieve rhythmic phrasing. In measure 6, the concluding measure of the first phrase, for example, move the right arm up on beat 1 and down on beat 2.

The four sixteenth notes in measure 7 are intricate. Gather them together in a single movement of the hand. Observe the placement of the slur and do not inadvertently add a slur between the second and third notes of this figure, or between the last sixteenth note and the first eighth note (see Ex. 22.17).

Ex. 22.17

In measures 11 and 12 it is also important to play the slurs as written. It takes gentle finger activity supported by the appropriate arm movement.

The fingering of the two-voiced chords in measure 3–4 and elsewhere has been a matter of much discussion. Some pianists recommend 3–1, 4–2, while others use their thumb: 3–1, 4–1, 3–1, 4–1, 5–2 (see Exx. 22.18a and b). The

Ex. 22.18a

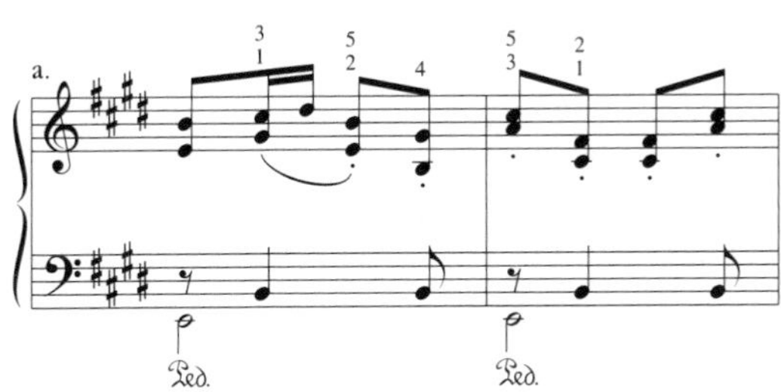

thumb can also be used in measures 7–9 and in the reiteration of these figures. The sixteenth notes in measures 38–41 are difficult to execute. If your hand is small it is possible to cut short the lower voices in the right-hand chords (see Ex. 22.19).

Ex. 22.18b

Ex. 22.19

If your hand is big enough, practice measures 38–41 as a tied exercise. Hold down the first, second, and perhaps the third fingers, and play F♯ repeatedly with the fourth; then do the same on G with the fifth finger. Franz Liszt laid great emphasis on tied exercises in order to free and strengthen the fingers so that they could articulate clearly even in restricted and difficult positions.

The same problem arises in the *Molto Allegro* section. Musically, however, the line in the left hand is more important here. The passage in measures 49–52 and its repeat are extremely difficult to play well. Try playing the octaves in alternate hands (see Ex. 22.20).

Ex. 22.20

Be careful about the brilliant, commanding rhythm in the last two measures: the second eighth note should not sound like the downbeat. Try to feel the rest, and thereafter a swinging rhythm that makes the next two beats strong—but not a downbeat (see Ex. 22.21).

Ex. 22.21

CHAPTER

23

Lyric Pieces VIII, Op. 65

Grieg paints with a broad brush in Op. 65. The first piece, *From Early Years*, is the most grandly conceived of all the *Lyric Pieces*. The last one, *Wedding Day at Troldhaugen*, is the longest. *Ballad* is incomparably the weightiest, expressively; its tempo indication *Lento lugubre* provides the setting for the Old Norse melody, the most ancient material in the collection. *Peasant's Song* is beautiful. The coloring of *Melancholy*, with its bold contrasts, is reminiscent of Edvard Munch. The only lively piece in the set is *Salon*.

No. 1, From Early Years

Grieg spent the happiest and best days of his youth in Denmark. It is an overstatement to say that *From Early Years* is distinctively Danish, but the first motive does have the rounded contours and dreamy quality of the Danish landscape. Privately you might think of it as "A Norwegian in Denmark." In any case, do not play it too straightforwardly or directly (see Ex. 23.1).

The form is ABA.

Measures 17ff. have a very Norwegian sound (see Ex. 23.2), which continues in measures 29–32. This dramatic, pianistic passage reflects the composer's impressions of Norway's rugged scenery (see Ex. 23.3).

The rippling sound in measures 50–57 is almost identical to the accompa-

Ex. 23.1

Ex. 23.3

niment in *At the Brook*, the last song in Grieg's famous cycle *The Mountain Maid (Haugtussa)*. This "brook" theme concludes the A section. The B section is a fetching, lively *springar* (see Ex. 23.4).

Ex. 23.4

In the recapitulation, the "brook" theme is broadened somewhat; then it fades away quietly and ends in silence—a rest with a fermata (see Ex. 23.5).

Ex. 23.5

The solitary voice that cries out in the coda gives added depth to the piece. Is it a sigh of longing for a vanished youth? (see Ex. 23.6.)

Ex. 23.6

From Early Years demands highly developed pianistic skills. The cascades of sound and the octave passages must be played with a full, rich tone (see Ex. 23.7). Some of the notes scored for the right hand can be played with the left (see Ex. 23.8). In measures 18 and 19 (see Ex. 23.2), taking the treble A with the left hand facilitates the playing of a smooth melody line.

Ex. 23.7

Ex. 23.8

Whichever way you do it, it is important to pay attention to the phrasing slurs. The long lines in the piece require a good overall plan. You might give the opening "Danish" part a *parlando* character. In the recapitulation following the *springar*, the dynamics and coloring might differ from the first iteration. Grieg's indication for the recapitulation is *cantabile*, which could call for an intensification; but you could do the opposite: use a more forthright sound the first time and then let the recapitulation be softer. Plan the dynamics leading up to the *fortissimo* in measure 41 and in the corresponding place in the recapitulation. Hold back a bit until the recapitulation so that everything has not been "said" the first time (see Ex. 23.9).

Ex. 23.9

The opening also requires smooth phrasing and flexible dynamics. Both the arm and the wrist should be relaxed (see Ex. 23.1).

The B section is almost dancelike, so here it is appropriate to articulate more clearly. Use a rather low wrist to achieve articulated slurs and clear tones except in the *crescendo* passages, where a heavier attack is required (see Ex. 23.10).

Ex. 23.10

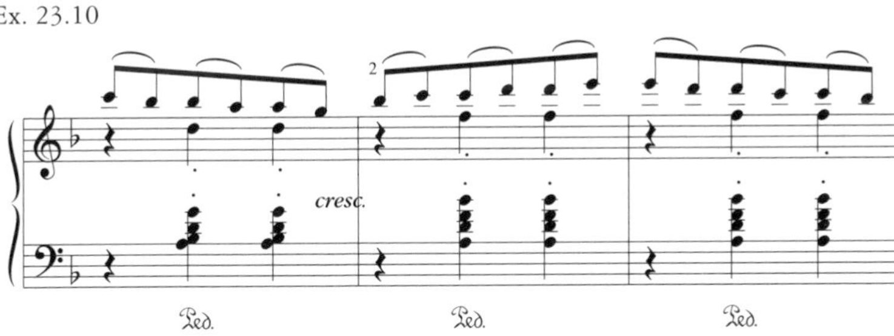

The repeat in the *Molto più vivo* section should absolutely be observed, as it provides an opportunity to add to the tension and the intensity the second time through. As in all dance pieces, the left hand controls the tempo and creates the desired drive. It is the conductor, and the right hand must obey with exact rhythm. It helps to think of the sixteenth notes as attached to the succeeding beat, i.e., like an anacrusis (see Ex. 23.11).

The introduction to the *springar* is very interesting. The solitary voice in

Ex. 23.11

the alto range sounding a B♭ is like an announcement, like the plaintive sound of a *lur* (an indigenous instrument that resembles an alpenhorn) proclaiming that something important is about to occur (see Ex. 23.12). This characteris-

Ex. 23.12

tically Griegian twist appears again in *Puck*, Op. 71, No. 3, where the "announcement" is again a B♭ (see Ex. 23.13). There is even a solitary B♭ in the A-minor Concerto (see Ex. 23.14).

Ex. 23.13

Ex. 23.14

In the *springar* the left hand has an interesting countermelody (see Ex. 23.15).

Ex. 23.15

To keep the rhythm in the right hand perfectly clear in the *fortissimo* part, starting in measure 77, support the fingers with a rhythmic impulse in the lower arm.

The eighth-note triplets at the end of the B section must be very lively and articulated. I recommend the fingering indicated in Ex. 23.16.

Ex. 23.16

Think of the repeat as continuing without interruption through the whole rest in measure 106. Let it end in the rest, in silence (see Ex. 23.17).

Ex. 23.17

From Early Years is a splendid piece. It deserves careful practice and performance.

No. 2, Peasant's Song

This is a truly beautiful and noble piece, despite its brevity and simplicity. Rarely does one find such a lovely melody united with such pure harmonies. It is a perfect entity, *semplice* in form and expression, with not one note too many or too few.

There are four voices throughout, which should be played with such transparency that we can hear the interplay between them. The melody as well as the other parts should be played with the strictest *legato*, which is accomplished by keeping the arm and wrist in gentle but constant motion.

Peasant's Song is singable in the best sense of the word, and for that reason it is important to "pause for breath" at the end of some phrases. Take time at the end of the sentence, as a singer would, but do not interrupt the flow of the music. Here, as elsewhere in Grieg's music, play the appoggiaturas fast.

With regard to coloration, first bring out the fine bass line that descends diatonically in measures 5–8 and more chromatically thereafter (see Ex. 23.18).

Ex. 23.18

Secondly, you can produce an organlike sound in measures 13–15 and 21–23 by emphasizing the bass in the descending octaves. In the conclusion, Grieg contrasts dark colors with light ones: the low A in the bass in measure 23 (see Ex. 23.19a) and the bright final chord in measure 26. The left hand is in the middle register, so hold it down to the end. The right hand is in the "xylophone" register and sounds better if it is attacked a little faster than the left hand (see Ex. 23.19b).

Exx. 23.19a and b

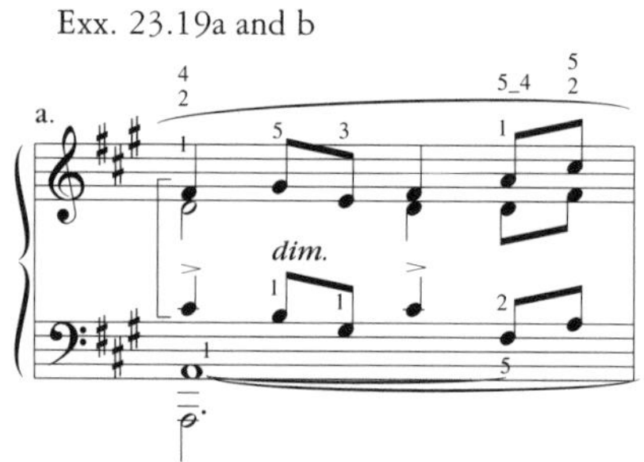

No. 3, Melancholy

This piece anticipates Edvard Munch: it is red, yellow, almost bloodlike. It is a depiction of agony, of a bottled-up despondency that rips and tears and from which there is no release.

The recitativic character of the introduction is very important in establishing the mood. The accompaniment is very simple, but sets the tone of the music—not dynamically, but by giving it intensity and adding depth to the phrasing. The bass line is like that of a cello or a bass section that is intensely involved in its accompanying role (see Ex. 23.20).

Ex. 23.20

At first, the right hand leads and must be played with a singing, intense tone. The whole arm must be intimately involved when playing the slow-moving, *legato* passages. The descending *portamento* in measures 7 and 13 may also be played with the whole arm. Do not allow the tempo to slow down too much in measures 8 and 9; if you "conclude" with every *diminuendo*, the piece will fall apart. Keep the music moving, like submerged streams that continue to flow even when they are out of sight.

Later the picture is reversed: the left hand leads while the right hand accompanies. The accompaniment figures primarily give the piece its melancholy, almost morbid, character, as if something repressed or imprisoned in these accompaniment figures is straining for intensity but is required to remain soft. It breaks out in the left-hand cadenza in measures 29–30 and 50–51. Do not play these octaves with two hands; they are supposed to be a little difficult, a little laborious, to yield the right expression.

The piece has many repetitions; vary the expression so that each iteration adds to the richness of the whole. *Tempo I* is somewhat orchestral in character. Do not make the *ritardando* too pronounced the first time, but in the conclusion both the rhythm and the volume can be reduced considerably. The melancholy subsides but it does not disappear. The sufferer merely drifts off into a troubled sleep.

No. 4, Salon

Not all of Grieg's compositions were inspired by Norwegian folk music. Grieg also was capable of being light and elegant, of writing character pieces depicting scenes far removed from folk life and folk instruments. The present piece depicts an elegant big-city salon with plush carpeting, palm trees, and

Victorian furniture. We overhear a snatch of polite conversation—perhaps between a man and a woman, or between two women concerning a man. The conversation is not profound, but animated, provocative, and descriptive. The flirtation, the seductiveness, the sophisticated naughtiness of the setting should be conveyed through a roguish interpretation of the piece. It should not be difficult to conjure up an interesting picture to think about as you are playing!

Keep the playing light in finger movements, arm use, and body movements. The posture of a ballet dancer is a good model for the outer extremities of your fingers. Play with ankles and toes, so to speak—as trippingly light and even as you can. When Grieg placed this piece between *Melancholy* and *Ballad*, he understood the need for a light intermezzo between those two heavy pieces.

The time signature is 6/8, so *Salon* is not a waltz in the conventional sense, but it should have the elegance of a fast waltz. The accompaniment moves in a triple rhythm with frequent rests on the first beat, emphasizing the lightness and the rocking character.

The first two measures are exceedingly light. Do not accent the sixteenth notes. They should be sparklingly clear and as articulated as possible, with the melody notes in between round and full (see Ex. 23.21).

Ex. 23.21

When there is a meaningful rest at the end of the phrase, e.g., measures 12–13 and 40–41, make it into a moment of expectation, in which one listens intently for what is to come. This device occurs in Grieg's earliest piano compositions and is typical of his music.

The *con moto* section, starting in measure 16, is full of syncopations and hemiolas; think in terms of three beats to the measure and accent accordingly. Just before the *a tempo* the melody becomes more concentrated and evolves into a little recitative in which the rhythm is totally altered (see Ex. 23.22).

With respect to *rubato*, Grieg has indicated *stringendo*, *tranquillo*, and *con moto* in addition to the initial *Allegretto con grazia*. Learn to play the piece with only the tempo variations specified by the composer before adding any of your

Ex. 23.22

own. There is room in *Salon* for one's own transitions and *rubati*. The numerous repetitions are an open invitation to vary the expression. Let the recapitulation tell a slightly different story each time it appears, with the *forte* a little louder each time, or the *pianissimo* extra soft the second time. Or the *tranquillo* can be even more peaceful the second time than the first. Do not overdo the *rubato*. These are cultivated people, and in such a salon everything must be in good taste, with no boorish exaggerations.

Salon is clearly not a dance that one dances, but a conversation about such a dance—in a suitable framework. It is a delicate little piece to entertain the audience, uplifting and much needed between its two somber neighbors (see Ex. 23.23).

Ex. 23.23

No. 5, Ballad

Black and brown Viking ships glide over the deep waters of the fjord. Is it a final journey, or is it the solemn sense of destiny of an entire nation that is reflected in *Ballad?* We sense a stately, elevated—but at the same time humble—attitude. One's mind, one's imagination, one's capacity to listen—all are put to their greatest test. There are not many notes, so they alone cannot convey the greatness. The way to the interpretation of *Ballad* lies between the keys, the notes, the lines. In this piece, as in no other, one is dependent on an intense inner picture. It need not be exclusively visual, but can also be a sound picture. You must leave the concrete dimension, the here and now, to play this piece.

The piece requires a free, warm sound and a smooth *legato*. Each note must be played with an unhurried intensity and preferably held—experienced—almost as if it were a part of the next note. An intense intimacy between person, hand, and instrument must coalesce into a single entity that encompasses the keys and the strings as well.

The opening eight-measure period is repeated with the melody in octaves, resulting in a little darker sound (see Ex. 23.24).

Ex. 23.24

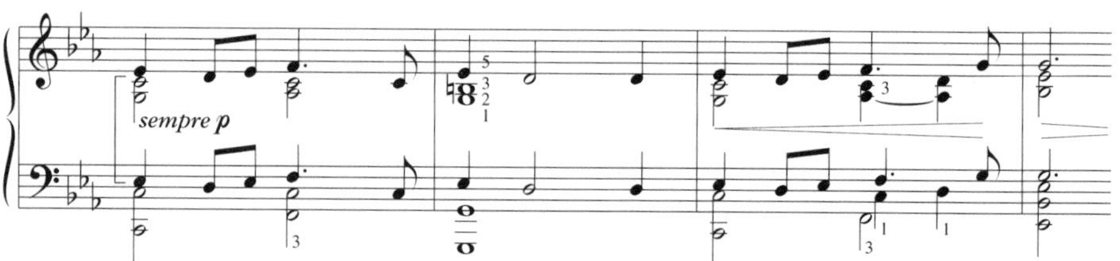

The contrasting section that follows is modal and slightly faster, with a *parlando* effect.

Tempo I contains a partial imitation and a *crescendo molto*, which anticipates the dense structure of the harmonies and imitations to come (see Ex. 23.25).

Ex. 23.25

Measures 33–40 are a repetition of the *poco mosso* section, with darker harmonization. The music has an undulating, swaying feeling and moves in a more *alla breve* fashion here.

Try to bring out the feeling of greatness, of vanished splendor, that permeates this piece.

No. 6, Wedding Day at Troldhaugen

This piece was originally called "The Well-wishers Are Coming" and is presumed to have been written to commemorate Edvard and Nina Grieg's silver wedding anniversary. They had invited fifty guests to Troldhaugen to help celebrate the event, and to their consternation 130 people showed up. The booming, buzzing confusion is reflected in the music as the well-wishers stream in from every direction, and the poor host doesn't quite know what to do. *Wedding Day at Troldhaugen* is a broad tableau—the longest piece in Op. 65—and it became so popular that Grieg would undoubtedly have been famous had he written only this one piece.

The scoring is not *alla breve*, but in many places Grieg has placed an accent over the third beat. Thus it is tempting to think that the *Marcia* called for in the main tempo indication applies to the half note (see Ex. 23.26).

Ex. 23.26

The piece has many mirrorlike effects. When the open fifths introduced at the beginning reappear a few measures later, they seem to have become distorted. Perhaps Grieg was thinking of the way an image becomes distorted when it is reflected in a fjord (see Ex. 23.27). When the open fifths reappear in measures 21–22, in A major, their character is different: this time they are like pliant drums (see Ex. 23.28).

Ex. 23.27

Ex. 23.28

The piece has a "terraced" feeling throughout—not *terraza* dynamics in the old sense, but in the sense of looking first to one side, then to the other. Perhaps on one side one sees people, on the other side nature (see Ex. 23.29).

Ex. 23.29

The middle section contains the famous sixteen-measure passage that sounds like a frantic race between the hands. This is where the guests—or perhaps the trolls—come swarming in, to the delight and alarm of the Griegs (see Ex. 23.30).

Ex. 23.30

The music now becomes virtuosic to a degree previously seen only in *March of the Dwarfs*, and it rolls over the piano with thundering brilliance (see Ex. 23.31).

Ex. 23.31

Everyone likes to play—and to hear—the four measures of solid chords that ring out like a rousing piano concerto. Play the notes simultaneously and equally loud, but with minimal back support (see Ex. 23.32).

Play the beautiful *Poco tranquillo* section as a duet. It should be rhythmic but not too loud. Think of it as a story: the wedding march has stopped, and now we are getting an artistic insert—a talk, a song, a duet, a diversion to elevate our minds and hearts (see Ex. 23.33). The whole passage is repeated like a mirage, like a shimmering dream reflected in the fjord—a multi-dimensional picture in B major. It provides a wonderful opportunity for the performer to shine (see Ex. 23.34).

Ex. 23.32

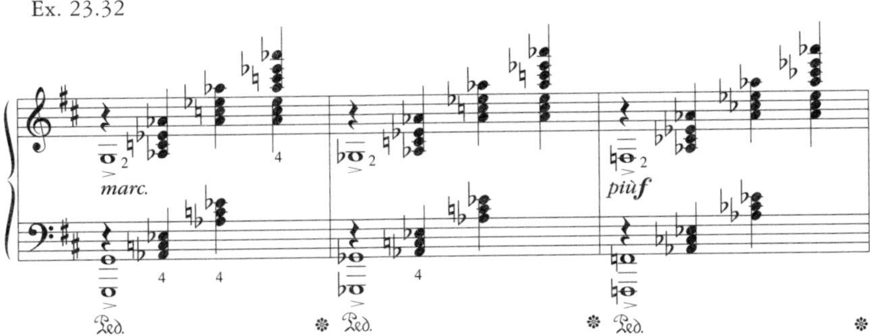

Ex. 23.33

Ex. 23.34

You need not be too rhythmic here, but do not use so much *rubato* that you lose the syncopated pattern: eighth note, quarter note, eighth note. Think about the syncopation accent in relation to the usual accent on the first beat. It must not be so strong that the downbeat gets lost, that it begins to sound like the downbeat (see Ex. 23.35).

Ex. 23.35

Measures 75–86 imitate the ringing of bells. Their impressionistic dimension can be brought out by holding the pedal down throughout the B-major and G-major passages and playing very softly.

Tempo I—the recapitulation of the opening wedding-day motive—can be a little softer than in the first iteration, perhaps *una corda*. The entire piece is now repeated. It is not always necessary that a repetition contain some development. Grieg may have been thinking of an ABA form with architectonic portal effect, a parallelism. In any case it is tempting to turn up the volume on the big chords the second time through (measures 151–54). The excitement grows even more in the passage immediately following (see Ex. 23.36).

Ex. 23.36

In the joyous conclusion, it can be difficult to maintain the rhythm, i.e., to keep the downbeat where it belongs. Remember that the heaviest attacks are in the left hand.

Experience shows that it is difficult to make the last sixteenth note in measure 163 short enough (see Ex. 23.37).

Ex. 23.37

Finally everything slowly fades away—from *piano* in measure 167 to *pianissimo* in measure 174 to *ppp* in measure 178. The last series of fifths is enchantingly impressionistic. (One is reminded of *Bell Ringing*, Op. 54, No. 6.) *Wedding Day at Troldhaugen* is without doubt one of Grieg's most successful compositions. As is appropriate for a wedding reception, it ends with a bang—a salute with cannons, champagne, and *fffz* (see Ex. 23.38).

Ex. 23.38

sopra
pp
ppp
fffz
Ped.
una corde
Ped.
Ped.
Ped.
Ped.
Ped.
tre corde

CHAPTER

24

Lyric Pieces IX, Op. 68

No. 1, Sailors' Song

None of the books of *Lyric Pieces* starts out more vigorously than Op. 68, with its rollicking *Sailors' Song*. The city of Bergen, where Grieg grew up, is a seaport, and as a boy he undoubtedly spent a lot of time on the wharf. His memories may be depicted in this piece. The *alla breve* scoring and the *Allegro vivace e marcato* indication tell us how to perform it. Maintain a strong, festive rhythm and a pronounced feeling of movement. Broaden out a bit in measures 33–36, and even more in measures 53–66—marked, in both cases, *poco a poco ritardando* (see Ex. 24.1).

Ex. 24.1

The fermata in measure 36 should be comparatively short, for there is more to come. The passage marked *a tempo ma ben tenuto* should be broader the second time than the first, so hold back a little in measure 33.

Most important in *Sailors' Song* is perfect coordination—absolute simultaneity—between the hands when playing the chords.

No. 2, Grandmother's Minuet

We go from *vivace e marcato* to *grazioso e leggierissimo*. What a contrast! The little dance trips along, light as a feather. The swinging rhythm conjures up a picture of petticoats and high-button shoes, as if Grandmother is saying, "Hey, look, I can still dance!"

The mood of this piece is somewhat similar to that of the *Gavotte* in the *Holberg Suite*, Op. 40. Perhaps you can imagine a hidden irony, a bit of roguish playfulness, in the *staccato* runs. Like the *Gavotte*, *Grandmother's Minuet* is charming and elegant, but with an undercurrent of sarcasm. With a knowing glance to one side, a raised eyebrow, and a disparaging comment spoken in a whisper, this minuet becomes even more interesting. It isn't as innocent as it looks.

The dance should, of course, be rhythmic, but there is nothing wrong with giving it a certain swing. For example, in measure 2, let the second beat come just a shade too late. The first measure can be construed as a long upbeat to the second (see Ex. 24.2).

Ex. 24.2

The anacruses should be fast and light. All the marked tempo variations—*ritardando*, *con moto*, *un poco stretto*, and *un poco ritardando*—take place within a very narrow range. Everything should be understated.

Measure 6 can be treated as an echo of measure 5. A similar echo pattern occurs a number of times (see Ex. 24.3).

Note the teasing *tenuto* accents—first up and then down—in measures 27–28 and 63–64—as if Grandmother takes a step to the right, then one to the left (see Ex. 24.4).

The questioning whole rests (measures 48 and 50) followed by an elegant

Ex. 24.3

Ex. 24.4

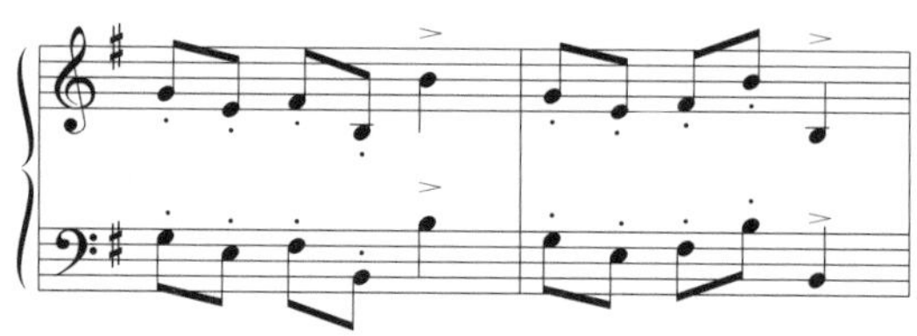

and expressive conclusion in *Tempo I* are very effective. Make the most of them (see Ex. 24.5).

Ex. 24.5

Variation of these roguish hints and witticisms—the mock refinement—make this piece an especially charming rococo miniature. Grieg may have been thinking about Landås, the stately old family home in the Bergen suburb where the Griegs spent the summer when Edvard was a boy. Several of his grandmother's silk dresses, suitable for the highest of high society, are still preserved there. The association was natural for him; make the piece come alive as an animated little conversation.

The fermata in measure 72 can be a little longer than the one in measure 36. The *staccatos* should be relatively short throughout, but the quarter notes should be a little longer than the eighths, giving you an opportunity to demonstrate that there is more than one way to play "trippingly" (see Ex. 24.6).

No. 3, At Your Feet

This piece expresses warm adulation, unqualified devotion. In the *Lyric Pieces*, it is often wise to hold back a little when the feeling is most intense. If you give it everything you've got, there is a danger of destroying the mood. In *At*

Ex. 24.6

Your Feet, however, there is no reason to hold back. Give it all the warmth you can muster, all the inner feeling suggested by the indications *molto espressivo*, *agitato*, and *appassionato*. The piece is genuinely Romantic in tone, rhythm, and phrasing. Even the attack should be executed by a pliable arm, relaxed at the elbow, wrist, and hand. Preliminary loosening-up exercises might be advisable if you feel the least bit stiff. One must be relaxed in both body and mind.

The accompaniment *quasi arpeggio* moves smoothly from chord to chord. The harmony consists mainly of chords that are not resolved; indeed, the first that is fully resolved is the A-major triad in measures 33–34 (see Ex. 24.7).

Ex. 24.7

Because of the harmonic suspension, think of the entire first part (measures 1–34) as one long, uninterrupted line. The chords in measures 10, 11, 14, 15, and 17, for example, are seventh and ninth chords, which do not come to rest but point toward a resolution yet to come.

Even the melody is somewhat fragmentary. It gropes its way through many suspensions and works its way higher and higher before finally dropping down again (see Ex. 24.8).

Ex. 24.8

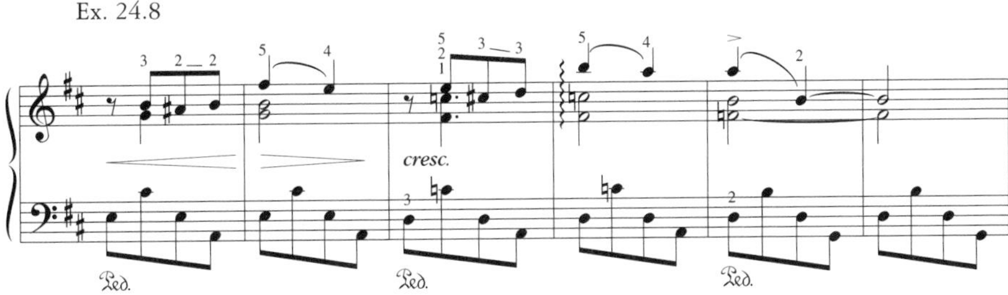

The *Più mosso* section presents a tender dialogue between a cellolike solo in the left hand (see Ex. 24.9) and an *agitato* reply in the soprano (see Ex. 24.10).

Ex. 24.9

Ex. 24.10

The middle section (starting in measure 63) is characterized by increasing inner tension. There are no tonic chords here. The suspense grows and grows and is not resolved until the D-major chord at the very end (see Exx. 24.11, 24.12a, and b).

Ex. 24.11

Ex. 24.12a

Ex. 24.12b

The *Più mosso* section uses mediant shifts as modulations. For example, the harmony moves abruptly from A major to F major in measure 35. It goes to A minor in measure 39, to C major in measure 43, and finally to an A-major chord in measure 59 (see Ex. 24.13).

Ex. 24.13

Everything is left hanging until the very end. The unresolved chords give the music a Wagnerian flow. Just what *At Your Feet* is trying to express must be decided by you, the interpreter.

No. 4, Evening in the Mountains

On the fair copy of this piece Grieg wrote, "To my dear Frants"—i.e., Frants Beyer, who was often his helper and supporter. Grieg first gave it the title *Cow Call*, and on an early version that he sent to Beyer he wrote, "Can be thought of as an evening in Utladalen (Skogadalsbøen)."

Evening in the Mountains, as the piece was finally called, is a high point among the 66 *Lyric Pieces*. In the first half, the unaccompanied melody sounds plaintively across a mountain meadow. One can visualize the whole landscape: the mountain, the forest, the grassy plateau. Perhaps the experience of a human being is also being depicted amid the enormous height and breadth of mountains that soar above the clouds and touch the sky. The mountains can give one an "ocean" feeling. One feels the nearness of the sea even though it is far away: earth, sea, and sky become as one. Try to convey some of that feeling of vastness when you perform this piece.

The eight-measure introduction is a long *lur*-like call on a single note, B, accompanied by a series of light steps in the left hand: someone has heard the *lur* sounding and runs to see it, to get a better view. The beginning is objective, but the coda is just the opposite. It is strongly dramatic and has a distinctly personal stamp: an outcry in the form of a canon depicts the fate of some human being.

As so often in Grieg's music, the melody in *Andante espressivo* requires a flowing *legato*. The sound should be as clear as a flute, as plaintive as an oboe. Use pedal sparingly in order to convey a sense of the pure mountain air. The phrasing is a little irregular, as indicated by Grieg's placement of the accent marks: first two-measure periods, then periods of irregular length in which the second beat is accented now and then (see Ex. 24.14).

Ex. 24.14

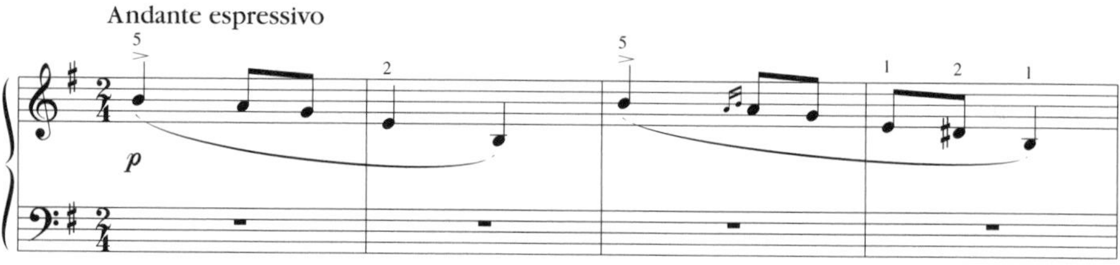

The *tenuto* in measure 22 can be produced with a small, hesitating arm movement; and the pattern of slurred and articulated notes that follows is important (see Ex. 24.15).

The excitement grows, then a gradual *più tranquillo* leads to a solitary,

Ex. 24.15

expectant B followed by an ingenious little pentatonic tune: A–B–D (measures 36–42). The B in the transitional measures (43–46) harks back to the pedal point of the introduction.

The melody in *Tempo I*, starting in measure 47, is identical to that of the *Andante espressivo*, but this time Grieg has added late-Romantic harmonization. In the denser texture of this section use a little pedal to enhance the *legato* in the left hand. The sound is enlarged and strengthened in this section. From a single willow flute it has grown to a full string orchestra. Beautiful chromatic counter-voices strengthen and underscore the melodic material at various points. *Evening in the Mountains* is a work of genius.

No. 5, At the Cradle

This little cradle song is simple, innocent, and lovely. The texture is mainly four-part. Even though the melody is in the soprano most of the time, the other voices must be clear. In measure 3, you can handle the trill better if you play the alto part with the left hand (see Ex. 24.16).

Ex. 24.16

The first eight measures can be played a little softer in the repeat, perhaps *mezzo piano* for the first iteration and *pianissimo* for the second one.

The middle section, starting in measure 9, is a lullaby, and a little shimmering fuzziness is in order. It is difficult to make the parallel thirds precise; try a tiny jerk of the wrist on each one.

The transitions in measures 23–28 show that Grieg is now a mature—indeed, elderly—man with long experience. He uses the perspective gained in the course of a long life to put the cradle song—that which happens at the cradle—in an infinitely deeper context. At this point your interpretation is put to its biggest test. This is perhaps the most important passage in the entire piece. It is daring in its modulation as it makes a long leap to the left on the circle of fifths: from an F♯ chord in measures 22–23 to a C chord in measures 25–26—a tritone leap (see Ex. 24.17). Then it shifts to E major via

Ex. 24.17

the mediant relationship, but this is actually a downward shift of a minor second, for the E-major chord rests on B in the bass in measures 28–30. These harmonic calisthenics are enormously dramatic, but do not be intrusive; indeed, they should be especially tranquil.

A more important iteration of the principal melody follows. Perhaps the child is sleeping and dreaming. Perhaps the person singing the lullaby notes this and smiles approvingly (see Ex. 24.18). Finally comes a coda, with a warm sound in the middle register.

Ex. 24.18

At the Cradle concludes with crystal-clear chords in a high register, in a mood of sleeping innocence; then, *ppp*, there is nothing but warmth (see Ex. 24.19).

Ex. 24.19

This piece requires a lively imagination. Listen to your playing, and observe what is happening with each phrase. Listen before you play, feel before you play, imagine before you strike the key.

No. 6, Valse Mélancolique

Tempo di valse tranquillo is not tranquil in the usual sense; its outward tranquility is disturbed by an inner unrest. We do not know the reality behind this piece, so we have to make up a story. Perhaps it expresses a teenager's anticipation of something that is about to begin. Or perhaps a woman has been unfaithful and is afraid of being found out. In the latter case, measures 38–53 could be understood as her lover telling her not to be afraid, that everything will be all right (see Ex. 24.20).

Ex. 24.20

Then perhaps she replies (measures 54ff.): well, if I am going to be found out, let us at least use the time we have. It is a hectic little love story; the deceit is not found out, but the disquiet returns. One must have this or some other suitable story in mind while playing *Valse Mélancolique*. But don't use my story. Write your own libretto!

Most modern editions omit the repeat sign, but the original score called for the first 149 measures to be repeated. However, the piece becomes terribly long, and the same music is repeated over and over again. It can become unbearably trivial and banal, or, if one's artistic imagination, vision, and imagination are equal to the task, absolutely spellbinding! *Valse Mélancolique* is one of the most extreme of the *Lyric Pieces*. It stands or falls on the creative capacity of the interpreter, for it can easily lapse into monotony. Unless you have a story in mind, it is difficult to bring this waltz to life.

Now and then there is room for a typical waltz tempo—for example, in measures 10–13 (see Ex. 24.21).

Note the many indications of *poco ritardando* and *stretto*, and make them different each time they occur. Be cautious at first, then gradually make them more pronounced.

Ex. 24.21

To make the parallel thirds clear and precise, especially in measures 31 and 33, play with a little arm support, giving a little impulse to each (see Ex. 24.22).

Ex. 24.22

In accompaniment figures in waltzes, the accents should not always be the same. The bass note must support the rest of the chord harmonically. It is the left-hand accompaniment that offers an opportunity to play with alterations in the rhythm from time to time—not, perhaps, in a typical Viennese manner, but with some of the irregularity to which the waltz lends itself. In Ex. 24.23, for example, one might prolong the second beats slightly.

Ex. 24.23

A little hesitation at the surprisingly disappointing resolution in measure 28 is very effective and stands in contrast to the real resolution in measures 36–37. There should be no *rubato* in the latter.

In measures 76–77, play the solo voice almost like a recitative, as, sobbing, it descends from A♭ to start its new "circle" waltz. (By "circle" waltz I mean that the motives and the waltz itself are somewhat circular melodically and with respect to form. The whole thing starts over and over again, tries to make progress, but is unable to break out of the circle. Seen from this perspective, *Valse Mélancolique* becomes an intriguing little description of an affair, or perhaps a picture of the dance of life as portrayed in a salon—in any case, a riddle to which there is no solution.) Use your thumb on the A♭ and keep the arm loose. Make the attack with the left side of the bottom joint, i.e., with the thumb at an angle (see Ex. 24.24).

Ex. 24.24

The piece concludes with a 21-measure coda that begins with a warm *crescendo* (see Ex. 24.25).

Ex. 24.25

The coda continues with a pastichelike lightness reminiscent of a ballet. The picture fades away, *Valse Mélancolique* is over. The associations we have suggested may sound silly off stage, but when you are performing they serve a useful purpose.

CHAPTER

25

Lyric Pieces X, Op. 71

Volume 10 of the *Lyric Pieces* is big and varied. These seven pieces of diverse character and differing keys are intermingled in such a masterful way that they can be played in succession, as a cycle. No. 3, *Puck*, is an infernally amusing little scherzo; No. 5, *Halling*, is the virtuosic high point; while No. 6, *Gone*, has a deep tragic and melancholy character rarely found in the *Lyric Pieces*. No. 7, *Remembrances*, the last of the 66 *Lyric Pieces*, is a reminiscence of *Arietta*, Op. 12, No. 1, the first one, now changed to 3/4 time and expanded harmonically. With this piece Grieg wraps a ribbon around all ten volumes of *Lyric Pieces*.

No. 1, Once Upon a Time

Grieg uses a Swedish folk song, *Ack Värmland du sköna*, and a Norwegian *springar* to create a Norwegian-Swedish contrast. The form is ABA—in this case, Swedish–Norwegian–Swedish. In the A section, as often in Grieg's music, sustain a smooth *legato* in the soprano voice in its duet with the fine bass line. Try to create long lines, being careful not to subdivide into two-measure periods. Vary the emphasis when motives are repeated. Pay close attention to Grieg's dynamic shadings: make a clear distinction between *piano*, *pianissimo*, and *forte* in the A section. Plan the tempos so that there are definite contrasts between *Andante con moto* and *Animato* and *a tempo tranquillo*. These tempo variations contribute to the plasticity of the A section, which can easily get too sedate. The rests in the second ending of the *Animato* section are very effective (see Ex. 25.1).

Ex. 25.1

The tempo relationship between the A and B sections is as follows: one beat in *a tempo tranquillo* = one measure in *Allegro brioso*, that is, a quarter note in A now equals a dotted half in B. This is just an approximation and need not be observed with mathematical precision; there is room for judgment. *Allegro brioso* implies that the music should be spirited and light—and as soft as a shadow.

Technically, it is not easy to execute the two voices in the B section—the quarter-note/eighth-note combination in the right hand. Try using some arm support, a flick of the elbow on each quarter note (see Ex. 25.2).

Ex. 25.2

In the hemiolas in measures 55–62, continue to feel the prevailing three beats in order to create an inner friction, a rhythmic tension.

Although the B section builds up to a powerful, driving *fortissimo*, the *pianissimo* passages are the most important. The *poco ritardando* in measures 60–62 should be broader in the repeat than the first time.

In measures 63–70, when the *springar* is played *fortissimo*, the accents on the second beat add immeasurably to the excitement. To keep the downbeat from getting dislocated and to keep beat 2 from sounding like beat 1, stress both beats.

Let the *springar* fade out steadily toward the fermata at the double bar, an expectant stillness (see Ex. 25.3).

Although Grieg has written "like the beginning," the recapitulation (mea-

Ex. 25.3

sures 78ff.) is the greatest interpretative challenge of the entire piece. Precisely because it is identical to the first section, give the Swedish folk song different coloring here. For example, the first time you might stress the soprano, to bring out the melody, but in the recapitulation, give a little more emphasis to the other voices.

No. 2, Summer's Eve

When you plan the tempos in *Once Upon a Time*, you must also be thinking of the tempos in *Summer's Eve*. The indication in No. 2 is *Allegretto tranquillamente*, in contrast to the *Andante* of *Once Upon a Time*. This relationship is important for Op. 71 as a unified whole. Moreover, in order to bring out the brightness and the pastel colors of a Nordic summer evening (when it never really gets dark), the piece should not be too slow.

The light, clear tone is achieved with a smoothly floating arm and a firm, biting fingertip. Articulate clearly! Grieg uses mediant shifts and chromatic alterations, both of which are invitations to varying coloration. The B♭-minor chord in measure 5 should not have the same tone color as measures 1–4 even though it is also *piano*. Whether it should be lighter or darker is up to you, but make it different. The same advice applies to measures 9–12, where the harmony moves up chromatically.

Do not worry about the "muddiness" when you use the pedal as indicated in the sixteenth-note figures in measure 14 and elsewhere. Grieg's music often contains impressionistic passages of this kind. Keep the pedal down, even in the long descending line in measures 16–19. The most important thing is to execute a good *diminuendo*, to play as if in the shadow of the top notes—*sur le ton*, as the French say. The sixteenth-note rest with the fermata at the end of this passage can be very effective, especially if you think of it as the goal toward which the passage points.

In *Tempo I*, use an extra bright tone in the soprano, as if you were imitating a flute, and emphasize the low bass notes in measures 28–31. In this way you can create a light-dark contrast, as in a Rembrandt painting (see Exx. 25.4a and b).

Exx. 25.4a and b

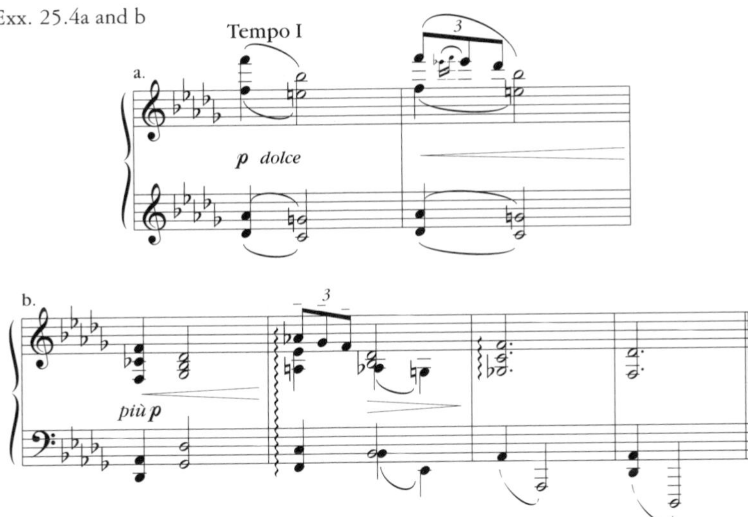

The balance of the piece consists of repetitions, which is an advantage when you are learning it but a challenge when you are performing it. Practice the same parts in various ways to come up with different harmonic emphases, different tone colors, to make the piece interesting onstage.

Always try to increase or decrease steadily, phrasing from the first to the last note. More than anything else, that elevates the performance of the *Lyric Pieces* to a high artistic plane.

No. 3, Puck

This is one of Grieg's signature pieces, which all young Norwegian piano students are expected to learn. It is devilishly hard to play with precision, and must be practiced for a long time in a regular tempo before it can be played quickly and lightly. Start with an even four-beat count in the left hand, *pp*, but with a lightning-fast *staccato*. This is quite a technical challenge. At the beginning I recommend the fingering shown in Ex. 25.5.

Ex. 25.5

The thirds and fourths must be precise, *staccatissimo*, but with the melody line prominent. The hand must be steady, but it is easier to bring out the soprano voice if the wrist is a little high. Try tipping the hand a bit to emphasize each of the top notes. Think of your fingers, hand, and wrist as members of a ballet troupe, working together with precision.

Measures 19–20, marked *forte*, must not be mistaken for the conclusion of the piece, marked *fortissimo*. Hold back a little so that you can really explode at the end (see Exx. 25.6a and b).

Exx. 25.6a and b

The middle section requires vigorous articulation in the left hand for clarity. The attack should be almost a *staccato*, but do not use too much weight or it will get muddy (see Ex. 25.7).

Ex. 25.7

The dramatic B♭ in measures 49, 51, and 53ff. is surprising both harmonically and melodically and sounds almost like a *lur*. The one in measures 53–61 is marked *pianissimo*, but in view of its long duration, the attack must not be too weak.

The most important element in *Puck* is the soft but audacious beat in the left hand. It is an effective little virtuoso piece, but it comes to life only when you master its technical challenges.

No. 4, *Peace of the Woods*

Many consider *From Early Years* (Op. 65, No. 1) the greatest and most important of the *Lyric Pieces*. Others think that honor belongs to *Ballad* (Op. 65, No. 5), and still others regard *Peace of the Woods* as the finest of the 66 pieces. Its title is ambiguous. The depth and darkness of a large forest constitute a drama all their own. If in addition you imagine human beings who are experiencing its stillness, you will get close to the mood of this piece.

The two opening chords set a bright tone, in contrast to the dark accompaniment that follows. Strike them in a bell-like manner, and sustain them with the pedal, but there is no need to keep the fingers firmly on the keys for their entire duration.

Practice the opening chords first. Then practice those at the beginning of *Tempo I*, which are the same chords set in relief by the open fifths in the left hand. Light and darkness are juxtaposed. Finally, practice the heavy, organlike chords near the end of the piece (see Exx. 25.8a, b, and c).

Exx. 25.8a, b, and c

In measure 70, the effect of the *ppp* chord on A is like that of a trumpet suddenly muted. If all the notes are to be sounded simultaneously, one's hand cannot be too loose, but even so I think the attack should be made with an upward, not a downward, hand movement. The following rolled chords are exciting. Try to make each one unique in some way: vary the dynamics, emphasize different parts of the chords (the bottom, middle, or top notes), or change the speed with which you play the arpeggio. Try various effects to see what works for you. Even the three B-major chords that conclude the piece should not be identical.

After you have practiced these chords, which provide a framework for the piece, go back to explore its range of sonorities. Measures 31–34 call for a brilliant foray into the descant register, while the impressionistic *pianissimo* passage in measures 57ff. is at the opposite extreme and requires plenty of pedal (see Ex. 25.9).

Ex. 25.9

Note next that the rests in the recapitulation (*Tempo I*) alternate between four beats and two. This alternation, if strictly observed, is very effective (see Ex. 25.10).

Ex. 25.10

Peace of the Woods must hang together in one line for the listener. The secret to making this happen is the accompaniment in the left hand. The eighth notes must be as even as possible, with an incessant drive, but they should not dominate the overall sound. There is room for *rubato*, *ritardandos*, transitions, and *strettos*, but you must always be cognizant of the accompaniment figure and its basic building block, the eighth note, and apportion these liberties in such a way that the flow of the phrases never stops.

The soprano voice should be as *legato* as possible. The middle voice should be significantly softer, but always variable. It should stay in the background, but when the melody gets louder it should follow suit.

It is easy to overstress the fifth of the chord in the accompaniment figure, because the broken chord begins with the fifth and then repeats it. Be aware that the root of the chord is the fourth eighth note; stress it to create a harmonically correct sound, especially in the *forte* passages.

Note the sequential shifting of the motives in measures 16–17 and 20–21. Do not color them alike, and do not treat them in the same way dynamically even though *piano* is the indication in both cases (see Exx. 25.11a and b).

Exx. 25.11a and b

The D-minor chord in measure 24 and the dominant seventh chord on G in measure 25 are somewhat of an afterthought, so it is appropriate to retard the tempo just a shade here. They anticipate some dramatic outbursts in the stillness of the forest, so there is need for a delicate sensitivity in the changing harmonies.

Tempo I provides an opportunity for a question-and-answer effect as the melody line alternates between a higher and a lower register. If you prefer, play the phrase as if it were an attempt to get out of some difficulty. Play it with a little anguish, a little *stretto*, but absolutely *tranquillo*.

The point of maximum depth—the dominant seventh chord on B—is reached in measure 71. The balance of the piece should be played like a coda.

You cannot play the *Lyric Pieces* unless you can conjure up suitable pictures and then let the music flow from them. This is very much the case with *Peace of the Woods*, which tests one's musical and poetic imagination but can also call forth one's poetic powers. Let the poetic conception be your goal and the focus of your practice. Then *Peace of the Woods* can become for you one of the most important of the *Lyric Pieces*.

No. 5, Halling

Except for those in Op. 72, this *halling* dance is the most virtuosic that Grieg has written. As always, it is important to practice it first in a fixed tempo. The most important interpretive consideration is the rhythm, particularly in the accompaniment. It is very easy to get sloppy, to play the accompaniment as triplets instead of the dotted eighth and sixteenth note. Because it is an ostinato figure, it deserves careful attention. Feel the dot, i.e., the note that is not played, or, alternatively, treat the sixteenth note as an anacrusis to the next note (see Ex. 25.12).

Ex. 25.12

Now add the right hand, following the rhythm of the left hand as precisely as possible. It is fun once you get the hang of it! If you can do this, you have made great strides.

Next, pay attention to Grieg's irregular accents in the right hand. The first two measures of each phrase have accents on the second beat, while the rest of the phrase has none. This swinging irregularity is exceedingly charming. Moreover, the accented beats should be *unequally* accented (see Ex. 25.13).

Ex. 25.13

Do not let this *halling* dance become too loud. The passages marked *piano*, *pianissimo*, and *ppp* make the piece jovial and fun instead of bombastic, and they make the *forte* and *fortissimo* passages much more effective by contrast.

Grieg's pedal indications are very important. Holding the pedal down where the score calls for it in measures 49–60 will create an orchestral sound (see Ex. 25.14). Measures 49–60 are based on one big chord, a dominant ninth in which the fifth is lowered to D♭ starting in measure 53. As you hold the pedal down, the sound of the D♮ will gradually fade away.

In measure 60, aim for the last note of the *glissando*, E, not the F on the downbeat of the next measure. This final E tends to get lost, so aim toward it and practice stopping on it (see Ex. 25.15).

Ex. 25.14

Ex. 25.15

In the *fortissimo* section that follows the *glissando*, the left-hand octaves are a challenge. Practice and prepare each octave, i.e., place your hand before you strike the keys and feel the distance. Repeat this exercise each time you plan to play *Halling*. When you feel secure enough, play the octaves with a swinging motion, without first feeling for them, but directly, "from the air." This technique produces a wonderful, free sound, but it should be your goal only after long practice with the more cautious technique. Practicing only "from the air" the wonderful sound for which we are striving is likely to become a cacophony of sour notes.

Meanwhile, the right hand, which alternates between fourths and octaves, should be practiced one voice at a time. Use a little extra lower-arm motive on the accented notes (see Ex. 25.16).

Ex. 25.16

Measures 69–76 should also be practiced one voice at a time, particularly the alto. I prefer to use fingers 3 and 2 rather than 4 and 2 on B♭ and G (see Ex. 25.17).

The following tempos are indicated in *Halling*: *Allegro molto*, *Allegro moderato e marcato*, and *Allegro molto* (*Doppio movimento*). The last two mea-

Ex. 25.17

sures are marked *Tempo I*, i.e., *Allegro moderato e marcato*. The opening measures should be lightning fast and the concluding measures even faster (*marcatissimo*). The body of the piece, however, should not be too fast. A smart, rhythmic sophistication is more evident in a rhythm that is not too hurried. For *Allegro moderato e marcato* maintain a steady beat, one that does not quicken.

Halling, Op. 71, No. 5, is an effective virtuoso number whether it is played in conjunction with the other works in the cycle or by itself.

No. 6, Gone

This piece bears the subtitle "In Memoriam." It may have been written in memory of someone who has died, or of a broken friendship, or of an unfinished composition, or of a relationship that has ended. Turn your imagination loose, and let your interpretation benefit from your mental pictures.

The piece has been the subject of much discussion. Norwegian pianist Fridtjof Backer-Grøndahl, who studied with Grieg himself, omitted No. 6 when he played Op. 71 because he thought it inferior to the other pieces in this opus. Russian pianist Emil Gilels, on the other hand, declared *Gone* the most important and the most interesting of all the *Lyric Pieces*. Other pianists have had differing opinions on this piece. It certainly cannot be denied that it is unusually interesting harmonically, with its chromatic series of $^6_4$ chords, unexpected altered dominants, and their resolutions.

Gone could have been written for the organ—which brings us to the main point in the interpretation of the piece. Play *legato/legatissimo* like an organist. Make the transition from one chord to the next almost a *glissando*. Release the pedal at the last possible moment, perhaps even a little too late. Your hands should move so smoothly from chord to chord that they never leave the keys. The fingertips must press firmly but gently against the keys, and the arm must be constantly in motion. The accented upbeats convey a feeling of a sigh (see Ex. 25.18).

The middle section is more positive. The lines move upward rather than downward, and the mood is not as depressed and depressing as in the first and last sections (see Ex. 25.19).

The resolutions via eighth-note runs can be executed with the pedal de-

Ex. 25.18

Ex. 25.19

pressed most of the time, so the major third slowly resolves to a minor third (see Ex. 25.20).

Ex. 25.20

One must strike a balance between playing in a completely even and static manner and phrasing so as to avoid becoming too obvious and overbearing. If the dreamy Romantic spirit is given free rein, *Gone* can become one of the most interesting and remarkable of the *Lyric Pieces*. It has great dramatic potential, in some places approaching Edvard Munch's *The Scream* in expressive power.

No. 7, *Remembrances*

Of the many waltzes in the *Lyric Pieces*, *Remembrances* is the most elegant. By echoing *Arietta*, the first of the *Lyric Pieces*, *Remembrances* becomes a backward glance over nearly four decades of Grieg's output. The feeling of reminiscence, of looking back with love and longing, permeates this piece. It is therefore important to observe Grieg's dynamic instructions, mainly *piano* and *pianissimo*, and to distinguish between them without making the *piano* too loud. I suggest that you attack with a downward arm movement when playing *piano*, an upward one when playing *pianissimo*. It helps to keep both arms moving freely in the process. The arms should move independently, however: often the right hand will be going down as the left hand is going up (see Ex. 25.21).

Ex. 25.21

As in the other waltzes, pay attention to the accompaniment, making sure that there is a balance between the melody and the afterbeats, and that the bass note is slightly louder than the afterbeats.

The modulations to D major, B♭ major, and then to E♭ major are very effective. Try to feel the shifts on the circle of fifths. You can enhance the effectiveness of these modulations if you regard them as raising the sound up from the fog, as it were, into a clearer, lighter sphere (see Exx. 25.22a, b, c, and d).

Exx. 25.22a, b, and c

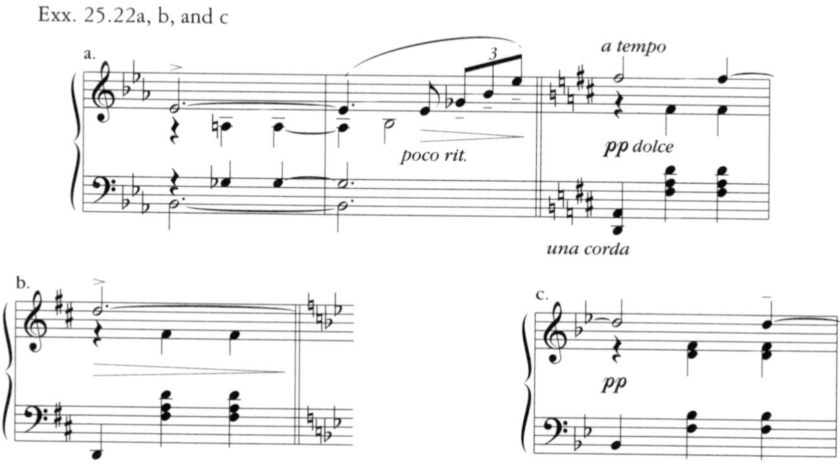

Note the similarity of the first and last notes of the piece: G with a fermata in both cases. Because the first G is a quarter note, it should be a shade more definite and brighter than the last G, which is an eighth note on the second half of the weakest beat (see Exx. 25.23a and b).

Ex. 25.22d

Exx. 25.23a and b

Play *Remembrances* with your fingertips close to the surface of the keys, both when the keys are moving downward and when they are coming up again. Add a bit of sophisticated pedal work and this piece becomes a real Griegian pearl. It is lyrical, tender, indirect, evocative, and impressionistic—a touchingly beautiful conclusion to a lifelong project. The ring is closed.

CHAPTER

26

Norwegian Peasant Dances (slåtter), Op. 72

The *Norwegian Peasant Dances* (*slåtter*; the singular form is *slått*) occupy a unique place in Grieg's production and in Norwegian music as a whole. These singular, uncompromising, beautiful, difficult, animated, lyrical, introspective, swaggering, tender dance tunes are so special that one would be hard pressed to find anything like them anywhere else in the world.

SOME GENERAL OBSERVATIONS

The melodies are not the invention of any one person—not Grieg or anyone else. They are an expression of the soul of the Norwegian people, the product of a lengthy process. They were passed down from person to person, from generation to generation, from fiddler to fiddler for centuries. They were written down for the first time near the end of the nineteenth century. According to legend, the early fiddlers first learned them from a water sprite, a mythical creature capable of appearing in many guises who was thought to dwell in the waterfall. They were originally associated with Thor, the Old Norse god of thunder, but over time each dance tune became identified with certain fables, legends, individuals, and fiddlers. An air of legend, of mystery, hovers over these tunes.

If you wish to play this great work, it is essential that you first study Johan

Halvorsen's transcriptions of the tunes for violin, made in 1901. It is also imperative to listen to these tunes played on Norway's national instrument, the Hardanger fiddle. Live performances of such music are given in Norway, where the folk-dance tradition is still alive. For those unable to visit Norway, recordings are available.

The composition of Op. 72 was very taxing for Grieg. At first he was not greatly interested in the project, for the melodies and harmonies were far removed from his previous writing. As time went on, however, he became more and more enamored of the task, and, he said, it "bewitched" him. But the environment in which he was working was not supportive—it was, in fact, negative. His wife, Nina, is reported to have said, "I don't understand these dance tunes at all. They are foreign to me." Despite these obstacles, Op. 72 is such a monumental achievement that everything Grieg had previously written for the piano may be viewed as a preparation, a forerunner to this great work. It is his crowning achievement for solo piano.

The oldest dance tunes—Nos. 16 and 17—date back to the eleventh century. Remarkably, all the tunes appear to have survived virtually unchanged through the centuries, partly because of Norway's geographic isolation and partly because the country was subordinate to Denmark for a long period. During the Danish rule, the gap widened between the continental cultural life of the cities and the living folk music of the rural areas. In the latter tradition, melodies were not written down but were transmitted orally from old to young, from experienced to inexperienced. In this situation the old melodies were preserved and to a certain extent developed—but in an authentic way—right up to the beginning of the twentieth century. By that time they were mature, ready to be written down.

In view of this history, it is not surprising that the musical language of the *slåtter* is unique and so far removed from the Romantic language characteristic of Grieg. The tonalities are for the most part Lydian; indeed, this is one of the distinguishing features of Op. 72. Thus the augmented fourth—the dissonant relationship D–G♯—is the trademark of these pieces. It is not a distinctively Norwegian feature, however, but appears in many parts of the world where there is original and genuine folk music. Grieg focuses on this interval, which in Hardanger-fiddle music is normally linear, i.e. melodically Lydian. He employs it harmonically, with D and G♯—i.e., the tritone, the *diabolus in musica*—often sounded simultaneously. In Grieg's version, therefore, the *slåtter* have a strongly Lydian cast vertically as well as horizontally. Let this fundamental feature be a guiding principle as you play them.

There is no direct evidence that Grieg conceived of the seventeen *slåtter* as a cycle, but he ordered them in such a way that they can be played as a cycle. In my opinion when they are conceived in this way—when they are played as a suite—they come into their own as the greatest national epic in the history of Norwegian music. The sequence of tonalities follows a remarkable pattern. Nos. 1–7 have D as their key note, a kind of D major, often with a raised—i.e., Lydian—fourth. No. 8 is in A. Let us call it A major, but the important thing is that the key note is A. No. 9 once again has D as its key note, and No. 10 has G. Nos. 11, 12, and 13 return to D, while No. 14 is again in G. No. 15 takes us back to D. Thus it is a tremendous surprise to find that Nos. 16 and 17 are in the key of F. (I write "the key of F" advisedly, for in all cases—be it F, D, or G—the tonality is almost Lydian.) Arranging the key notes in sequence, we find that the Dorian mode hovers over the set as a whole. In this mode, the root tone is D, with G as the subdominant and A as the dominant. After touching on and establishing them (in Nos. 10 and 8), Grieg returns to the key of D, and we could be left with the feeling that the whole set is basically in the key of D were it not for those last two *slåtter* in F. F is the reciting tone, the tuba tone, in the Hypodorian mode. That Grieg consciously intended to intimate the Dorian mode is far from certain, but when playing the pieces one should be aware of this aspect. The ordering of the tonalities underscores the modal character of these dances; think of it as Dorian stage lighting subtly illuminating the whole.

When you play Op. 72 as a complete set, pay special attention to the beginning and the conclusion. Be a little cautious with the tempo and expression in No. 1 so as to create the feeling that the dances gradually emerge, that they rise up like the land out of the sea. Play No. 1 in a restrained manner, softly: one should not play all one's cards in the first dance. The opposite advice applies to No. 17, or perhaps even Nos. 16 and 17. Because they are in the key of F, the tuba tone of the Dorian mode, they have an unreal and unexpected, archaic sound. When the cycle is performed as a whole, the expression in the last two pieces should be rather mild. This is relatively easy to achieve in No. 16, but in No. 17 it is necessary to hold both the rhythm and the volume in check. Look upon No. 17 as one last resonating offshoot of this great work. The powerful nuances can be communicated inwardly and subtly rather than outwardly and directly.

The main difficulty with playing all the dances as a set is that at first hearing they seem quite similar. Therefore, look for a low point and a high point. For a low point it is natural to choose No. 8, *Myllarguten's Wedding March*, which should be played in a tender and restrained manner. Create a peaceful mood by producing on the piano a sound similar to that of the Norwegian *langeleik*, a zitherlike instrument. The most dissonant of the dances is No. 13, *Håvard Gibøen's Dream at the Oterholt Bridge*. The extremely strong dissonances in the last part of this piece bring to mind Bartók's arrangements of Hungarian folk tunes. The *fortissimo* section of No. 13 can be the highest high point of the set, with the dissonances emphasized and even exaggerated. The identification of high and low points is not enough to hold the work as a whole together, but it will help.

Note the bounciness of No. 2, the stately dignity of No. 3, the jaunty, swinging character of No. 4. And one could hardly imagine anything more contrary, more obstinate, than No. 6, which sounds like a distinctly Norwegian portrayal of a decidedly untamed shrew. The most remarkable dance of all is No. 11, *Knut Luraasen's Halling II.* My recommendation is that this piece be played relatively calmly. Grieg's indication is *Allegretto tranquillo*, but pay attention to the *tranquillo* so that your listeners can pick up some of the intricate articulation and surprising rhythmic shifts with which this piece abounds. The melody revolves around various tonal centers and is not easy to hear at first. Once you grasp the basic character of the piece, you may conclude that it is one of the finest in the entire opus. It is useful to have this structure in mind when you play No. 11.

It is easy for the *slåtter* to become too heavy, too massive, probably because they are difficult. With those that are technically demanding, one is tempted to pound out the beat just to keep control. But that is not the way to play these dances, for folk dancers are usually light-footed young people. No. 12, *Myllarguten's Springdans*, is full of youth and excitement. Play it bouncily and animatedly, as if it were being danced by a well-conditioned nineteen-year-old. You need a sparse sound and fingers in top condition.

No. 14, *The Goblins' Bridal Procession at Vossevangen*, is surpassingly beautiful. The bewitching mood at the beginning serves as an introduction to the remainder of the set. Increase the depth and weightiness of your playing in Nos. 14 and 15, then lighten the color as you bring things to a close in Nos. 16 and 17.

The ideas and advice offered here may seem confusing, disorderly, and unsystematic for those who do not play the entire set of *slåtter*. But when you perform Op. 72 as a unified whole, these ideas can be of considerable help and inspiration, as they have been to me.

"Performance practice" has become a popular and overused expression that appears in many contexts. The day is long past when one could play Baroque music as it was written. A pianist who plays the rhythms as they appear in the score will not get very far. No, one must study the performance practice of the Baroque period, insofar as we are able to reconstruct it, and we must try to transfer some of this technique to our modern instruments. The same is true of Chopin's mazurkas. Nobody would dream of playing them exactly as Chopin wrote them—with a steady 3/4 beat from beginning to end!

The situation is the same with the *slåtter*. Listen to the country fiddlers playing the *springar* and the other Norwegian dances! At first you may have the same experience that I had: I simply couldn't understand the rhythm. The fiddlers were keeping time by stomping their right foot, but how could this stomping help them when the beats were always uneven? Later I discovered that different fiddlers used different beats, and that there were differences from one district to another. Especially in western Norway, the rhythm of the *springar* has become very subtle and complex. The three beats in the measure are of different lengths: the second one is the longest, and the third is quite short and leads into the first beat of the next measure, almost like an upbeat. I once recorded several of the *slåtter*, alternating with two country fiddlers, who played the same tunes on the Hardanger fiddle. Their rhythms seemed to be totally different from those in my score! I finally understood that the piano is a totally different instrument from the Hardanger fiddle, and that in Grieg's arrangements for piano the rhythm had to be more regular. When I tried to incorporate some of the fiddlers' flavor I was very clumsy and could not even stomp out the beat, much less play the pieces. Finally I suggested that the fiddlers and their wives dance while I played. Little by little the rhythm of their dancing found its way into my playing, especially in the 3/4 time of the *springars*. As in Chopin's mazurkas (and also in Bach and in early Baroque music) *rubato* is individual.

I found that it is possible to incorporate the irregular *springar* rhythm in some of the dances, in places where Grieg has notated equal quarter notes. When the left hand has a more elaborate part—with rapidly moving eighth notes, for example—it is more difficult to achieve and often results in harmonic muddiness. One passage that lends itself to a *springar* rhythm is the *fortissimo* section of No. 2, *Jon Vestafe's Springdans* (see Ex. 26.1). The music

Ex. 26.1

preceding and following this section does not lend itself to such treatment because of the complexity of the left-hand part. In No. 5, *The Prillar from Os Parish*, it is more difficult to vary the rhythm, but it can be done. The right hand has both eighth notes and triplets, but in measures 1–16 and 35–42 the bass part consists at times of quarter notes and it is possible to make the second beat a little longer.

In No. 12, *Myllarguten's Springdans*—an especially bouncy *slått*—you can prolong the second beat throughout measures 1–26 (see Ex. 26.2). This can also be done in measures 27–50 if you can play the bass like quarter notes with anacruses in between.

Ex. 26.2

Measures 1–19 and 23–41 of No. 13, *Håvard Gibøen's Dream at the Oterholt Bridge*, also lend themselves to a lengthened second beat (see Exx. 26.3a and b.).

Exx. 26.3a and b

In No. 16, *The Maidens from Kivledal*, rhythmic alterations must be made very carefully. However, just a little emphasis—a mere hint of a lengthening—on the second beat rather than the first adds an incredible measure of charm to this dance. It will help you to visualize the shy, heathen maidens of Kivledal as they frolic on the meadow.

One need not employ a *springar* rhythm in all the pieces mentioned. These are some of the places in Grieg's settings that lend themselves to modification consonant with the folk-music tradition in which the tunes originated. It is a matter of individual preference, and you must decide which passages to modify in this way.

In playing the Chopin mazurkas, it is customary to play dotted rhythms differently depending on whether they are written as a dotted eighth note followed by a sixteenth note or as an eighth note followed by a sixteenth rest and a sixteenth note. Traditionally one is permitted to exaggerate the latter pattern a little, and give the music a little more swing. Something similar occurs in Op. 72, especially in the *hallings*. In the passage from No. 4, *Halling from the Fairy Hill*, shown in Ex. 26.4, one might give a little extra swing to

Ex. 26.4

the highest A by extending the sixteenth rest a tenth of a second. The same pattern occurs in No. 13, *Håvard Gibøen's Dream at the Oterholt Bridge* (see Ex. 26.5), and in No. 5, *The Prillar from Os Parish* (see Ex. 26.6), and can be modified to give the rhythm a special twist.

Ex. 26.5

Ex. 26.6

At the beginning of No. 9, *Nils Rekve's Halling*, one might play the left hand quite loud in contrast to the right hand, which leaps up from the *staccato* octave and lands on the open fifth a split second too late. Think of the left hand (the walking dance) as the boy, the right hand (a more swinging dance) as the girl (see Ex. 26.7).

Ex. 26.7

When you are familiar with the *springar* as it is typically played in western Norway, you will instinctively note other passages where the rhythm can be subtly altered. After transcribing these pieces as played by fiddler Knut Dahle, Johan Halvorsen wrote to Grieg that Dahle's rhythms were like trout: just when you thought you had them they slipped away. Since it was impossible to notate them precisely, you must read between the lines.

In addition to the Hardanger fiddle, the pianist should be aware of another indigenous Norwegian instrument, the *langeleik*. The dances in Op. 72 were not performed on it, but you should have its sound in your ears in order to bring out the Old Norse flavor that permeates these pieces. Some passages evoke the image of a tern flying in the fog, of people hovering specterlike in the billowing mist. Some would call these passages "impressionistic," but to Norwegian ears they are reminiscent of the zitherlike sound of the *langeleik*. See, for example, the beginning of No. 3, *Bridal March from Telemark*—especially the passage in Ex. 26.8. You can enhance the *langeleik* effect by holding down the pedal (see Ex. 26.9).

Ex. 26.8

Ex. 26.9

No. 8, *Myllarguten's Wedding March*, sounds almost as if it had been created for the *langeleik*, especially the beginning (see Ex. 26.10a). The same is true of measures 14–16 of No. 11, *Knut Luraasen's Halling II* (see Ex. 26.10b).

Exx. 26.10a and b

Other passages that appear to echo the *langeleik* occur in No. 13 (see Ex. 26.3a), No. 16 (see Ex. 26.11a), and No. 17 (see Ex. 26.11b).

Exx. 26.11a and b

Let the sound of the *langeleik* be your model as you play these tender passages. It will help you to achieve a delicate, slightly veiled, incredibly soft sound, like a hidden, delicate undertone, which can enrich the entire set. When one performs Op. 72 *en suite*, the task of introducing sufficient variation in the seventeen dances seems almost insurmountable. That is when this *dolce* element—with its subtle allusion to the sound of the *langeleik*—becomes very important.

The *slåtter* contain many trills and other figurations, which are easy to produce on the Hardanger fiddle and the *langeleik*, but not, unfortunately, on the modern piano. It is especially difficult to make them soft enough. The figurations are decorations that embellish the melodic line but must not be intrusive. Keeping them light is more important than whether they are played on the beat, before the beat, or midway between two notes. In No. 8, *Myllarguten's Wedding March*, Grieg has indicated that all the figurations are to be played on the beat, at the same time as the bass note. That is fine for No. 8, but I doubt that the same instruction should be applied to the embellishments in No. 1, which seem subtle and light (see Ex. 26.12).

Ex. 26.12

In No. 2, *Jon Vestafe's Springdans*, you might use one kind of trill in measure 50 and another in measure 52 (see Ex. 26.13). In No. 3, *Bridal March from*

Ex. 26.13

Telemark, I play embellishments on the first beat *on* the beat, those on the second beat *before* the beat. I also play the trills *on* the beat and the inverted mordents *before* the beat (see Ex. 26.14).

However, this matter cannot be reduced to a set of rules. It is one of taste, of personal preference. Bach spoke of *le bon goût*—a knack, a sense on the part of the performer achieved after long and careful study. You must develop your own musical sense, and find your own guiding principles. For me embellishments executed *on* the beat convey weightiness, gravity, solemnity, whereas those executed *before* the beat express elegance, lightness, lightheartedness. A

Ex. 26.14

trill between two melodic notes adds connectedness and pliancy; it fills space (see Ex. 26.15).

Ex. 26.15

Grieg wrote in the Preface to Op. 72 that his goal was "to raise these works of the people to an artistic level." This "artistic level" is especially evident in their polyphonic cast. The arrangements do not make use of such advanced devices as complex counterpoint or fixed ostinato voices. Rather, Grieg has written snatches of countermelodies here and there, melodic fragments that illuminate the melody and emphasize the thematic material. They are also the principal source of sonic variation in the *slåtter*. Time and again one has the opportunity to emphasize the tenor, the bass, or the alto voice, sometimes to make it the dominant voice for a while, sometimes to provide momentary contrast to the melody in the soprano. Use your imagination—and your magnifying glass—and you will find endless opportunities for variation, passages where you can bring out hidden melodies or melodic fragments. Do not bring out exactly the same parts each time you perform. One time you can bring out the bass, another time the tenor. Try to emulate the country fiddlers, who exhibit admirable freedom in their playing, varying their performance in countless ways even though the melodic material remains the same.

THE SEVENTEEN SLÅTTER

We turn now to detailed comments about each of the seventeen pieces constituting Op. 72. However, the general comments and suggestions above are the most important and useful things for the interpreter of these pieces. Orient yourself in terms of these overarching principles. Because one's performance should be characterized by freedom, individuality, and personal taste, the general concepts are more important than the details.

No. 1, Håvard Gibøen's Bridal March

Establish a firm rhythm from the very beginning of No. 1. In the pattern in the bass all the notes are played on the afterbeat, and the danger is that they will be construed as occurring on the beats. Feel the rests, and play the notes lightly with an upward hand movement. Then create an unbroken dynamic line all the way from measure 3 to the *fortissimo* in measure 18 (see Exx. 26.12 and 26.16).

Ex. 26.16

Starting at the upbeat to measure 19, the melody is in the alto voice. In this register it can be played in a quite clear and articulated manner (see Ex. 26.17). In measure 21, when the melody is repeated *pianissimo* an octave higher, you might use a little pedal. The parenthesis in measure 22 signifies a broken chord (see Ex. 26.18). The interesting pedal point on G in measure 23 can be emphasized a bit to enhance the melody, which is here repeated in the alto voice.

Ex. 26.17

The *fortissimo* passage that begins with the upbeat to measure 27 requires chords of hardened steel (see Ex. 26.19).

If you wish to emphasize two voices simultaneously, keeping a low wrist makes it easier to articulate clearly. Try this in Ex. 26.20.

Measure 46 is virtually impossible to play as written (see Ex. 26.21a). I divide it up as shown in Ex. 26.21b.

No. 1 ends as it began: from measure 53 to the end it has that same bass

Ex. 26.18

Ex. 26.19

Ex. 26.20

Exx. 26.21a and b

pattern with notes only on the afterbeats. Once again, the rhythm must not be allowed to shift. The ending sounds as if the piece is slowing, but the tempo should remain more or less the same to the very end (see Ex. 26.22).

Ex. 26.22

No. 2, Jon Vestafe's Springdans

The two introductory measures establishing the bouncy rhythmic pattern in the bass were composed by Grieg. In Halvorsen's transcription the piece begins with the melody that appears in the soprano in measures 3–4 (see Ex. 26.23). The pattern in the bass is quite sophisticated, with a little stress on the

Ex. 26.23

third beat. Do not let it become a strong dynamic accent, or it will dominate and quicken the tempo. But it is fine to have a tiny little *sforzando* within the *piano* dynamic level in measures 1–16 (see Ex. 26.24).

Ex. 26.24

The *sforzando* on the third beat in measure 18 followed by *subito piano* in measure 19 is very effective. This pattern appears frequently in the *slåtter*, i.e., a *crescendo* leading to an accent on what would otherwise be a weak beat, and then an abrupt *piano*.

Measures 23–28 have an interesting countermelody in the left hand. The descending chromatic scale is familiar to us from a number of other works, notably Op. 66. Bring it out here, too.

The first part of the recapitulation—measures 31–34—can use a little more pedal than the opening measures. The rest of the piece should be played with very little pedal (see Exx. 26.25a and b).

Exx. 26.25a and b

Starting in measure 76 it is very difficult to emphasize the melody properly because it lies buried in a welter of other notes. As a last resort, to bring out the middle voice, try extending your finger and holding it straight down (see Ex. 26.26).

Ex. 26.26

The grand, virtuosic *finale*, beginning in measure 81, should be played incisively and cleanly. Bring out the chromatically descending octaves in the left hand in measures 81–86 (see Ex. 26.27).

Ex. 26.27

Jon Vestafe's Springdans should be played as if it were a matter of life and death. Jon Vestafe, from Tinn in Telemark, was imprisoned on suspicion of murder. At his trial, he asked to be granted one last wish—that he be allowed to play a *slått*. He played this *springdans* so dazzlingly that he was set free on the spot. So: play for your life!

No. 3, *Bridal March from Telemark*

This piece is marked *Alla Marcia* and is scored in 4/4 time, but Grieg's one-measure introduction has an *alla breve* character. However, the tempo should not be fast. To the contrary, there must be time to execute the numerous figurations and rhythmic subtleties. It helps to create a swinging plasticity if you think in terms of two beats per measure rather than four (see above, Ex. 26.14). The exceedingly lovely melody in the tenor voice can be emphasized a bit in measures 2–4 and 6–8.

Starting in measure 10, marked *dolce*, the sound may be quite tender, but make sure that all the voices are heard. The relation of the tenor voice to the soprano is especially important. Measure 11 creates a strong feeling of harmonic friction—like a narrow place in a river. In the case of a river, the narrowing holds the water back, interrupts its forward flow. Something like that occurs harmonically in measure 11—and then in the next measure it breaks loose and resumes its course, so slow the tempo just a bit in the "narrowing" in measure 11 (see above, Ex. 26.8).

The middle section, which starts at the upbeat to measure 14, is a military march attached to the bridal march (see Ex. 26.28).

The most grandiose feature in the piece is the ostinato bass figure. It creates a nice effect if you let it get gradually louder, but not farther than *mezzo forte* the first time through. At the repeat, do not start out *pianissimo*, but continue *mezzo forte*, and this time take it to *molto forte*, almost to *fortissimo*. That creates a longer line (see Ex. 26.29).

There is enormous dynamic contrast between measures 28–29, marked *pianissimo*, and measures 30–31, marked *fortissimo* (see Exx. 26.30).

Ex. 26.28

Ex. 26.29

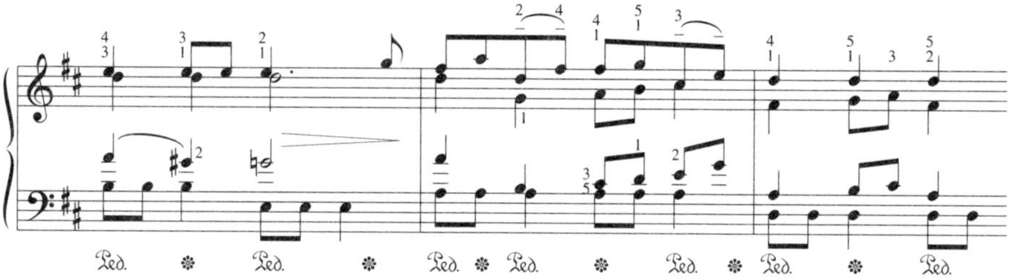

Ex. 26.30

The coda should be played transparently, so your listeners can follow the movement in all four voices (see Ex. 26.31).

Ex. 26.31

This beautiful bridal march from Telemark is very fetching, very dramatic. In Norway it is sometimes called "Brudens tårer" (The Bride's Tears). This wedding was not just a happy occasion!

Norwegian Peasant Dances (slåtter), Op. 72

No. 4, Halling from the Fairy Hill

What is most distinctive about this piece is its rhythmic pattern. Leave a little space between the first and second beats in the left hand, and give a little accent to the syncopated beat. Coordinate this carefully with the rhythm in the right hand, which leaps into the air on the third eighth note. The result is exciting and elegant. Your fingers and your thoughts must be those of a frisky young person! (see above, Ex. 26.4.)

The placement of the *sforzando* in measures 11 and 21 is also important (see Exx. 26.32 and 26.33). All these things work together to create a vibrant rhythm in which the accents occur at the most unexpected places—everywhere except on the first beat!

Ex. 26.32

Ex. 26.33

The transition to the middle section can be very effective. The solitary A in measure 28 is like a note blown on a Norwegian *lur*. Strike it in a swinging manner with pedal, depress the key silently, release the pedal, then alternate between pedal and depressed key without pedal. This will produce a vibrato effect, as if the sound of the *lur* were echoing across the valley (see Ex. 26.34).

The middle section, composed by Grieg, is polyphonic and four-voiced. In this piece and in No. 7, *Røtnams Knut*, the note values in the middle section are double those of the rest of the piece.

With respect to expression, there are at least four different possibilities to employ at various times. Measures 29–36, marked *espressivo*, should be *legato* (see Ex. 26.35a). When this phrase is repeated an octave higher in measures

Ex. 26.34

Ex. 26.35a

37–44, use more pedal and emphasize the soprano voice a little more (see Ex. 26.35b). The *poco mosso* section should perhaps be played more transparently, using a slightly lower hand, raised fingers, and little weight (see Ex. 26.36). The recapitulation is darker and more weighty. Emphasize this quality by stressing the octaves in the left hand (see Ex. 26.37). The coda sounds good *sempre* pedal (see Ex. 26.38).

Ex. 26.35b

Ex. 26.36

Ex. 26.37

Ex. 26.38

It is important to have a wide range of tone colors at your disposal when you play the *slåtter*, especially if you play them as a complete cycle. Unless you vary the coloring, they will sound too much alike and boring for your audience. With a lot of coloring, Op. 72 can be especially interesting.

Tradition has it that this dance was originally sung to one Brynjulf Olson by a *hulder*, a troll. With a mischievous and fetching smile, she is said to have sung, "Near the top of the mountain you will find your ox." She was beautiful—and suddenly she was gone.

No. 5, The Prillar from Os Parish

Here, as in the previous piece, Grieg wrote two introductory measures to establish the rhythm that prevails in the counterpoint (see Ex. 26.39). As always in a *springar*, pay special attention to the second beat. Make use of the conflict between the accent on beat 1 in the left hand and the slight stress on beat 2 in the right (see Ex. 26.40).

Use a little pedal on the repeat an octave higher (see Ex. 26.41). The afterbeats in the left hand must be precise (see Ex. 26.42).

The left hand controls the rhythm from measure 23 to the coda. It is both a supportive rhythmic factor and an illuminating melodic-contrapuntal line in contrast to the soprano voice (see Ex. 26.43).

Ex. 26.39

Ex. 26.40

Ex. 26.41

Ex. 26.42

In measures 37 and 38, give the rhythm an extra swing by lengthening the sixteenth rests (see above, Ex. 26.6).

The last two measures sound like an addendum. This ending is reminiscent of Norwegian folk ballads, which often end with something like, "That's what he said" (see Ex. 26.44).

Ex. 26.43

Ex. 26.44

No. 6, Myllarguten's Gangar

This music is the most cantankerous imaginable. The musical elements are so completely thought out, so spicy, so brilliantly arranged. The resulting polyrhythms and polyphony are difficult to bring out, and one must also pay attention to the articulation, the ties, and the slurs. Even though nothing seems to fit with anything else, one must maintain an uninterrupted beat in the left hand (see Ex. 26.45). In measures 7–8 the rhythm resembles hemiolas with an added beat.

Ex. 26.45

Starting in measure 23 the accents are incredibly interesting. At first the left hand has accents on beat 1 in contrast to various unexpected patterns in the right hand (see Ex. 26.46). Starting in measure 27, the left hand has accents on both main beats, while those in the right hand vary, as before. In addition to the contrary, complicated, contorted accents, there are descending octaves in the left hand (see Ex. 26.47).

The beat in this masterpiece must be as solid as the Rock of Gibraltar. The

Ex. 26.46

Ex. 26.47

sturdier and more exaggerated it is, the greater is the impact of the many surprises scattered through the piece.

Near the beginning there is a direct imitation of the Hardanger fiddle, with the D and the A imitating drone strings (see Ex. 26.48). Play the A's in the alto voice as *legato* as possible, ideally with no space between them. The A will then be sustained, in contrast to the articulated voice above and the short, percussive monotone below.

Ex. 26.48

No. 7, Røtnams Knut. Halling

It was said of the Knut after whom this piece is named that "he was both wild and tame." The implications for its performance are obvious. Once again, the accompaniment starts on an offbeat, creating confusion and making it difficult to establish where the downbeat is. Be sure to feel the rest clearly. Play the fifth lightly, with an upward movement. Note the unexpected and irregularly placed accents (see Ex. 26.49).

Ex. 26.49

The *subito piano* shown in Ex. 26.50 is very effective. In measures 19–23, the left hand introduces some good contrary motion (see Ex. 26.51). The recapitulation features pedal points in the left hand and asymmetrical accents in the right (see Ex. 26.52).

Exx. 26.50 and 26.51

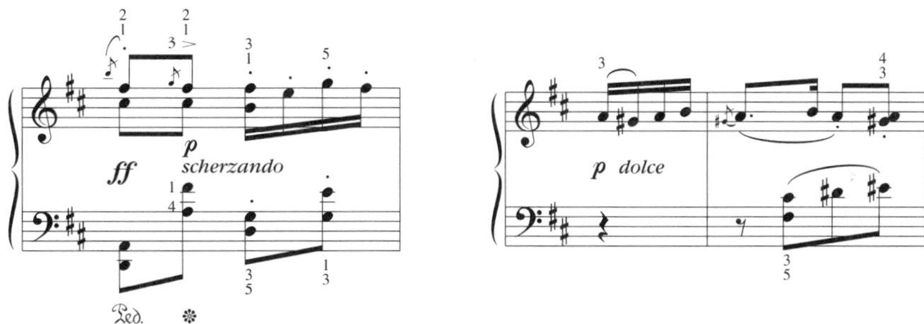

Ex. 26.52

The middle part, in doubled note values, is the longest section in the *slåtter* composed by Grieg. It creates breadth and scope in the landscape; suddenly things are not so concentrated, so compressed. There is time to breathe, to broaden out, to shape some longer lines. Emphasize the pedal points starting in measure 87 (see Ex. 26.53).

Measures 87–94 may be played transparently, perhaps with a lowered wrist and fingers held relatively high, creating a sound like a reed organ. Play *legato* and with very little pedal. When this passage is repeated an octave

Ex. 26.53

higher, in measures 95–102, the sound will be enhanced if you play a little more gently and use more pedal (see Ex. 26.54).

Ex. 26.54

The polyphony in the recapitulation is very effective (see Ex. 26.55).

Ex. 26.55

Grieg was a master of instrumentation. When he presents the melody in octaves, try to achieve a *dolce* effect, a sound that soars rather than stomps. Give some preference to the soprano voice to brighten the music in contrast to the dark sound in the left hand at the end (see Ex. 26.56).

Ex. 26.56

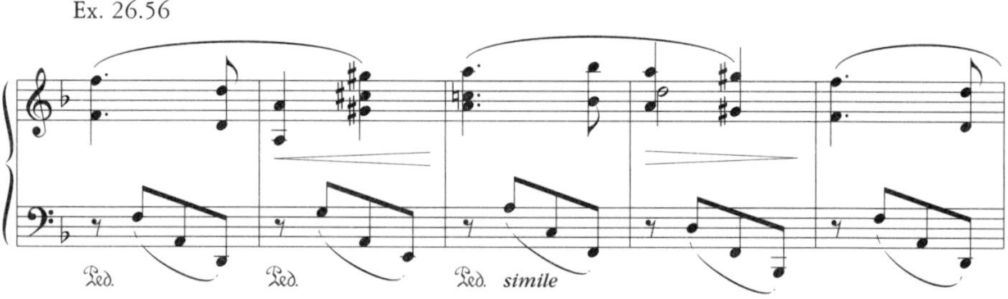

Røtnams Knut is the showiest number in Op. 72. Knut had a reputation as a fighter and a troublemaker. He was said to be the strongest man in Hallingdal until the new pastor came to the community. One day when Knut was drunk and quarrelsome, the pastor told him to leave. Knut declined, held onto the door frame, and refused to budge. But the pastor was even stronger: he threw him out, door frame and all!

No. 8, Myllarguten's Wedding March

The legendary fiddler Myllarguten wrote this wedding march for his beloved Kari, who jilted him to marry someone else. It is said that the plaintive motive in measures 13–14 and 17–18 represents the distraught lover sadly calling out her name (see Ex. 26.57).

Ex. 26.57

The piece is an absolute pearl. It is very beautiful in its restrained sorrow. Play it reverently, but without losing the inexorable rhythm that continues throughout. The sound of this piece is similar to that of a *langeleik*. The attack can be handled in various ways, but maintain a light touch. Only the tips of your fingers should touch the keys. Try to feel the keys' upward movement more than their downward movement to achieve sensitive playing. A countermelody begins in measure 50 (see Ex. 26.58).

Ex. 26.58

Myllarguten's Wedding March is like a slow movement in the middle of the set—the axis of the cycle, in a way, the piece around which the other sixteen revolve. Take plenty of time before you start, and when you have finished allow sufficient time for it to sink in. It is the still water, the quiet forest, the meditative heart—and a fleeting glimpse of the inexorable march of fate.

No. 9, Nils Rekve's Halling

This lively *halling* gets the second part of the cycle off to a rousing start. It is marked *Maestoso*, so it should not be played too fast. As so often in the *slåtter*, varying accent patterns create polyrhythmic relationships between the hands. A repeated ostinato bass figure provides the foundation for the dance. The Lydian tinge in the melody is employed harmonically. The first bass chord is the Lydian D and G♯—an augmented fourth—sounded simultaneously. So the *halling* is Lydian vertically as well as horizontally (see above, Ex. 26.7).

The many *forte* accents can become overpowering. Focus the accents on the melodic line. In the opening, this means accent only the soprano voice. If you are playing *Nils Rekve's Halling* by itself you might do it differently, but within the context of the whole set, softening the accent pattern here provides some variation and helps avoid a steady diet of harsh accents.

Measures 11–14 contain some simple but effective counterpoint in the form of descending scales with nice echo effects (see Ex. 26.59).

Ex. 26.59

The bass notes are divided interestingly in measures 21–24: a pattern of 2 + 2 alternates with one in which all four eighth notes are accented (see Ex. 26.60).

Ex. 26.60

As in No. 5, in *Nils Rekve's Halling* the left hand sets the pace both rhythmically and melodically-contrapuntally in the last part of the piece. Follow the lead of the left hand in both tone color and rhythm (see Ex. 26.61).

From measure 31 on play the left hand *staccato*, like a soft bassoon, so it

Ex. 26.61

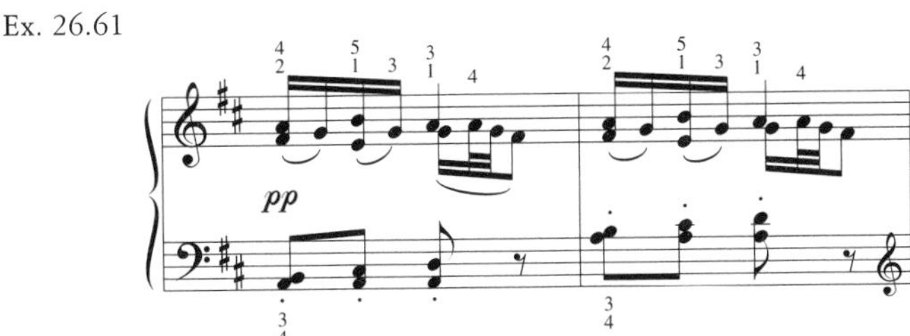

does not get too heavy and muddy in the low register. As always in Grieg's music, the final anacrusis should be short. If it is played at the last possible moment, it lends excitement to the conclusion (see Ex. 26.62).

Ex. 26.62

No. 10, Knut Luråsen's Halling I

This number is wonderfully effective whether you play it by itself or as part of the cycle. Within the context of the whole cycle it comes across as youthful and refreshing. Once again Grieg chose an almost primitively simple accompaniment, but a very interesting polyrhythm results from the differing patterns in the two hands (see Ex. 26.63).

Ex. 26.63

At the beginning, as well as later in the piece, the top note of the chords should come out clearly, and the chords must not be thick and flabby. Especially when in the higher registers—in the second and third octaves above middle C—a strong, vigorous fingertip is needed to produce a sparkling *staccato* (see Ex. 26.64).

Ex. 26.64

The accompaniment in measures 26–34 is a stroke of genius. This glorious ostinato is like a man repeatedly swinging a scythe (see Ex. 26.65).

Ex. 26.65

The unexpected accents both preceding and following measures 37–43 (see Exx. 26.66 and 26.67) are difficult to execute without destroying the primary rhythm.

Ex. 26.66

Ex. 26.67

The articulation in the coda is ingenious with its ties and slurs of varying lengths and, in measure 46, an abrupt *sforzando* brutally placed in the middle of a soft passage. Try to execute it without disrupting the principal rhythm.

The *stretto* at the end is very effective. The last three chords are precise and resilient. They are marked *fff*, so make them as loud as you can.

This *slått* is sometimes called "Hjerki Haukeland," and therein lies an interesting story. Hjerki was engaged to Øystein Lurås, a brother of Knut Lurås from Telemark. But she broke her engagement and went off to Bergen to marry a ship's captain. She had received a beautiful silver Telemark belt from Øystein as an engagement present, and she had the audacity to wear it on her wedding day. But the young fiddlers from Telemark were not about to take this insult lying down. Knut Luråsen composed a *halling*, and he and his brother went to the wedding. Knut played the *halling*, and Øystein asked his former fiancée for a dance. As they danced, he cut the belt with his knife and left. Hjerki was not hurt, but presumably she learned that it is dangerous to play with the affections of fiddlers from Telemark.

No. 11, Knut Luråsen's Halling II

This piece is perhaps the greatest, most important, most complicated of all the *hallings*. Its overall impression is of something unreal, irregular, balladic. The clue to finding the predominant mood lies in the pedal points—first on D, then on A (see Exx. 26.68a and b). Later the accompaniment changes to open fifths and more elaborate bass figures (see Ex. 26.68c).

Exx. 26.68a and b

Ex. 26.68c

This *bourdon*, bagpipe character, which resembles the sound of the drone strings of the Hardanger fiddle, should be heard as something inexorable, unifying. Rhythmically these components are very simple, almost stereotypical, but in this dance their structure is subtly articulated and subdivided (see Ex. 26.69).

Ex. 26.69

The *scherzando* section, marked *forte*, incorporates a sophisticated hemiola rhythm. It contrasts with the first part of the *halling*, which is basically duple (see Ex. 26.70).

Ex. 26.70

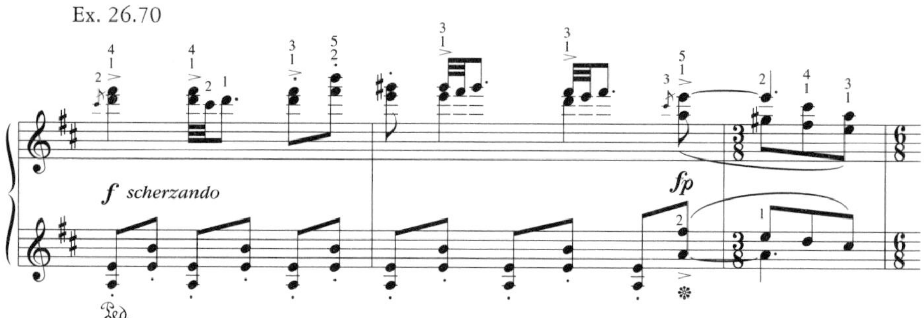

Do not slow down in measure 28. But measure 31, which serves as a transition to the *tranquillo* section, can tolerate a slight *ritardando* (see Exx. 26.71a and b).

The *tranquillo* section is marked *dolce*. To produce a *cantabile* effect and let

Exx. 26.71a and b

the melody sing out in the soprano voice, keep the wrist and the fingers relaxed.

In measures 32–37 let the left hand lead. Maintain a steady rhythm and slowly increase the volume as you move toward the *forte* in measure 38 (see Ex. 26.72).

Ex. 26.72

The *tranquillo* passage in measures 41–44 features a duet at an interval of a tenth between soprano and tenor. Keeping your wrists rather low will help you bring out these two voices.

In measures 45–48 it is very difficult to bring out the melodic line because it is sandwiched between the other notes in the right hand. The melody is played mostly by the second, third, and fourth fingers; it helps to keep them rather straight, almost rigid.

Measures 49–52, marked *fortissimo feroce*, are followed by a more conciliatory coda *a tempo tranquillo*. Within this quieter passage, bring out the *rin-*

forzandos on weak beats in measures 59 and 62, more with expression than with the degree of loudness. Take a little time, create a transition (see Ex. 26.73).

Ex. 26.73

The conclusion calls for a steady *diminuendo*, but even here Grieg has introduced irregular counterrhythms. The last three measures incorporate a sophisticated interplay between triple and duple groupings (see Ex. 26.74).

Ex. 26.74

No. 12, Myllarguten's Springdans

The most important element in the interpretation of this piece is to use the irregular *springar* rhythm described earlier, for *springdans* is just another word for *springar*. Clarity is important. Use very little pedal, as figurations and trills occur frequently. Practice without pedal to begin with, then gradually add a little as needed.

If you have difficulty with the left hand in measure 26, bend the thumb and turn it inward; then play the A with the nail and the upper B♭ with the edge of the first joint (see Ex. 26.75).

Ex. 26.75

The accompaniment in the second half of the piece tends to turn into a series of triplets instead of the dotted eighths and sixteenths called for in the score. Make the sixteenth notes very short, almost like anacruses.

This dance is sometimes called "Igletveiten," after a fiddler who was said to be just as skilled as his famous contemporary, Myllarguten. One summer he took a lesson from the fiddler Håvard Gibøen, and he agreed to cut some hay in return. On his way home, he realized that in the process of cutting the hay, he had forgotten the *slått* he was to have learned. He went back and learned it again—and this time he remembered it.

No. 13, Håvard Gibøen's Dream at the Oterholt Bridge

Tradition has it that Håvard Gibøen was on a trip, and on the way he lay down to sleep beside the Oterholt Bridge. His dream was this *springar*.

The mood ranges from very tender to the sharpest, harshest dissonances imaginable. The first part may be played in a *langeleik* style, with a gliding, flowing rhythm in the left hand. When the melody is repeated, *staccato*, with embellishments, play without pedal. The soft, swaying, *legato* passages contrast with the short, snappy, *staccato* ones many times throughout the dance, like a dialogue.

The reach in the right hand in measures 19–22 is difficult at times. Try playing the recurring A with the left hand (see above, Ex. 26.5).

The chords in measures 23ff. tend to get too heavy. Play sparsely and bring out the melody in the soprano voice. In measures 39–41 the melody tends to get lost because it is in the middle voice. Straighten the second and third fingers. But keep the arm loose, otherwise you will not be able to bring out the melody (see Ex. 26.76).

Ex. 26.76

In measures 42-45 do not let the chords on the afterbeats in the left hand distort the rhythm. Let the right hand control it here. Beginning at measure 46, however, the left hand should lead both rhythmically and dynamically as you build toward the *fortissimo* in measure 54. Be careful to bring out the interesting articulation in the right hand in measures 48–53 (see Exx. 26.77a, b, and c).

Exx. 26.77a, b, and c

Bring out the ascending line in the bass in measures 51–53. The dissonance in the *marcato* passage that begins in measure 54 is razor-sharp, excruciating, and *fortissimo*! Bear in mind that this is the dissonant high point of the cycle. Play with a booming, pounding rhythm; pull out all the stops. Keep your fingers close to the keys, the closer the better. A *fortissimo marcato* should not be played from three inches above the keyboard, but needs an intense, direct attack from close range. That will give you a wild, macabre sound without any extraneous noises.

The counterpoint in the left hand is brilliant. It first pounds away in octaves, then leaps over the melody and sparkles like lightning above a churning sea (see Exx. 26.78a and b). Old Thor cannot be far away!

Measures 62–71 constitute a graceful little coda for this *springdans*. Articulate the right hand, but listen to the rhythm in the bass.

No. 14, The Goblins' Bridal Procession at Vossevangen

According to legend, the goblins were holding a wedding at Vossevangen. A little fiddler—a goblin, of course—in a pointed red cap led the bridal proces-

Exx. 26.78a and b

sion. As it begins one can see a mountainscape, perhaps a picture of Vossevangen. Then the music describes the little forest pixies who appear in the distance, come closer, pass by, and disappear.

The introduction, in a free tempo, is lovely. In Nos. 4 and 7, Grieg created two-measure introductions using the accompaniment figure and added a middle section of his own invention, employing doubled note values. In No. 14, as if inspired by all the preceding *slåtter*, Grieg has gathered some of the thoughts and feelings from those dances and expressed them in a captivating way in the introduction. A beautiful rolled chord followed by a series of crystal-clear notes in a high register create a bright mood. There is no doubt that the weather at Vossevangen is sunny and clear! In contrast, the chromatic figure starting on C in the tenor voice should be played in a singing *legato*. The rests can also be very effective (see Ex. 26.79).

Ex. 26.79

The sixteenth-note triplet at the end of measure 1 is the upbeat to the *slått*, which is marked *Allegretto*. From this point forward maintain an absolutely even tempo, a *gangar* ("walking dance") rhythm—not rigidly metronomic, but even in a human way, suitable for walking. The *Allegretto* must not be too fast for you to make a clear rhythmic distinction between two thirty-second notes followed by a sixteenth and a sixteenth-note triplet. This distinction is often blurred, with the pattern in measure 3 being played just like the one in measure 4 (see Ex. 26.80).

The dotted quarter notes in the left hand establish the *gangar* rhythm and give the dance its form, its architecture. The right hand follows along. Execute a steady *crescendo* in measures 8–11 to a *forte* at the beginning of

Ex. 26.80

measure 12. Note the *piano subito* at the upbeat to measure 16. Here the *gangar* rhythm is still controlled by the left hand, but in the descant register. Instead of providing a foundation for the harmony it has the effect of a mirage. Still, it must be perfectly even. In measures 24–37 the *gangar* rhythm becomes more direct, almost pounding (see Exx. 26.81a and b).

Exx. 26.81a and b

Note Grieg's minute notation of the articulation with slurs and weak-beat accents in measures 38–41 (see Ex. 26.82). Bring out the hemiolas in alter-

Ex. 26.82

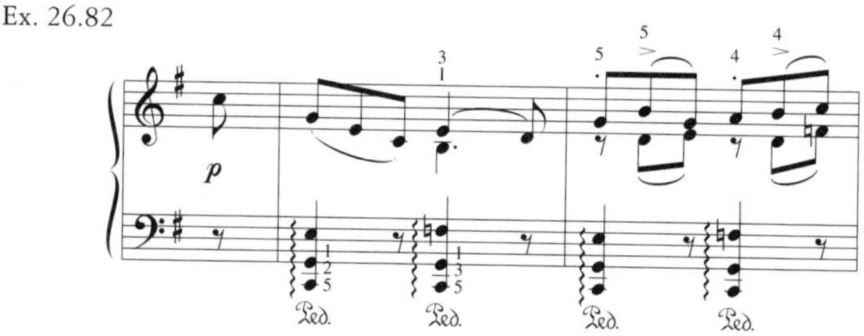

nate measures, starting in measure 43, against the duple pattern in the other voices (see Ex. 26.83).

In measures 32–37 the same motive is repeated three times. Measure 34 is more melodic than measures 32 and 36. See the chord progressions in Exx. 26.84a, b, and c). The harmonies are not pure, but are based on secondary

Ex. 26.83
Exx. 26.84a, b, and c

relationships. The sonority here can be a little gentler and rounded off, perhaps a *quasi cantabile*. In measures 32 and 36 we have only triads, so perhaps the sonority can be more direct.

In the upbeat to measure 38, as in the previous instance, the *piano subito* is effective. At this point the counterrhythms become even more sophisticated, including not only hemiolas but also irregular accents, on such beats as 2 and 5. The pattern varies from measure to measure, with interesting contrasts between duple rhythm and hemiolas. Pay attention to articulation. *Staccatos*, accents, and slurs are important in the interpretation of this piece.

Measures 54–63 constitute a kind of coda, a *sortie*. The music dies away, the *slått* is coming to an end. Try to produce three types of sonority: a "warm" sound in the first octave, a brighter one in the second, and an austere one in the third (see Ex. 26.85).

Play the concluding arpeggio as softly as you can, yet clear as crystal and with no *rubato*.

Ex. 26.85

No. 15, The Skuldal Bride

The story of the Skuldal bride is dramatic. The young lady in question was the most beautiful girl in the valley, and her father insisted that she marry an old man, whom she did not love, so that his farm and her father's might eventually be joined. She asked for and received a most beautiful bridal attire—a colorful national costume with elaborate trimmings in silver and gold. On her wedding day she donned the dress and suddenly disappeared. Choosing death rather than a miserable life, she leaped into the waterfall and drowned.

The Skuldal Bride is the dramatic high point of Op. 72, the pinnacle of majestic pride, *maestoso e marcato*. Play this sturdy piece broadly but not too fast. Its wealth of rhythmic and harmonic subtleties are in danger of getting slighted if the tempo is too quick. Like the previous piece, No. 15 is a *gangar*. In *gangars* the dotted quarter notes must be absolutely stable, of equal length throughout the piece. They provide the skeleton, the framework on which the piece is built (see Ex. 26.86).

Ex. 26.86

Once again Grieg employs hemiola effects concurrently with a continuing duple rhythm in the left hand.

The accents on weak beats that we observed in No. 14 appear again, but here they are introduced at the very beginning and become more and more prominent as the piece proceeds. Practicing the two pieces alternately will point up the differences in accent patterns and articulation.

In measures 16–57 Grieg uses hemiolas with great frequency. Measures 16–18 consist of one measure of hemiola, one in duple time, then one in duple time with counterrhythms in the left hand. *Il basso marcato*, with the right hand playing a more accompanying role, adds to the interest (see Ex. 26.87).

Ex. 26.87

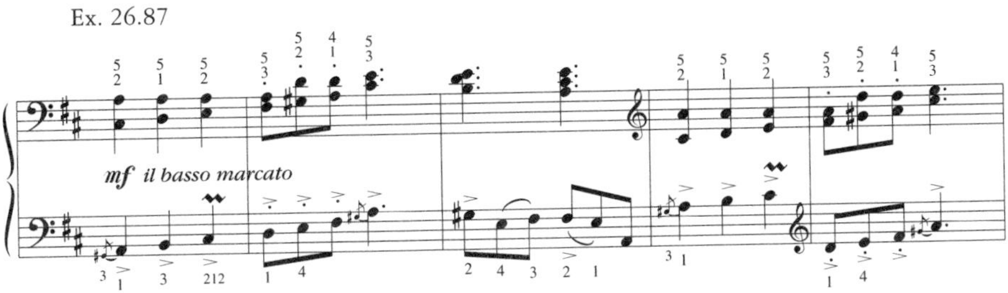

The dissonances become harsher and harsher, with numerous seconds (including minor seconds) and sevenths. The chords bring to mind Bartók and Kodály. That is not surprising, for they had studied Grieg's Op. 72. The rhythms clash sharply and accents explode at unexpected places. The whole process reaches its culmination in the *marcatissimo fortissimo* section that begins at measure 39. Both the duple and the hemiola rhythms must be precisely maintained (see Ex. 26.88).

Ex. 26.88

Try to vary the sonority in measures 35–38. Measures 36 and 38 should not sound like echoes of the preceding measures, but they can be a little softer, like answers to a question. Grieg has implied such a contrast with the differences in the left hand in alternating measures, but it can be underscored with a little lighter attack in measures 36 and 38 (see Ex. 26.89).

The *marcatissimo* section ends with a *subito piano* in measure 43 and some clever articulation in the right hand. As in *Knut Luråsen's Halling II*, there are also a few measures in 3/8. Even when playing softly it is imperative to feel and communicate the polyrhythmic elements (see Ex. 26.90).

The rolled-chord accompaniment in measures 54–58 creates a somewhat bizarre effect before the bass part changes to a more *legato* pattern with a pedal point on E. It moves to a pedal point on A before finally cadencing in D major.

Ex. 26.89

Ex. 26.90

The coda, *piano dolce*, begins with the upbeat to measure 68. Play it like a reverberation, a winding down. The last part of the coda alternates between G chords and D chords. This plagal effect is further reinforced in measure 82 by a brief excursion into G minor. The tenor note, D, emerges from this chord alone, like a solitary *lur*, before the final chord is sounded *pianissimo* in the home key of D major. To be sure that the D still sounds in measure 83, stress it a bit when it is struck in the preceding measure (see Ex. 26.91).

Ex. 26.91

Keep a relatively low wrist in the last part in order to bring out the polyphonic features. A heavy touch tends to make all the voices sound alike. As in the previous piece, the chords must be played clearly and precisely. Thus your hand must be quite rigid so the triads will be as crisp as possible. But combine a rigid hand with a flexible arm so the sound does not get hard.

No. 16, The Maidens from Kivledal. Springdans

After the long series of pieces in D, G, A, and then D again, the cycle receives a new harmonic and tonal twist as it moves to F major for the last two pieces.

As previously stated, F is the tuba tone in the Hypodorian mode, i.e., the note on which the priest—after all the preparations, all the preliminaries—proclaims the gospel. That is the position in which Grieg placed these two versions of *The Maidens from Kivledal*, and that is their role if the cycle is played in its entirety.

The story associated with these two *slåtter* concerns the last two heathen girls in Seljord, a small town in Telemark. One Sunday morning they sat on the mountainside during mass and played so beautifully on the ram's horn that the congregation listened to them instead of to the priest. Soon the entire congregation left the church to stand on the hillside and listen to the lovely sound wafting across the valley. The priest remonstrated and argued, but to no avail. Finally he resorted to ecclesiastical power: he had the two girls condemned. One of them was dashed against the cliff and turned into a moss rose, the other became a column of stone. And to this day, according to the legend, they can be seen in the Kivle valley of Telemark.

Nos. 16 and 17 are the oldest tunes in the collection, and both the melodies and the harmonies have a Medieval cast. After a two-measure introduction, No. 16 begins with a plaintive melody in the soprano voice that is repeated several times. Try to achieve a crystal-clear tone, and make the melismas and embellishments as light as feathers.

Measures 15–22 are rhythmically interesting, with dotted-eighth and sixteenth notes, triplets, duplets, some notes with slurs, some with *staccato*. Articulate precisely. The simpler the accompaniment in the left hand the easier it is to work in rhythmic variations in a natural and flexible way. As with *springars* generally, the second beat can be lengthened slightly at the expense of the third (see Ex. 26.92).

Ex. 26.92

At measure 22 the forward progress of the music suddenly stops. The figure in the right hand of the next measure is a *lokk*, a type of folk tune associated with the calling of farm animals. It imitates a ram's horn, and with each of its four iterations, the harmonization and embellishment vary (see above, Ex. 26.11a). Play the arpeggios in measures 29–31 before the beat. Start them soon enough so that they fit in naturally between the beats, and vary them each time (see Ex. 26.93).

Note the elegant articulation in the principal melody, both at the begin-

Ex. 26.93

ning and in the recapitulation (see Ex. 26.94). The afterbeat in the melody in measures 8, 12, etc., is more harmonic than melodic. Play it as if it were a sounding of a drone string on a Hardanger fiddle. On the piano we can produce such a tone by playing it much softer than the rest of the notes.

Ex. 26.94

In the concluding phrases Grieg brilliantly combines Medieval and Romantic harmonic elements. The authentic Old Norse rhythm is combined with the descending chromatic line—an unmistakably Romantic touch—that Grieg so dearly loved (see Ex. 26.95).

Ex. 26.95

The piece ends in F major, but even as you bring it to a close there is room for a little swinging *springar* rhythm, a final little reminder.

No. 17, The Maidens from Kivledal. Gangar

If we view Op. 72 as Norway's great national musical epic, there are certain implications for the way we perform No. 17. Although Grieg sometimes calls for *fortissimo*, it is better to treat *ff* as *forte*, or *rinforzando*—more as an expression of strong inner tension than of outward power. Let me offer one final suggestion to tie the whole cycle together: In connection with No. 1, *Håvard Gibøen's Bridal March*, I advised being a little cautious with the tempo and expression so as to create the feeling that the dances gradually rise up like the land out of the sea. The varied richness that emerged from the sea in No. 1 has been present in various fascinating ways in the fifteen *slåtter* that followed; now, in No. 17, it is about to sink below the horizon again. Thus conceived, the second musical depiction of *The Maidens from Kivledal* takes on new meaning. One can imagine this *gangar* being played in the gathering twilight, or at the end of the rainbow: its sounds envelop us as the *slåtter* disappear into the sea whence they came.

All of Grieg's sophisticated compositional devices are present in this piece, but they are hinted at, suggested, rather than flung in our face. In some passages you can use a little pedal—for example, in Ex. 26.96, where the right hand illuminates the overtones of the B♭–F chord in the bass—rather than differentiate each individual interval.

Ex. 26.96

Measures 31–34, marked *pianissimo*, can be the softest passage in the entire cycle. Hushed down, smoothed out with shimmering pedal, it is very effective as the dynamic low point. Then Grieg gives this *slått* another Romantic touch with a descending chromatic line in the bass voice (see Ex. 26.97).

Ex. 26.97

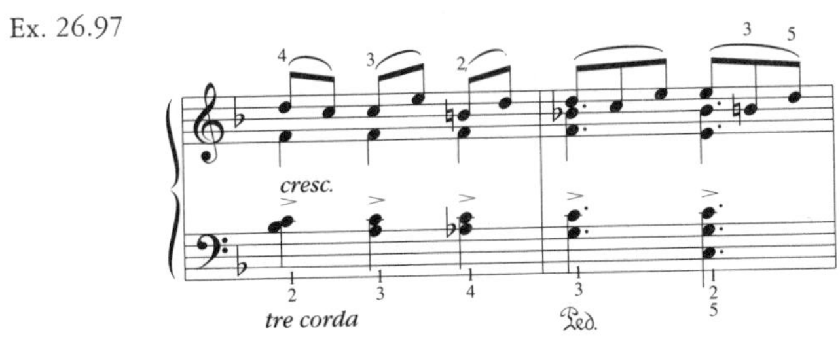

There are contrasting rhythms of various kinds, but the basic duple beat must be present at all times. Don't let this *gangar* turn into a syrupy little piece in which the underlying rhythm drops out of sight.

The tempo slows down a bit at measure 39, *tranquillo*, and stays at that level for the remainder of the piece. Such a systematic modification of the rhythm differs from an arbitrary, uncontrolled romanticizing of it. A hemiola rhythm appears in contrast to the underlying beat in measure 39 and elsewhere (see Ex. 26.98a). Sometimes the rhythmic pattern is varied through the use of slurs, ties, grace notes, and unexpected accents (see Ex. 26.98b).

Exx. 26.98a and b

The many embellishments call for a good deal of active finger work. Try to create an echo in measures 13–14 and 17–18. I recommend that the trills in measures 16 and 18 be fingered 2–4–3. The slurs in measures 20 and 22, followed in both cases by accents on beats 5 and 6, contend with the underlying rhythm—as if the hemiola rhythm were challenging the duple *gangar* rhythm for dominance.

The beautiful coda is essentially modal, although it has some chromatic passages. It rests on a pedal point on F and an inverted pedal point C that finally resolves to F in the next-to-last measure. The open fifths should be slightly stressed. The coda serves as a marvelous conclusion to this great cycle. The sound came from the mountain (the maidens playing the ram's horn), and it returns to the mountains.

It is possible to play the *slåtter* as individual pieces, but the effect will never be as overwhelming as that of the entire set as a cycle. When playing the whole set, there are many more things to bear in mind beyond what appears on the printed score. Many details of each piece come to life and are enhanced, and many things must be modified when viewed in relation to a larger whole. Each kind of performance has its own rewards, but you must perform the whole cycle to get "the whole Norway."

CHAPTER

27

Moods, Op. 73

We have come to Grieg's last opus for piano and the next-to-last in his entire oeuvre. Not all the pieces in Op. 73 are late, however. No. 5, *Study (Hommage à Chopin)*, was sketched at the same time as *Folk Song*, Op. 12, No. 5. The only complete composition that comes after *Moods* is *Four Psalms*, Op. 74, a choral work.

Op. 73 brings up a problem that Grieg wrestled with much of his life, that of larger vs. smaller musical forms. The bulk of his output consists of miniatures of various kinds. Grieg often regretted this, because he wanted to write more extended forms—symphonic works or longer works for piano. Indeed, he himself often felt some aversion for the endless stream of *Lyric Pieces.* He knew that they were skillfully crafted, but when they "swarmed forth from every nook and cranny," as he once said, his feelings were ambivalent. On the one hand, he knew that as a miniaturist he was an absolute master. On the other, he felt an urge to write longer works, but he knew that his long preoccupation with miniatures prevented him from doing so. That is probably why he decisively terminated the series of *Lyric Pieces* with Op. 71, calling the last piece *Remembrances* and using the same theme he had used in *Arietta*, the first of the *Lyric Pieces*. Thus he definitively concluded this part of his task and announced to his publisher and his friends that there would not be any more *Lyric Pieces*.

In thus "closing the circle" on the *Lyric Pieces* Grieg may have hoped that this decisive act would stop the miniatures from swarming and free him to compose a larger work. No doubt he looked back longingly to the *Piano Sonata*, the *Piano Concerto*, and the *Ballade*, perhaps also to the three sonatas for violin and one for cello. He had also written a symphony, though he declared that it must never be performed. One can only speculate about what Grieg was thinking at this point, but my guess is that he aspired to write a major work. For that reason I firmly believe that the *Norwegian Peasant Dances*, Op. 72, should be regarded as a cycle. Viewed in that way it is the biggest cycle and the longest piano work written in Norway.

The pieces in Op. 73, *Moods*, are longer and broader than the *Lyric Pieces*. The longest ones are No. 2, *Scherzo-Impromptu*; No. 3, *A Ride at Night*; and No. 5, *Study (Hommage à Chopin)*. No. 4, *Folk Tune from Valdres*, is reminiscent of the arrangements in Op. 17. No. 1, *Resignation*, and No. 6, *The Students' Serenade*, are similar in form and concept to the *Lyric Pieces*, but harmonically they are closer to Op. 66, *Nineteen Norwegian Folk Songs.* No. 7, *The Mountaineer's Song*—the last piece in the set—is a tribute to Norway's impressive mountain scenery and a marvelous piece all by itself. The affinity of No. 7 to Op. 68, No. 4, *Evening in the Mountains*, is evident in the single-voice passages, but the harmonies, impressionistic surfaces, and abrupt key changes are more reminiscent of Op. 54, No. 6, *Bell-Ringing*. The sturdy little melody is a *lokk*, a type of folk tune associated with the calling of farm animals. The extensive use of echo effects gives it an introspective character, however, and in the process it acquires a deeper perspective. The unique blend of simplicity and greatness makes *The Mountaineer's Song* a worthy conclusion to Grieg's works for solo piano. It is a national-Romantic, hymnlike tribute to the rugged beauty of his native land. The format is larger than that of most of the *Lyric Pieces.*

No. 1, Resignation

Op. 73 starts off on a folkish note as we first hear a solitary B that is like the sound of a horn, a *lur*, resounding across the valley. Try to make it resonate, to vibrate, using the following technique: 1. depress the pedal before you attack the note, 2. play the note, 3. depress the note silently and release the pedal, 4. depress the pedal and release the note. Then alternate between 3. and 4. and the effect will be similar to a vibrato.

The opening note is followed by a sinuous, somewhat chromatic melody in the right hand that is given additional depth by the accompaniment. Create a dialogue between the hands (see Ex. 27.1).

Ex. 27.1

Cantabile suggests a flowing *legato*, which requires a relaxed arm and intense contact with the keys. Listen carefully to the even pace of the eighth notes in the left hand (see Ex. 27.2).

Ex. 27.2

The accompaniment, which is somewhat Romantic-chromatic, contains a number of pedal points (see circled notes in Ex. 27.1).

A series of sequences leads to the first high point on a $\frac{6}{4}$ chord in F major (measures 15–16). The descent that follows has a folkish cast owing to the tritone effect created by the proximity of B and F in measures 17 and 18 (see Ex. 27.3).

Ex. 27.3

When the $\frac{6}{4}$ chord in F is repeated it is followed by a triplet figure that reaches high E in measure 23 before descending. A verbatim repetition of measures 2–4 at *Tempo I* is followed by an impressionistic passage: a long ascending passage with pedal despite the chromatic progressions. If it is played softly and lightly, with good support in the bass on the octave E, pedal may be used throughout (see Ex. 27.4).

The conclusion (measure 39) begins with Grieg's specialty, a dominant thirteenth chord. It is followed in measure 41 by a seventh chord on A, with

Ex. 27.4

a suspension, resolving first to the major third, then to the minor third of the chord. The suspensions are resolved gradually and chromatically in a manner similar to that used in Op. 66 and elsewhere. The concluding chord in E minor can be given a folkish color like the opening B to emphasize the unity of the piece.

No. 2, Scherzo-Impromptu

This piece quickly became popular and was arranged for violin and piano as well. It is a peppy salon piece with a bit of a folkish flavor and some echo effects. Take sufficient time in the *piano* passages so that the echo can be heard. This does not mean to play more slowly but to set the passage in relief (see Ex. 27.5).

Ex. 27.5

The middle section starts out like a little question-and-answer duet between the bass and descant registers (see Exx. 27.6a and b).

Ex. 27.6a

Maintain a feeling of continuous movement in measures 36–58. The rests must of course be observed, but try to create the feeling that the music con-

Ex. 27.6b

tinues to flow. Both the *stringendo* and the *rallentando* should be done as gradually as possible.

It is permissible to take a few liberties with the rhythm in *Scherzo-Impromptu*. In measure 4 and similar passages, a slight delay before striking the syncopated quarter note keeps the piece from becoming too stiff. It should not be exaggerated but done subtly (see Ex. 27.7).

Ex. 27.7

An augmented version of the theme appears in measures 93ff. (see Ex. 27.8).

Ex. 27.8

Resist the temptation to play the *Scherzo-Impromptu* too fast. Plan to have the *Molto vivace* section, starting in measure 106, a little faster than the rest of the piece. *Tempo I* in measure 116 then means return to the *Allegro capriccioso* with which you began. Think of the relationships between and among the various tempos.

No. 3, A Ride at Night

This piece depicts the scariest of scary rides—like the one in Washington Irving's *The Legend of Sleepy Hollow*. It must have very long lines, but you do not have the luxury of thinking only about them. The tempo is quite fast, and the rhythm is complex. If you think only about the long lines, some of the rhythmic details may get lost. On the other hand, if you are too preoccupied with the rhythmic complexities you are likely to lose sight of the long lines. Without the long lines, *A Ride at Night* is unbearable—but without the rhythmic pungency the piece loses some of its bewitching, devilish character. The dominant rhythmic idea is the relation between consecutive measures with the varying patterns indicated in Ex. 27.9. The hemiola pattern in measures 3–4 and elsewhere is especially troublesome!

Ex. 27.9

In measures 25ff. we have eight iterations of the same rhythmic pattern: a quarter note followed by a half note. The danger is that the pattern will get twisted so that the half note begins to feel like the downbeat. Be sure to put enough emphasis on the quarter note to preserve its character as the first beat of the measure (see Ex. 27.10).

Ex. 27.10

With chords as precise as possible and an incisive rhythm, you will set the right tone for the piece. It then remains for you to execute a gradual *crescendo*, building up to a thundering *fff*, then a gradual *diminuendo* with rests as indicated—so that you imperceptibly reach total silence at the end of the first section (measure 133). This effect requires discipline on the part of the performer—not to *crescendo* too soon, not to miscalculate the *diminuendo*, and not to slow the tempo while reducing the volume.

Note the periods in measures 109ff. This section begins with a percussion-like figure—alternating fifths and octaves (see Ex. 27.11). The next period begins with a rest, which should be regarded as beat 1, and the tied chords as beats 2, 3, and 4. If you feel an impulse in the rest it will influence your attack in measure 114 (see Ex. 27.12).

Ex. 27.11

Ex. 27.12

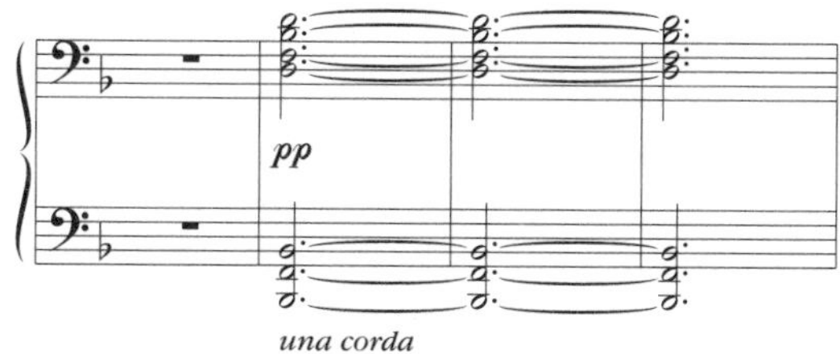

The beautiful middle section (measures 151ff.) can be construed in various ways. It can be played as an augmented form of the four-measure dance at the beginning of the piece, making it a little bizarre. When you play it, you can emphasize either its beauty or its bizarre character. I favor the latter interpretation and try to create a trollish atmosphere, as if a bewitchingly beautiful troll maiden were lurking behind the notes. Each phrase in this section begins with an accented upbeat marked *fp* tied to the measure that follows. This interpretation will be enhanced if the eight measures following the upbeat are played in its shadow. They should not be colorless—shade them as much as you wish—but listen to the sound of that accented upbeat as you play the rest of the passage.

Later the melody becomes *ben marcato* (measure 183) and is given a bizarre and remarkable *staccato* accompaniment. This section acquires a unique character if you use virtually no pedal, but try to play the melody in the middle voice *legato* in contrast to the *staccato* accompaniment. That is not easy to do, but it is interesting.

In the concluding section it appears that Grieg has been thinking about the sound of a *staccato* accompaniment in contrast to a *legato* melody: note the *staccato* on beat 3 in measure 204 (see Ex. 27.13). It is the last one in the section; thereafter the tone becomes progressively milder. The music melts away, as if it were disappearing into the fog over a mountain lake before the deviltry starts all over again. The hemiola effect in the middle section should not be as pronounced as in the faster first section.

The next question is whether the recapitulation should be identical to the opening. You can think of the piece as a conventional ABA form and let A = A, thereby framing the whole with two sturdy pillars. (Compare *Wedding Day*

Ex. 27.13

at Troldhaugen, March of the Dwarfs, Røtnams Knut.) Or you can provide a wholly different treatment the second time. You might be prepared to do it various ways and to decide onstage—following the mood of the moment—whether to play it *maestoso*, to create a naturalistic tableau, or to make your second ride at night an especially wild one, to make the furies even more furious than before—more *agitato*, more *feroce*, *fff*. However you play it, make this piece festive. Use a pounding left hand, incisive rhythms, and lightning-fast *staccatos*—including the last one *pianissimo* in measure 361.

No. 4, Folk Tune from Valdres

Trees, mountain lakes, and grassy knolls can look surpassingly idyllic by day but dangerous in the dark. This folk tune, depicting a daytime scene, is one of the finest pearls in Grieg's entire corpus. It closely imitates the *langeleik*, an indigenous Norwegian folk instrument similar to a zither.

The piece opens with a gentle pedal point on E♭, then an inverted pedal point on A♭, which eventually yields to chromatics in a manner similar to that in Op. 66. Otherwise it is clean, wispy, and sparse in sonority and expression, almost like Op. 17. Everything is muted and soft, with the accents not too prominent. No matter how softly you are playing, no matter how muted, you must distinguish between *ppp*, *pp*, and *p*. This is possible only if you go from *ppp* to *pp* and then *p*, not the reverse. I also recommend that in playing the *ppp* and *pp* passages you use an upward movement—in contrast to the beginning, which is a very soft *piano* but is played downward with firmness in the cushion of the finger. *Andante* 2/4 is not terribly slow. The pastoral character is disturbed if the triplets are not slinky enough. Let your touch be as gentle as a cat's paw (see Ex. 27.14)!

Ex. 27.14

The fingering is not easy, but no matter what fingering you choose, you must have a pliable wrist and a leading elbow that gives the fingers a little help preceding the triplet figures. In measures 7–9 and elsewhere you might try to get a kind of humming effect in the right hand and bring out the descending chromatic line in the tenor voice. The last figure in measure 4 sounds more like an accompaniment than those preceding it. Even though the slur goes all the way to the end of the measure, the melody actually concludes on the A♭ preceding the bass clef sign. What follows is an echo effect, so it should be softer (see Ex. 27.15).

In the *a tempo* section, measures 13ff., use a lighter and brighter sonority. The melody is innocent, unaffected, but the *dolcissimo* part absolutely must have a *subito* effect. Take plenty of time on the arpeggio, which Grieg has marked *tranquillo*. Try to achieve a humming effect, and bring out the sadness in measure 19 (see Ex. 27.16).

Exx. 27.15 and 27.16

Measures 20–25 are like a chorale. Use a somewhat darker color, and keep the music soft and warm.

No. 5, Study (Hommage à Chopin)

Many of Grieg's character pieces can be described as mood pictures. To create the appropriate atmosphere for them the interpreter must have plenty of imagination, an attentive ear, and a curious mind that goes beyond the notes. Despite the amount of practice required, it is exhilarating to find a real pianistic challenge. One delights in playing such works as the *Sonata in E Minor*, the *Holberg Suite*, *Pictures from Folk Life*, and *Brooklet*.

No. 5 of the present opus is another virtuoso number that is invigorating for both listeners and performer. It is not a "study" in a negative sense but could almost be called *quasi impromptu*. The runs are Chopinesque in that they are all melodic, but they must be fast and smooth, and the fingering must be as even as possible. The triple rhythm requires good coordination between the hands. Practice both hands precisely and evenly. To develop the finger attack, hold one note down and actively play the one next to it with just finger movement. Some parts could also be practiced with finger *staccato* in order to develop a lightning-fast reaction in the fingers. Most important, however, is the rolling, circling hand movement: if this motion becomes too pronounced, the articulation suffers. The biggest problem is with the second finger. It must be used constantly, and it is always in danger of playing too softly. Be especially aware of it, therefore, almost as if you were trying to emphasize the third and sixth sixteenth notes. The emphasis disappears because of the fast tempo but it will increase the clarity. As with etudes generally, you can practice it according to Cortot's principles with various rhythms and preparatory exercises. For example: stop on the first note and play the next two fast, then play the first two notes fast and stop on the third one. Or practice 6 + 6 notes fast and stop on each sixth note, i.e., twice in the measure, or practice whole measures fast but stop on the first beat of each measure. Tied exercises are also helpful. For example: hold A♭ and E and play F, or hold E and F and play A♭ and C. Do the same with other similar figures. Thereafter, to master the etude you must practice it slowly, then gradually increase the tempo, perhaps with the help of a metronome. Increasing the metronomic tempo one notch per day over a period of three or four weeks should be sufficient for learning it the first time or recovering it after not playing it for awhile.

The cascades of sound in measures 34–37 are virtuosic and brilliant. With active fingers and a free arm they will resound in an almost Lisztian manner. Musically, these figures have a quixotic *agitato* character, and the *pianissimo* effects are wonderful (see Ex. 27.17).

Ex. 27.17

No. 6, The Students' Serenade

This beautiful, singable piece is in a late-Romantic style. At the time it was written, Norwegian students were ardent representatives of the idealism and nationalistic spirit that in a few short months would lead to independence from Sweden. Some of this youthful fervor is expressed in *The Students' Serenade.*

Note that measures 6–8 and 13–16 are interludes of lesser importance. Play measures 27–29 and 30–37 somewhat muted, the rest of the piece *cantabile*. The 6/8 rhythm has a rocking feel that comes out best with a relaxed arm. Think of each eighth note as being connected with the quarter note that follows, not the reverse. Quarter + eighth = choppy; eighth + quarter = upbeat phrasing and a naturally forward-moving line (see Ex. 27.18).

Ex. 27.18

Use some Romantic *rubato*—"take and give back"—in measures 17–26, marked *poco più mosso*. The goals of the phrases are the upbeat to B on beat 2 in measure 18, then the next main beat. Thereafter play with a falling gesture, which is not difficult if you think of two or three measures as constituting a single entity. Free yourself from the tyranny of individual note values and think in terms of several measures at a time to feel an impulse that first rises and then falls. The richly varied chromatic harmony provides many opportunities to bring out contrary voices—for example, the bass line in measures 28–29 (A–G♯–G–G♯–A) echoes the soprano line in measures 27–28.

No. 7, The Mountaineer's Song

L. M. Lindeman's transcription of the tune on which No. 7 is based appends the following text: "The troll lady called out to the man, 'Listen to me! Get dressed and fetch your gun. Shoot the bird—but don't shoot me, for if you do you will have bad luck as long as you live.'" This unique piece is Grieg's farewell to the piano and to instrumental music in general. In many ways the present piece points toward *Four Psalms*, Op. 74, his last opus. It is a heartfelt and solemn tribute to Norwegian folk music and Norwegian nature. The affinity to the folk tradition is especially evident in the frequent use of pedal points. The principal melody is almost pentatonic and has a rather archaic sound. In measures 7–10 Grieg uses chromatics in a manner especially reminiscent of Op. 66. He is illuminating, coloring the folkish material in an expressionistic way, thereby heightening the drama. In measures 11ff. we are again given a pure representation of nature. Imitations between the two voices remind one of a natural horn, i.e., a valveless horn that produces only the notes in the natural harmonic series. With a well-executed *diminuendo* you can create the impression that the sound is gradually fading away beyond the horizon. Measures 51ff. repeat the opening measures, framing the picture, which portrays the landscape.

The Mountaineer's Song is a splendid stylized drama that is distinctively Norwegian. Three times in measures 15–38 a statement is shouted out *fortissimo* and the answer comes back from nature *pianissimo*. Nearness and distance are united in the same space. Measures 36–44 take us deeper and deeper into space as the same motive is repeated in progressively higher registers in *pp*, *più pp*, and *ppp*. The practical implication, of course, is that the *pianissimo* in measures 36–37 must not be too soft if the volume is to be decreased in the two iterations to come. The idea, here and elsewhere in the piece, is to create the impression of sound rapidly disappearing in the distance. Use a lot of pedal—at least as much as Grieg has indicated. It will not result in an objectionable degree of impressionistic veiling of the sound if you give it a good foundation in the open fifth in the left hand (see Ex. 27.19).

Ex. 27.19

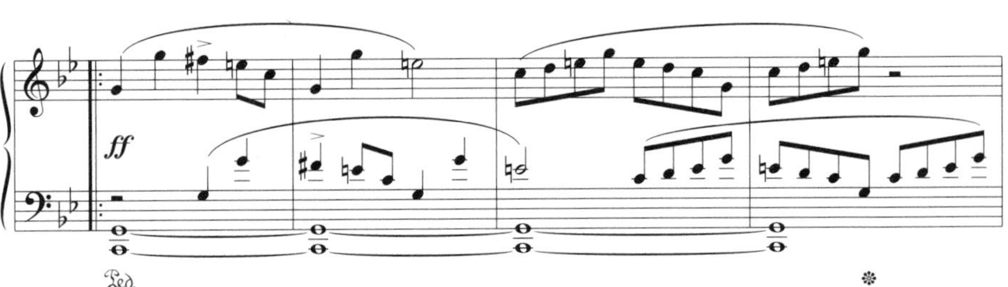

The single-voice transition in measures 45–50 is a very personal statement in the middle of the nature drama. Grieg has taken a page out of *Evening in the Mountains*: a *lokk* solo that can be varied and enhanced in innumerable ways. It is important that it be carried forward evenly to the *forte* in measure 49. At this point it should be given a reverberating, almost vibrato effect.

The recapitulation, starting in measure 51, is like the introduction and is characterized especially by the pedal point on D. The moving line in the lowest voice shuffles from half note to half note. The repeat need not always be observed, but the breadth and majesty of the landscape depicted in *Evening in the Mountains* are enhanced if measures 15–63 are heard twice—assuming that you are presenting it not just as another folkish piece, but as a song performed in honor of a nation. Give the *lokk* in the coda the character of a bright, friendly, happy product of Norwegian folk culture, brilliantly presented against the background of a C^9 chord (see Ex. 27.20). Then, *ritardando*

Ex. 27.20

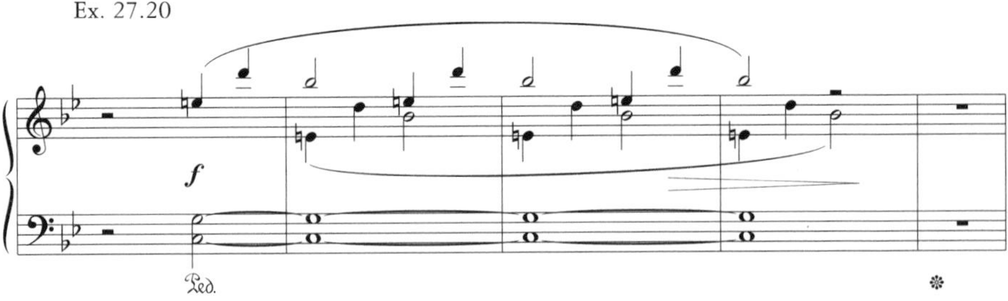

e morendo, there is a melancholy sigh as the same chord (but with a lowered third) is sounded in a lower register, and the piece finally comes to rest, *pianissimo* and *più lento*, in G minor.

Evening in the Mountains is a testimonial, Grieg's declaration of love and gratitude for the folk music that inspired him and for the rugged mountain landscape that was the backdrop for all his major works. Do your best to communicate the picture that he sought to share with all of us in this, his last composition for piano.

TITLE INDEX

Listed items are compositions or arrangements by Edvard Grieg except as otherwise indicated. Compositions without opus numbers are identified by the EG numbers assigned in the C. F. Peters edition of *Edvard Grieg: Complete Works*. Page numbers of the principal discussion of each composition appear in boldface.

Einar Steen-Nøkleberg, Professor of Piano at the Norwegian State Academy of Music in Oslo, has presented concert series of Grieg's complete piano works in Europe and the United States and has won several prestigious prizes for his performances of Grieg's music. He is editor of the new Henle edition of the complete piano works and has recorded them all on the Naxos label.

William H. Halverson is editor of *Edvard Grieg Today* and cotranslator of *Edvard Grieg: The Man and the Artist*, by Finn Benestad and Dag Schjelderup-Ebbe, and *A History of Norwegian Music*, by Nils Grinde. He has also translated 130 song texts in the C. F. Peters edition of Grieg's *Complete Works*.